Thought

A Sight to New Life

by
B. K. ASHOK

Translated by
**B. K. Shyamaly (Chembur, Mumbai)
Patrisai (London)**

An imprint of
B. Jain Publishers (P) Ltd.
USA — EUROPE — INDIA

THOUGHT – A SIGHT TO NEW LIFE

First Edition : 2009
2nd Impression: 2011

All rights reserved. No part of this book may be reproduced, stored in a retrieval system or transmitted, in any form or by any means, mechanical, photocopying, recording or otherwise, without any prior written permission of the author.

© with the author

Published by Kuldeep Jain for
HEALTH HARMONY
An imprint of
B. JAIN PUBLISHERS (P) LTD.
1921/10, Chuna Mandi, Paharganj, New Delhi 110 055 (INDIA)
Tel.: 91-11-4567 1000 • Fax: 91-11-4567 1010
Email: info@bjain.com • Website: **www.bjainbooks.com**

Printed in India by
J.J. Offset Printers

ISBN: 978-81-319-0781-8

Preface

THOUGHT – A SIGHT TO NEW LIFE

Should we not ask ourselves the question "What is life?" "Why are we here?" Do we exist just for the sake of our livelihood, or to pass an examination or carry on some business, or bring up children? To become too involved in such a mechanical life is to live a degraded life. Can we even call this living? Whilst you may achieve fame, wealth, position, etc, what is the use of these achievements if our minds are filled with fear, hatred, stress, tension and depression? Whatever stage you may be at in your life, whether young or old, you must aspire to create a better world in which people may experience bliss, peace and immortal love for each other. Good management of one's life can be such that it brings with it an unending mystery. However is it essential to understand, discover and attain an elevated life.

However, to understand this one needs to have a refined intellect and the formula to attain this is self-observation. The impact of the mind and senses on our being is the major obstacle in our life. Nowadays, we do not lack the basic necessities such as food, clothing and shelter and all other comforts, but the one thing which we do lack is knowledge. Life is full of bad habits. The major cause of psychological poverty is mental instability. Our minds are conditioned with strong attitudes based on traditional beliefs from our family, society and the country in which we live. Man cannot overcome these negative attitudes unless he wakes up and develops insight and a spiritual awakening. Life is changing at a very fast pace due to the effects of information technology and luxurious lifestyles. There is strong competition to progress but stress and impatience have made man depressed. Can life become easy, simple and happy? Can man walk on a happy and prosperous road to achieve excellence in life?

In the 21st century, where there is a mingling of cultures in the world, information technology has reduced the distance between countries. The distance to the moon and the sun has come closer, but what about the distance between the hearts of mankind? Today, on one side we are reducing the gap between people of different countries, and on the other side we are endeavouring to remove the differences between America, Russia, India and China. But are we successful in bringing about an attitude of brotherhood amongst the people of different countries? The psychological distance is widened because of hatred and jealousy. A lack of values in life has brought about a huge gap in the minds of people within families, society and the country at large. Indeed, the distance in relationships between family members is several times wider than the distance from the earth to the moon.

The question arises as to whether this is due to a lack of material prosperity in the world at large. Nowadays, we find that people of many countries have reached the height of material prosperity. Their homes are filled with luxuries and comforts and yet they still face obstacles in their lives. We find that depression, stress, insomnia, suicide, divorce, etc are all on the rise in many developed countries. It has been discovered that the major cause is a lack of spiritual awakening and spiritual values in life. We need to understand that the foundation of a harmonious family, society and nation and world is man himself. The character of a man is manifest through his soul. Man is not just made up of the sense organs. It is the mind that activates the senses and it is through these senses that thoughts, imagination, desires, etc are manifest. You are aware of this mind. It is the intellect which discriminates between positive and negative thoughts and makes a judgment. The mind and intellect are within the soul. In other words mind, intellect and sanskars are the powers of the soul. Man tries to experience the soul by coming out of his materialistic pleasures into a peaceful and happy spiritual life. This becomes possible when there is a revolution in transforming ones attitudes and behaviour. It seems as if man is longing for a prosperous life and yearns to enter into a golden future in the 21st century. The one and only path remaining is spiritual knowledge and a value-based lifestyle. It is not possible to find solutions to serious problems in life simply by understanding our behaviour. Indeed it is not possible until such time that we change our attitudes and lifestyles through a spiritual awakening.

Today, beliefs in elemental sciences, human science and medical science are deteriorating day by day. We are now entering into a world of atomic energy. We are moving into a new phase from the material to the immaterial where psychological and spiritual sciences are emerging. Mind and thought power have an impact on life's interactions. Scientists have discovered subtle atoms called neutrons which are both inside and outside the body and the planet and move faster than light. Scientists have discovered that these atoms collide with each other. A mathematics philosopher "Andreodrosk" discovered a new formula through which he identified a neutron-like atom called 'Saison' which collides with brain cell neurons to activate them. According to the elemental philosopher, "Rader Ford", atoms have an impact on human blood vessels. The neutron 'minedrino' was also discovered. Without spiritual awakening a happy and prosperous life cannot be achieved. This scientific truth cannot be overlooked.

This book is a living book in which each page mirrors the fears, struggles, carelessness and unending problems unknowingly created by man. You will find alternative remedies to these problems. You will also find in this book the author's goal to find solutions to the depth of life as its roots are spread internally in man's habits and attitudes and there within lies a lack of values in his life. Through this book, the author has made every effort to bring about transformation in our thoughts and in our life in the hope of finding a superior and happy life.

THOUGHT - A NEW DIMENSIONAL VIEW

Do we need to ask ourselves the questions "What is life? What is the purpose of our existence?" Is it simply to earn our bread and butter or to pass academic examinations, or just to go about our daily business or give birth to children, only to then become weak by becoming increasingly trapped in an excessive mechanical life. Can this be called life? Although you may earn fame, wealth, position etc, in spite of these attainments what will happen to the soul? A mind filled with fear, stress, tension, depression and suspicion, etc is an unfulfilled life. You may be at any stage of the life cycle, for instance, old age or youth, but you need to search for such a life that is beyond negative emotions. Wherever you find yourself in society and whatever duties you are performing, life should be without struggle with the ability to fulfill all responsibilities without running away from them. So ask yourself whether your life is one of complete bliss, immortal, peaceful and filled with true love. Undoubtedly the perfect life is one of being wonderfully harmonious in all aspects, filled with unlimited and yet mysterious events. Firstly one has to understand life in order to discover its secrets and finally to achieve it.

This book is a "Book of Life". Within its pages are a reflection of your inter-relationships through which you will attain divine insight into realizing your own fears, confusion, struggles, obstacles and unlimited problems, all of which have been self created through ignorance. This divine insight provides the key to resolving all problems. The purpose of the author in writing this book is to enter into the depths of the problems of life and to emerge with the solution.

The root cause of all problems lies deep within the unconscious mind which manifests as bad habits. In addition to these, there is also a great lack of virtues in life. The outcome of a stressful and peaceless life is a plethora of bad habits, ignorance of knowledge of the soul and an unhealthy life style. This book contains various chapters through which the author has endeavored to bring about a great revolution in our thinking, by transforming our lifestyle and thereby building a superior and blissful life.

The author, BK Ashok, has surrendered his life to this Godly Service for over 25 years. He has devoted his life to bringing about spiritual awakening in mankind and has carried out extensive research into meditation. He has written over thirty articles on spiritual topics which have been published in various magazines; Gyan Amrit, World Renewal, Amrit Kalash, Gyan Veena, Path-Pradashak, to name but a few.

Permanent Address: Pandav Bhawan, Mt Abu, Rajasthan
Today, when life is filled with luxuries, comforts, materialistic prosperity, unending desires, the thirst for true happiness, peace, bliss has created confusion in man.

Stress, tension, fear, a peaceless life did not exist in the past. Besides being successful, the writer has also inculcated both moral and spiritual values. Throughout this book the writer has presented a solution to the problem from a new spiritual dimension which is greatly appreciated.

**With best wishes from,
B K Nirwair
(Chief Secretary)**

Foreword

The meaning of life is to experience newness. To cease learning something new and experience the same is a worthless existence. Secondly, inculcation of values in life is essential and these can be achieved through experience. The human intellect has a plethora of questions on the purpose of life and how to inculcate values. The answers to these questions have been discovered by Rajyogi Brahma Kumar Ashok through his book "A Sight to New Life". He is on his way to give us an experience of love, wisdom, purity and of his constant effort to experience God as "Satyam – Shivam – Sundaram".

Those things which are useful and bring happiness are extremely valuable in life. They are valuable because they fulfill our needs. Needs are not only materialistic but also spiritual. To achieve this, a realization of the soul and God is essential. To inculcate these values you need to develop a strong willpower and transform yourself by overcoming your weaknesses.

In this respect, the author wishes for a better world where there is the spirit of brotherly love and a true path to reach that place. He truly wishes for a new world, a heavenly place here on earth.

With lots of good wishes from
Dr. Harish Shukla

Publisher's Note

"An unexamined life is not worth living", said Socrates. He also said, "Know thyself." *"Thought"* the book is a wake-up call amidst growing global competition. Provocative and stimulating, the book asks us: Maybe we are rich or well-heeled, but– are we inwardly happy? It is time to be honest with ourselves, and not to take oneself for granted. It is a long and lonely road to self-improvement, but the rewards at the end are worth the gruelling trial that our quest will face, when we have to achieve victory against all odds.

Self-knowledge makes us fearless and daring and "Fortune favours the bold". For the young especially it is time to take yourself in hand. "Faint heart never a fair lady won." "Nothing ventured, nothing gained." It's high time the young specially take up this book as their Bible of sorts, and with unrelenting zeal and commitment make a success of their life and vocation. "Sweet are the uses of adversity," said Shakespeare. When we face hostile and inhospitable climate, it will be time to prove this saying. *"Thought"* is a pep talk, a "man-to-man talk" in which the author shows how to face our most fearsome battles and emerge victorious against the odds. It's an invitation to be introspective and reflective, to really weigh the values one has embraced and after mulling over it to decide once and for all what do we want.

Kuldeep Jain
C.E.O., B. Jain Publisher's (P) Ltd.

Contents

Foreword ix
Publisher's Note x

CHAPTER 1 – THE MELODY OF SILENCE IN LIFE

Close Relationship Between Silence, Introspection and Speech	2
The Source of All Talent is Silence	3
Verbal Silence Brings Relaxation of the Heart	4
Silence is Comparatively More Authentic than Speech	6
What is the Reason Behind Incessant Talking	7
Today the Right Direction Towards Silence Has been Lost	9
Relationship Between Silence and Mercy	9
Check What is Important Whilst Conversing	12
All Sense Organs Must Be Passive to Make Silence Meaningful	13
The Importance of Introspection and Silence	14
External Silence Helps in Bringing About Inner Silence	17
Learn to go Beyond Thought to Experience Silence	17
Obstacles on the Path of Learning	18
Ways to Implement Silence in Life	21
Learn the Art of Being Silent	22

CHAPTER 2 – TRUE SUCCESS

The Foundation of Achieving Success	28
Soul Analysis	34
The Mystery of a Successful and Blissful Life	36
Failure is a Temporary Means to Analyze the Soul	36
Keep a Distance from Negativity and Always Keep Faith in God	40
Elevated Work Capacity	41

Reasons for Success	42
Hard Work is the Key to Success	44
Understanding Behaviour	46
Strong Will Power is Also Essential in Life	47
New Meaning of Success – Right Character	49
Obstacles to Success – Greed	56
Responsibility	58
What is Self-Confidence?	61
Misuse of Powers on the Path of Success – Miracles	67
Hope for Life	70
The Power of Concentration	76

CHAPTER 3 – ATTITUDE

What is Attitude?	79
How to Create Attitude	81
How to Inculcate a Good Attitude in Life	82
Negative Attitude is Universal	83
Insulting Others is a Means of Praising Oneself	85
Difference Between Positive and Negative Attitudes	87

CHAPTER 4 – BALANCE IN LIFE

Passive Emotions	111
Recognise the Powers of the Soul	112
Balance – the Foundation of a Beautiful Life	113
What is Balancing? – How Much is Required	115
Balance is an Internal State Which Comes Through Practice	116
Be the Ruler of Your Mind	117
Creation of the Mind and its Understanding is Necessary for Success	118
Unconscious Habits	124
The Foundation of All Expectation – Soul As the Adviser	128
Self Control Means Decency of Self-Discipline	131
Resolves Become the Second Nature of a Human Being	132

CHAPTER 5 – THE POWER OF DESIRE, THOUGHTS AND ACTION IN BUILDING FATE

Action	140
Rules for Action	141
Impact of Thoughts	145
Different Aspects of Thoughts	151
Desire and the Power of Desire	152
Formula for Desire and Purpose	154
Lack of Soul Awareness in Life	156
The desires of the Mind Can never be Fulfilled	157
Don't Allow Desire to Become a Need	160

CHAPTER 6 – THE BASIS OF HAPPINESS IS UNSELFISH CHARITY

What is Happiness?	163
Forget the Past and Look To the Future	164
Cultivate the Habit of Being Happy – Healthy Attitude	164
Is It Possible to Remain Happy For Ever?	166
Can Happiness be Achieved Through Knowledge and Meditation	166
Unselfish Service is the Key to Happiness	167
Impact of Happiness on the Body	169
Cheerfulness in Life is Just as Important as Breathing	170
The Outcome of Charity is Happiness	171
Whatever We Give We Get the Same in Return	175
Happiness Also Depends on the Way You Give	176

CHAPTER 7 – FORGIVENESS AND SYMPATHY

How to Enter Into the World of Sympathy	180
Thousands of People are Searching for Sympathy	181
Sympathy is a Must Regardless of Whether the Person is Capable	183
To Find Fault With Others is an Obstacle to Sympathy	184
People Are Ignorant of the Philosophy of Right Work	185

Reasons Behind Undesirable Actions	186
Man's Viewpoint is to Find Fault in Others	187
To Act Differently is a Challenge in Life	189
Man Becomes a Deity Only After Being Hurt	189
Forgiveness is the Greatest Jewelry	191
To Forgive and Forget is the True Solution	193
Benefits of Forgiveness	195

CHAPTER 8 – THE GREATEST BEAUTY OF LIFE IS LOVE

Materialistic Love	198
Why do People Love Wealth	199
Spiritual Love	207
Whatever You Wish for yourself, Wish for Others	210
Love Without Effort	210
Love is an Art, Learn It	213
The Last Leap to Achieve Complete Love - Perfection	214
To Surrender to God is to Experience Newness	217

CHAPTER 9 – UNSELFISH ACTION IS THE FRAGRANCE OF LIFE

The Philosphy of Action	223
Man Lives with the Expectation of the Impossible	223
What is the Next Step to be Free of All Problems	224
What is the Secret of Detached Action?	225
Detachment and Practice is Essential	226
Which Actions are Desirable?	229
What are the Different Forms and Colours of Action?	229
Action Without the Desire for Reward is Possible	232
Cultivate a Playful Attitude	233
Life is Energy	235
Can all Actions Become Acting?	235
Action Can Become Joyful	236
Emotions are More Important than Action in Life	237
Realisation of Action Without Reward is Essential	238
Perform Conscious Actions and Be Neutral	239
'I' is an Egoistic Notion	241

Think – Everything is Happening on its Own   241

CHAPTER 10 – TOWARDS A STRESS-FREE LIFE

How to Increase Resistance Power to Stress?	251
What is Stress?	252
Freedom from Thought is the Key to Overcome Stress	256
The Basis of a Stress-Free Life – Overcoming Fear	261
How to Overcome Anger	261
How to Reduce Stress	262
The Difference Between Knowledge and Being Knowledgeful	263
The Path of Fearlessness – Raj Yoga Meditation	266
The Difference Between Soul and Body, Knowledge and Experience, the Foundation of Fearlessness	267
Golden Rules for a Stress-Free Life	269

1

The Melody of Silence in Life

Generally, it has been observed that the majority of people take the literal meaning of silence to mean verbal silence. But suppose your mind is preoccupied with innumerable negative thoughts such as jealousy, anger, etc. Although you may be verbally silent, you may not be experiencing inner silence. This state, in fact, could be quite harmful. If a pressure cooker is filled with water and is kept on the boil, after some time the pressure in the cooker increases and may burst due to the excess pressure within. A similar situation arises when a person remains verbally silent but whose mind is filled with negative thoughts. The term "silence" has a deeper meaning. It is an inner state whereby the mind is filled with positive thoughts, well-wishing thoughts, remembrance of God, thoughts which help to inculcate divine virtues and those which elevate one's life.

Nanak Dev rightly said that "Eternal peace can never give internal peace, though many ages may lapse".

Mahatma Buddha said "A fool cannot become a saint just by remaining silent, but one who tries to overcome the vices and maintains balance is a true saint".

Ved Vyas stated "It is good to remain silent rather than to speak meaningless words. It is better to tell the truth rather than to be silent and even better to think positive and speak of spiritual things."

The purpose of silence is to free the mind of its stream of negative thoughts and endless desires. Silence can be experienced only when we succeed in overcoming all our desires and expectations. It is far better to remain silent and then to speak meaningful words for one minute than to speak empty words for hours on end. Real silence is experienced when there are no bad habits, negative addictions, egoism or selfish attitudes. In this state one maintains peace, bliss and freedom from wasteful thought.

The following clarifies this state of deep inner silence:

"Where verbal speech is lost, where thoughts and emotions are lost, where universal peace, might and bliss are overflowing through vibrations, in this state of mind the soul experiences silence by going into its depths. This is exactly what silence means"

Close Relationship Between Silence, Introspection and Speech

Introspection is when there is no noise pollution, or fictitious man-made rules, where there is no-one to influence our mind by bad habits. A peaceful garden, a beautiful mountain or a beautiful lake can also be regarded as introspection. Thoreau rightly said:

"Introspection is your best friend with whom you can always be with".

Definitely, "no-one other than introspection is your true friend, but until your mind is also ready to be friendly with"

Sarviyan said, "Introspection helps in union with God."

Fairbanne said "One who can't become introvert can never take the taste of the society".

If desires, expectations and tears are twin sisters, then introspection, silence and speech are twin brothers. These have a unique relationship between each other. Just as the importance of the day is highlighted by the night and white chalk can be seen on a blackboard, in the same way both silence and speech have a deep relationship in our lives. If silence and introspection are life's school, then speech is its colour. As silence and speech are inter-related so, too, they travel in parallel with each other in both life and in the universe.

The Source of all Talent is Silence

According to Vinoba Bhave, "Silence and introspection are supreme friends of the soul".

Franklin said, "No-one better than an ant can teach us because it remains silent".

Locokit said, "Silence is a tree on which you get fruits of peace".

Silence is the beauty of the soul. Whatever is superior and elevated in human life is the expression of art. Progress is the outcome of the power of silence. If you wish to become aware of your life, universal mysteries and truth, then become silent.

The great people of today who have been successful in achieving their aim in life and have used these achievements for the welfare of others, only succeeded due to experiencing inner silence and introspection. These famous people spoke with such mercy that every word became eternal and immortal inspiring many people throughout the ages.

Throughout history we find great people who spoke with great respect and were successful in every aspect of their lives. Whether from the field of religion, science, spirituality, art or culture, they will be remembered for all time because they had experienced true silence deep within. They emerged with innovative and divine ideas, thoughts and discoveries through the power of silence and introspection.

If we turn back the pages of history we find that all great people's words contained the truth because they valued silence. They are just as popular today as they were say, 2000 to 2,500 years ago. Buddha, Mahavir, Jurthust, Lao Tsu, Jesus

Christ, Shri Krishna, etc, to name but a few such great people. Mahavir remained silent for about 12 years; Buddha devoted 6 years to experience silence, Lao Tsu experienced silence in a very elevated form. Jesus used to leave his disciples for short intervals to go to a mountain to experience silence and introspection. Shri Aurobindo experienced a higher consciousness which was the outcome of silence. He remained in silence from 1926 to 1950. In the last days of his life he would remain in silence for hours and hours. Only a few people who had subtle vision could understand the silence of Shri Aurobindo.

Saint Raman also used to remain in silence. People used to realize the 'self' by coming into his company. The great poet, "Wordsworth" used to remain in silence for long periods of time and would admire the beauty of nature. In complete happiness he would admire the daffodils for hours on end. He gives all the credit to this experience to silence itself. Gandhiji, the father of the nation, threw out British rule from India on the basis of silence. He praised the importance of silence and tried to implement it into his life in a practical way. He proved to everyone how strong one can become and how the power of the soul can be increased by the power of silence A very well-known teacher of Taksh-Shila, founder of India and the foundation of future India, had experienced silence and introspection. And last but not least, the famous personality, 'Chankya', is the outcome of silence. Sikander, too, was impressed by Chankya and he could not stand in front of him as his silence was so powerful.

Verbal Silence Brings Relaxation of the Heart

In our daily lives we often use our tongue to speak more than our hands and legs. If we would have used our hands and legs more than our tongue, our fate would have become brighter. If you want your life to be melodious, it is necessary for you to learn the art of silence. Generally, a person needs only to speak that much which is necessary. If it becomes necessary to speak, then let his speech be concise, like a telegraphic message. At the end of the day, a person comes to the conclusion that 80% to 90% of speech is meaningless. If we can get our work done by speaking only one word rather than ten words, then we must practise this. One who is not a devotee of introspection will always interfere unnecessarily in other people's lives. Your speech should contain maximum information with minimum words and should inspire and motivate people to do something useful. But remember that it is better to remain quiet rather than utter meaningless words.

Sticks and stones can break your bones but words can break your heart and relationships. Your speech should be simple, sweet and polite. Speech should be meaningful and such that it does not hurt anyone's feelings but rather uplifts people. Truth in speech and politeness can be several times more valuable than diamond and pearls and will be appreciated by everyone.

In today's world, the right to speak should be given to those who understand the language of silence. In Shri Aurobindo's institute, shree mother always used to say that if any one remained in deep silence for seven days, he would be considered capable of speaking for one hour. And if he wished to speak for one day, then he would need to spend one year in silence. One who speaks more loses faith from people all around him. Such people are simply 'talkative'. Usage of abusive words indicates that you fail to understand the usage of right words. Speech is mortal and silence is one of the divine qualities. One of the great thinkers "Pascalan" said, "If people in the world remain silent, then at least 70% of the problems can be solved."

Disputes can be solved by mutual understanding. But the root cause is verbal. If you want to extinguish the fire of anger in a person, then you should pour the water of silence and peace on him. This remedy relieves both yourself and other person from the pain for days, months and years.

Nowadays problems, war, disputes, etc are increasing at an alarming rate. The tongue speaks out and later on gets involved in many problems and the person feels guilty and thinks "I wish I had remained quiet." Silence keeps a control over our tongue. The minute speech goes out of control, our interaction becomes bitter. This again can give rise to serious negative results spreading severe consequences. In history, if Anand had not made fun of Chanakya, then the Magad Empire 'nand' would not have been destroyed. Similarly, in the Mahabharata if 'Draupadi' had not insulted Duryodana, she would not have been abducted by Duryodana.

Agatsya said "When we are insulted it is extremely painful and we challenge that person who insulted us but try to see your own foolishness and ask yourself whether you insult others in the same way.

Silence is Comparatively More Authentic Than Speech

In a society it is impossible to speak honestly and with sincerity in most situations because the moment we start talking, we become more aware of customs, culture, formality, bondages, etc. If we keep these conventions in mind, purity in speech and truthfulness start to decline. Because as soon as we start talking, we start looking at others and gradually our mind speaks out as to what the other person wants to hear. Such speech pollutes the character of a person. Words such as "I am mistaken" or "please forgive me" etc. are hardly ever used by silent people.

Silence is authentic only when alone. Silence is truth.. As soon as silence spreads in soul, it starts to experience aloneness in a crowd. That is why divine and positive thoughts can never make anyone lonely. The person who learns the art of remaining silent need not go to a mountain top or bank of a river or forest. A silent person becomes so engrossed in himself that he realizes the truth of the universe. One who thinks of making others happy will fall into a trap of complications. This can become one of the main causes for people becoming untruthful, disloyal and hypocritical. The biggest difference between a simple man and a great person is how they implement silence and introspection into their daily lives. Politicians are simple people who live in a crowd. That is why they make a mess of their life. Whereas, a person who is living with silence and introspection reaches the height of virtues and depth of experience and is known as "Great".

If eight hours of sleep was not necessary, then man would have spoken continuously for twenty-four hours. It seems as if it is very difficult for a person to be free from continuous speech. If one bathes in the ocean of silence, then he achieves a depth of experience. His experience is as if his life has become enlightened. The music of silence starts vibrating in his heart and he experiences bliss. Thus, the soul receives the food of divine might from this silence.

What is the Reason Behind Incessant Talking

There are many reasons behind incessant talking. Speaking can sometimes be in the form of a dialogue or a monologue. Man cannot remain quiet. In general, man speaks in his daily life for the following reasons:
- Habit
- Due to a feeling of uneasiness or helplessness
- Due to endless desires, expectations and fancies.
- Through responsibility towards work
- Through mercy in order to provide valuable advice.

Generally people speak for two main reasons. Firstly, due to desires and expectations, or as great souls who speak with mercy. The former speaks because of a feeling of helplessness, whereas the latter becomes helpless in remaining quiet. The former cannot remain alive without talking, whereas the latter's speech is the outcome of silence. Suppose you are walking along a road and you meet a friend. If your friend doesn't greet you by saying "Hello, Hai", then you would feel insulted. At that moment, you don't realize that there may be a good reason why he does not talk to you. It may be that he is experiencing silence at that time. It could be that by remaining silent he can express love through his eyes, but you may not have understood his language of silence. Silence can be manifest as a welcome regard. But today, understanding is lacking in people and they are failing to understand the language of silence. Just as respect and insult, hatred and love, anger and silence, etc are opposites, similarly silence can be used as an answer to a question. Many times, remaining silent can be used as a form of communication and which may signal 'yes' to a question.

If you want to inculcate elevated human values and spiritual values, it is not sufficient simply to understand what, when and where to speak, but is also essential to learn 'when to remain quiet'. Rightly said by Jayshankar Prasad, 'It is not right to speak everywhere and every time. Sometimes silence does not create any harm". The language of silence is losing its importance. We have confined ourselves to only speaking words.

Today our understanding of silence is not as deep as it should be.

If anyone remains quiet we assume that he has not given importance to our question or we think that he is a fool, not to understand anything. His quietness in our presence creates an uneasiness within us. We are unaware of the fact that many people talk more in reality. Some believe that people will not understand if he doesn't talk. That is why he speaks such wasteful things. Such people may initiate arguments, debates and leave a strong impact of anger and foolishness on the minds of scholars. Like an intelligent gardener doesn't grow plants on an infertile land, similarly, a clever washerman doesn't wash clothes in dirty water. Because by doing so, time, money and energy is wasted. In the same way, great people are not interested in meaningless talk, negative arguments and unnecessary debates. This way, they economize their mental strength by remaining silent and polite. If they discover any weaknesses in themselves, then they accept that weakness and take advantage of the golden chance to understand themselves. The power of acceptance saves a man from anger, stress and egoism. This is the reason to economize time and mental strength. Thus, a silent person makes use of this economized strength for transforming himself and using it for the welfare of others.

Today the Right Direction Towards Silence Has Been Lost

In reality, all important questions of life have their answers in silence. But, regrettably, today the language of silence and its purpose is losing its importance. If anyone of us becomes quiet, there can be many meanings behind it. People can remain quiet due to several wrong reasons such as:

- To insult someone.
- Bernard Shaw said, "The best way to show disregard is to keep silence"
- When people become depressed, they become silent.
- Sudden fear or confusion can make a person quiet.
- When a person is in a very angry state, he becomes speechless.
- Sometimes excess anger reveals one's foolishness, so it is better to remain quiet.
- Many times, people remain quiet because they are ignorant about the answers to questions asked. At the same time, they don't want to appear ignorant to others. They don't want others to underestimate them in any way. Now you decide what they should really do in such a situation if they hadn't remained quiet.

In conclusion, we can say that we have associated all the wrong assumptions with our quietness and true relationship is lost from the melody of silence.

Relationship Between Silence and Mercy

Many people just get carried away by perpetual talking and assume that if they don't talk to others they will not be considered as a merciful and soft-hearted person. People think that if they talk, it shows their love for others. But truly speaking it is not so. Just as we see clouds everywhere in the sky, in the same way wasteful thoughts and negative thoughts are like clouds, which are spread throughout the human mind. Man feels uneasy until he speaks out or throws all his wasteful thoughts out of his mind. Whatever is within you is manifest through words and it is these very thoughts that have made you feel uneasy.

The other person is not really important to you but you want an excuse to talk with someone. You use the other person like a dustbin. If you pay attention to yourself, you will understand that many times you are not talking for others' benefit but you want to vomit out your inner feelings. If you feel that you have overcome your anger or uneasiness or feel light after talking to someone, then how can the other person benefit from your talking? Just think for a while, these wasteful thoughts were making you heavy and uneasy, then can the other person experience peace? No, absolutely not. You always speak for your own personal benefit. If you don't find someone to whom you can talk, then your dialogues change into a monologue. In other words, you start talking to yourself.

Today, all of us are connected with different forms of media such as newspaper, radio, TV, etc. These are various sources of news that are made available to us. People are aware that the news which they have read in the morning is read by others also, but still, people take great interest in listening to the same news and making others listen to the same things from morning till night. If you think that by talking to others you are showing your love and mercy, then you are absolutely wrong. You have wrongly certified your love. But those who know about love in depth agree with this statement that when two lovers meet, they become speechless and communicate silently. If we speak out of habit or desperation, then definitely this will neither benefit us nor the world in any way. Certainly if beneath the silence the fragrance of speech is flowing, then the other person will benefit. Where there is no cloud on the sky of the heart, where the sky is quiet, there is no uneasiness or impulse to talk and you will start looking to the welfare of others. In a true sense, your speaking would then become merciful and worthy. All important and beneficial thoughts of this world arise because of silence. In the same

The Melody of Silence in Life

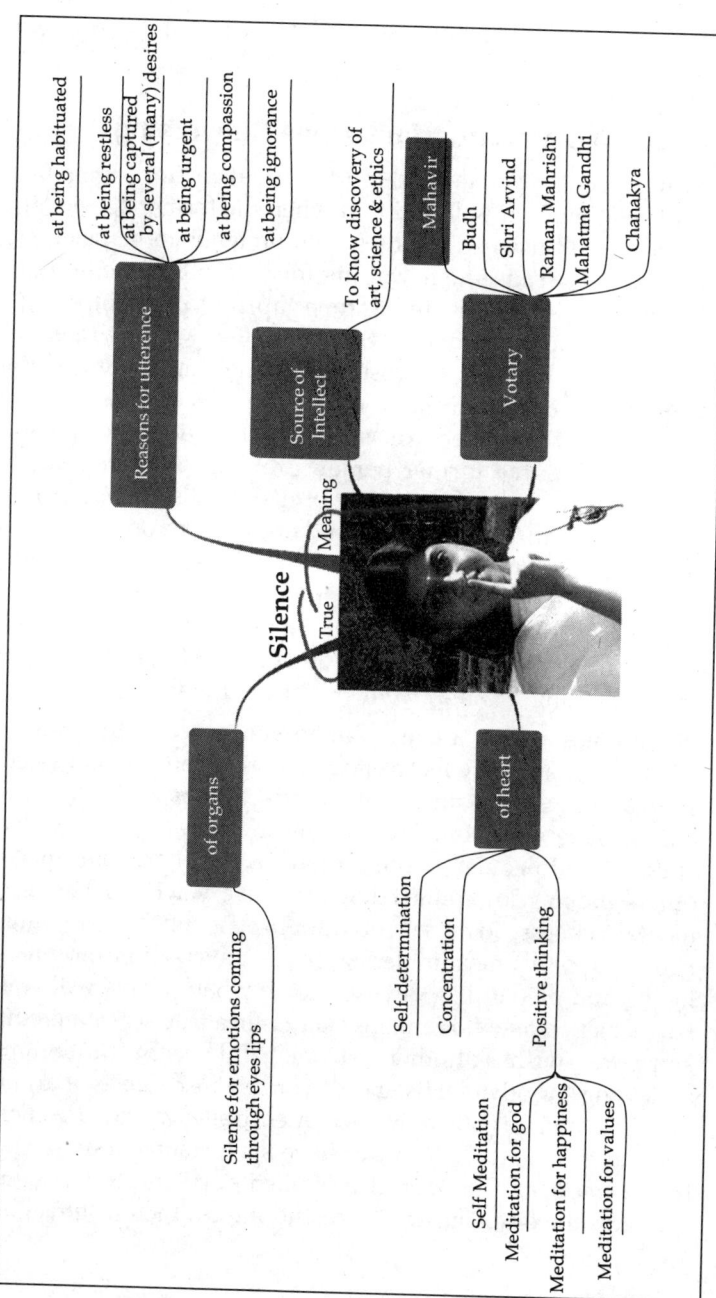

Silence — True Meaning

Reasons for utterance
- at being habituated
- at being restless
- at being captured by several (many) desires
- at being urgent
- at being compassion
- at being ignorance

Source of Intellect
- To know discovery of art, science & ethics

Votary
- Mahavir
- Budh
- Shri Arvind
- Raman Mahrishi
- Mahatma Gandhi
- Chanakya

of organs
- Silence for emotions coming through eyes lips

of heart
- Self-determination
- Concentration
- Positive thinking
  - Self Meditation
  - Meditation for god
  - Meditation for happiness
  - Meditation for values

way, if a person becomes silent, he can become loving and merciful.

Check What is Important While Conversing

You have to be neutral and pay attention to group conversation. You will find that when the former speaks, the latter doesn't listen. The latter only pretends to be listening. He is quiet because he is waiting for you to become quiet so that he can start talking. In this time gap, he is planning exactly what he can say when his turn comes. Many times, he interrupts in between because he becomes impatient and the former is compelled to say that "you first listen to what I am trying to say and then you speak." When the latter person starts talking, the former person pretends to listen. At the same time, he is on his way to preparing his speech. If one person is talking continuously and doesn't give any chance to the other person, then the other person says "O Brother, today you have really bored me". It could be that from tomorrow onwards the other person may not come in contact with him again. To listen to each other's speech is like a mutual understanding or an agreement between both.

Many times during a conversation you may be surprised at what is said and may feel as if the other person is unbalanced, simply because the subject about which he is speaking does not resonate with you. That is why the so-called, "Educated and cultured people" in our society become bored and make others bored. Gossiping takes place every where. This is a mental sickness. So those who want to experience silence must rise beyond this meaningless gossip. Conversation should be loving and merciful. A day will come when people will realize that a person who remains silent is in a true sense merciful and a well-wisher of others. His merciful speech can become a blessing for others. His speech comes out because of an inner necessity. But others will experience silence from his merciful speech. Your speech can have such tremendous power that it can open the door of unlimited opportunities. If your speech is the outcome of silence and mercy, then its effect on the other person is beneficial. And this is how we should communicate with others.

All Sense Organs Must Be Passive to Make Silence Meaningful

Silence doesn't mean just keeping the mouth closed. It would be appropriate if other senses are also passive at the same time. Let us take our eyes. It is the eyes that can speak more than the tongue. Those who know the language of the eyes are more capable of exhibiting their inner emotions through their eyes. It is through your eyes that a person can speak out. It is your eyes which reveal whether you love or hate the other person. If you want to show anger, you gaze at the other person. By doing so, you have shown much anger. Similarly, a person can show anger, lust, greed, enmity, friendship, revenge, etc. through their eyes. Gestures can be shown by the hands. Body language came into existence from the West. They believe that you can find out the nature of a person from his behaviour, from the way he walks, sits, stands, etc. Your perfect identity is the way you speak and your expressions reveal more than how you dress. Some people not only listen through their eyes. One who can read body language can read your lips and can know what you are speaking. Today, we find such people who can tell the colour of your dress through touch. Beethovan was deaf but the whole world knows the wonderful lyrics contributed by him to music. In other words, those who want to go into the depths of silence should not talk waste, not only through the tongue but not by any of the other senses either.

It is rightly said by psychiatrists that our intellect holds numerous differing attitudes. That is why in order to make it clean, people should go on a diet to reduce wasteful thoughts. On the long journey of the soul, there is the impact of wasteful thoughts and attitudes upon it.. The intellect is surrounded by the dirt of wasteful thoughts. Psychologists believe that our brain consists of six to seven crores of cells and each cell consists of crores of attitudes. The whole universal knowledge can be gathered and registered in the human intellect. Thus, it can be concluded that the original nature of the soul is hidden because of infinite attitudes which are like rust on our intellect. The rust has to be cleared. That is why a devotee needs to practise "silence" for several days. He needs to meditate and bathe in the ocean of truth so that his intellect becomes clean and pure.

That is why to become a successful person, silence plays a vital role. Silence means there is no waste either internally or externally because while speaking, mind and intellect play a vital role. Many attitudes are adopted by the mind and intellect every second. If a person goes on speaking the same thing again and again or after reading newspaper makes others listen to him, this really does cause harm as his time is wasted and he is projecting his own rubbish onto the other person.

The Importance of Introspection and Silence

If a person observes his speech during the whole day, then he will find that about 90% is waste. Even if you had never spoken, still your life would have moved on. Always remember, those things which are of no use to anyone shouldn't be related to anyone. It is certain that it will not bring benefit to anyone. Always speak less and only when it is necessary. Let others speak of wasteful things but change this waste into something meaningful. Do not accept wasteful thoughts into your intellect. If you accept one wasteful thought it can give birth to innumerable wasteful thoughts. If you give one wasteful speech, you will have to speak of many more things to prove it. Peace and happiness can spread in the world if people do not create any problems by speaking unnecessarily. Sometimes you speak out and land yourself in trouble because the other one reacts. However, to settle disputes, we have to speak and in this way, once again we become involved in the cycle of speech.

- According to Vidur, "We should talk only as much as is practically necessary. It is of no benefit to speak more than necessary even if your words are magical and

meaningful.
- According to Talmud, "One who speaks too much is one who commits sin."
- Jutrun said, "When can there be true introspection? When you rise up from a narrow-mindedness."
- Aabis said, "External silence is not true silence. Tension should not enter the mind when remaining silent."
- Silence has endless power contained within it. A silent person is generally strong. Often, circumstances may not be in one's favour but still one does not lose inner peace, respect and sympathy.
- It is through inner silence and peace that your inner strengths increase and remain in safe custody. These strengths are used by intellectual people for creative purposes both for society and oneself. The balance of speech, mental equilibrium and intellectual understanding can be achieved and controlled only through the practice of silence.
- Those people who set high goals in their lives possessed knowledge, virtues and inner power in abundance. In the absence of these, silence and introspection cannot be attained.
- One of the great preachers of silence, Gautam Buddha, used to become silent very often during a debate. Swami Vivekananda used to say "If, due to any reason the discussion increases, then you have destroyed your balance of mind."
- There is a very famous expression, "Barking dogs seldom bite". "Clouds that roar never rain." If there is depth to a river it flows peacefully. Great people always have a very soft voice. That is why the first sign of a strong person is patience and sincerity.
- The greatest teacher is silence, because a silent person listens passively when being insulted and makes others realize their mistake simply by remaining quiet.
- Silence is one of the greatest virtues because it not only saves mental strength but also physical strength. That is why a person who speaks more feels tired and weak at

the end of the day. Whereas, a person who is silent feels healthy and strong in comparison to a talkative person. Even a mountain climber has to remain silent to conserve energy. A person who expects to reach a mountain top or attain success in life must inculcate this quality of silence.

- A silent person creates an island of peace around him dispelling the vices.
- To remain physically healthy, one has to eat a balanced diet and have adequate sleep. Similarly, to gain mental health, positive thinking, silence and introspection is necessary.
- When materialistic happiness proves to be an illusion, when all happiness seems to be meaningless, when we make new friends, find new alternative ways to feel happy and still fail to attain true happiness, then the only option remaining is silence and introspection which are pure waterfalls of the soul whose one drop can transform a person by destroying the impact of desires and greed of many births.
- Silence and introspection have the capacity to bring about the desired result, so that a person can achieve success due to his well developed intellect regardless of unfavourable circumstances.
- All great people accepted the importance of introspection and knew that when a person becomes tired of material happiness and excitement due to depression, disappointment and various mental upsets one becomes trapped in a whirlpool of negativity. In this situation he has once again to consume the medicine of nectar of introspection and silence. This is the medicine which brings inner power.
- It is through introspection and silence that a person can gain invisible and subtle strengths such as thought power, will power, action power, power to tolerate, power to discriminate, power of concentration, etc.
- Each one of us through divine vision can experience reality. Because the voice of endless desires and aspirations are so high the original voice of the soul which is soft is unheard. The vibration of divine power in life is always

soft and generous. If you want to experience it and produce it on this earth, it is necessary to practise silence and introspection.

External Silence Helps in Bringing about Inner Silence

In a real sense, the meaning of silence does not just mean keeping quiet. The correct meaning of silence is a state of mind whereby one is free from thought, a state whereby both speech and thought become passive. However, in the initial stages we have to start with external silence. The reality is that these two are not two different aspects. Both external and internal aspects are inter-related. Like thirst is felt internally and we pour in water from outside and the thirst is quenched, in the same way external silence can help in stopping our wasteful thoughts.

Many times the thoughts which are going on inside are a way of rehearsing what one is going to say. A candidate thinks many times at the time of an interview before answering and if we analyze his thoughts we conclude that some thoughts are for preparation for the future and other thoughts are due to past unfulfilled desires. His thoughts may include, "This should have been done, but it was not," "This answer was to be given but a wrong answer was given," etc. If a person remains calm, then slowly and gradually his habit of talking reduces. The more you talk, the more your mind is activated. If a person remains quiet in between for short periods, then it shows he has broken the backbone of wasteful thoughts. For example, if any person sits in a pose with crossed legs for two days and suddenly starts walking, at that moment he is unable to walk. He will stand up to walk but will fall down.

Learn to go Beyond Thought to Experience Silence

To experience silence you should have a pure and stable vision whereby you become free from thoughts without analyzing silence. A psychiatrist from the West invented a way to analyze thoughts as a solution of mental illness. He accepted this path because it is through analysis that the root cause can be identified and a solution could be found. But the conclusion arrived at was that the problem exists before the thought process. Merely by understanding anger, jealousy, etc, these mental vices cannot be destroyed. In the same way, by mental analysis, internal weaknesses cannot be destroyed. As one problem is solved another ten different new problems come onto our path. That is why, it is not worth getting involved in this analysis by thinking, "Why and from where have these thoughts come? Or "How did these thoughts come?" etc. For this, you do not have to analyze but instead become neutral and soul conscious.

Here the important question is, "Should we look through our intellect? No, because if we look through the process of the intellect, then effort is involved. The medium through which we can observe ourselves is the intellect, through thought and time. We have a stock of past accumulated knowledge, experience and habits, which are in the form of remembrance. For example, if a query arises in the mind, or if any difficult circumstance, situation or person comes in front of us, then our brain tries to find a solution through its cells. The intellect starts making a decision and all these activities are performed by the intellect through the process of silence.

Our passive mind can gallop ahead with so many things that it can retain around five hundred years of life's dramas, which will be impossible for the brain to analyze. That is why it is not necessary to analyze anything. The original nature of the soul is to be neutral and it is through this neutrality that we have to see the world. For this, what shall we do? We have to passively watch the stream of thoughts which are entering into our minds. We have to learn to observe these thoughts without reacting.

Obstacles on the Path of Learning
- Lack of patience and peace
- Complications in decision-making and analysis.

◈ Unreadiness to accept our reality.

Lack of patience and peace
After twenty-five to thirty or forty years of age people begin to lack the power of tolerance. Man gets trapped in various problems in life and becomes exhausted. If you observe you will notice that patience and peace of mind are most essential qualities. We often tell our children to patiently complete their lessons in school, but if we ourselves have to remain silent for two to four days, we are unable to do so. We become impatient to get the expected results. We behave exactly like a child who buries a mango seed in the soil and digs the soil twice a day to find out whether the seedling has grown.

Complications in decision-making and analysis
The moment we start self-introspection or the minute thoughts start coming we forget the main purpose and get trapped in self analysis. We have to observe our thoughts passively. By exercising willpower, you will find within a few days that you are successful in achieving your set goal.

Along with this, the question may arise as to when we should observe ourselves because in today's world people are more conscious about gratification of the senses. That is why the value of time plays an important part in one's life. It is necessary for man to earn his bread and butter through a business or employment or profession, but hardly gives any time for practising silence. If man's intellect would have developed, then he would have seen how death destroys all his plans. If this truth is experienced by a human being, then he will not find excuses to devote his time to the practice of silence.

Unreadiness or fear to accept our reality
This is the third stage of self-introspection which is the most difficult. This process has some important barriers because the minute you start observing your thoughts silently, there starts a cyclone of thoughts in your mind. Mind consists of a number of experiences and memories of happy and sad moments, unfulfilled desires, etc. There are unlimited

expectations which are seen on the upper layers of the mind. It is the eyes which can see the world through words, forms, pictures, etc. in different births. In a mind in turmoil one is confused thinking "Am I such a person?" People consider me as a nice person and an incarnation of peace, but in reality I am an angry person. People assume me to be a soft spoken and polite person but I am very rigid, ill-mannered and egoistic. All these have an impact upon the mind. You become elated due to false praise, whose colour starts vanishing slowly and gradually. The impression made by a person starts to break down. At that time, he starts feeling guilty and for the first time in his life realizes his inner ugliness.

Now the shadow of silence is not yet seen and neutrality has not yet been experienced. On the basis of other people's views, we start making false images of our own personality. To the extent that husband and wife, father and son or neighbours, etc know us, to that extent we behave well in their eyes and hide the rest of our weaknesses. In this way, man runs away from reality and becomes trapped in a false image. In the process of observation he becomes so nervous that the soul feels insulted and depressed and gives up the practice of silence. He tries to maintain his old image but is unable to keep the facade to hide his ugliness.

You must have seen that when a cat attacks a pigeon, the pigeon closes its eyes because by doing so the cat will not be seen. But it is not like this. By not looking at the cat it does not mean that the cat has disappeared. By closing your eyes, you cannot escape from reality. Yes, by closing the eyes the pigeon was under the wrong impression that the cat has disappeared but it comes and takes hold of the neck of the pigeon. Today, people are also facing the same problem. Some people drink alcohol and close their eyes; some keep themselves busy by watching TV or any other form of entertainment. If you want to save yourself from this cat or wish to be cured of a disease, then the only path is through introspection and silence. You will have an opportunity for introspection. If you notice your state you will come to know yourself but by overlooking this, you cannot cure yourself.

The true residence of the soul is in introspection and solitude. Solitude is man's true nature. It can never be proven otherwise. Then why should we hesitate to accept it. The journey of this birth also started on one's own.

Right from the beginning of the universe until this birth, we travelled alone. When we go to sleep, or take a bath or perform any action, we are alone. Then why not experience relaxation, silence and bliss by becoming introvert and silent as is the true nature of the soul.

All human talents in any field can be developed and gained in this world by experiencing silence and introspection. One can choose a high ambition in life and achieve success because he gets the blessings of attaining a divine intellect from God in this higher state of mind, due to which, in a very short time, he experiences truth and mystery of life and universe. He gains this experience which no other person gains by reading books for years. His experience is as if cool rays of light falling are from a fountain and he becomes healthy and prosperous. His is then filled with satisfaction and excitement.

Ways to Implement Silence in Life

Silence is the key to success in life. That is why if silence is inculcated by willpower, then you can successfully achieve the set goal and values. Start this on any particular day in the week, and then gradually spend some time to experience silence. The moment you remain silent, at that time the impact of the mind also decreases. Within the mind you will find not only evil, but noble thoughts too. The good qualities are several times more powerful in comparison to evil.

Cease talking for some time. You can stop all external media such as the radio, TV, books, etc, which stimulate the mind. In the initial stages internal commotion will increase but gradually it will start to decline because the mind realizes that the soul is the king. The soul is using strong willpower to remain in silence, and then you can enter into the peace of the soul.

The next practice is from time to time throughout the day to sit quietly without judging for a few minutes and feel the inner peace. It so happens that right from morning until night we get involved in a thousand thoughts such as yes, no, comparisons, analysis etc. We are in a state of collision every second and it acts as a barrier in experiencing the might of the soul. For this, you have to make effort to stop the thoughts which are going on within by remaining silent. You have to create a space in between two thoughts and try to remain in that space. In this state of thoughtlessness, you will feel the silence and experience the true nature of the soul. Practice at least one hour every day remaining in the state of non judgment. Go on increasing this process.

Learn the Art of Being Silent

It is not necessary to go to the forest to experience silence. It is necessary to develop your understanding for experiencing silence. Just keep in mind that you need to save yourself from wasteful talk and this will benefit others also. For this, indifference to what is going on around you and within yourself is required. The mind remains stable in all situations, whether it is anger or jealousy, partiality or impartiality, friendship or rivalry, the meaning of indifference is that we are not taking any interest in the thoughts that are going on in our mind. Let us experiment with this. Let us be neutral and learn to see our thoughts. Let us not help our mind when thoughts are going on or the mind starts speaking. Become neutral towards them. Tell your mind such things as "you can speak as much as you wish, I have no interest in you". Therefore keeping all obstacles at bay keep on practising this procedure with willpower, patience and silence. After some time thoughts will start to reduce. The deeper your practice, the less time it will take to implement this practice into your life. :

By becoming free from thought, soul consciousness and neutrality are dissolved in silence and peace. Here there is no need to go anywhere or to anything because the soul, which

The Melody of Silence in Life

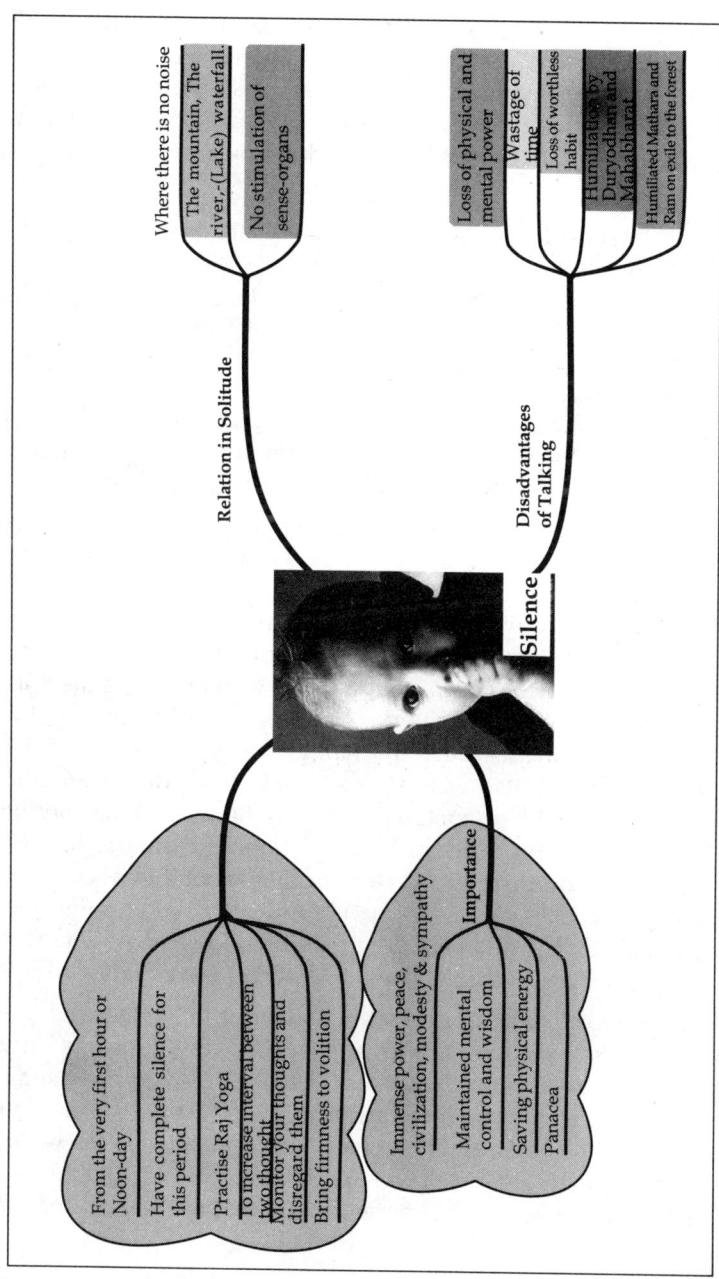

is a point of light, becomes merged in God, who is the Ocean of Love. Like Rargull in sweet sap water. Neutrality and indifference are, too, thought powers which will start to take birth within you. This will prove useful in helping to stop the process of continuous talking which is going on internally and externally.

You have to be in silence for some time and end all your wasteful thoughts. This is possible only when you seriously implement it in your daily life. In this world, all great people that we find are the result of silence. If there are any shortcomings in a successful life, then the only reason is that we have lost the power of silence. You can wash your dirty mind with the pure water of silence. But today, we have lost the art of being silent. We are busy right from morning until night in gossiping. We either talk with others or talk to ourselves.

Before going to sleep at night go into silence and remember God for one hour. Go to sleep in this state of thoughtlessness. It is your dream that spoils your consciousness by waste thoughts. So early morning during sunrise, you can clean your mind by keeping silent and remembering the Ocean of Peace, God. Remember to be in silence while walking along the road or while doing routine work. You may face difficulties in the initial few days because the habit of waste thoughts is not only deep but also vast. Remain calm from the inside and there should be no instability of any thought. You may be anywhere, in the office or in your shop. The minute you are silent, that moment is elevated. In that silent and aware moment bliss will arise within you. Now all types of body consciousness start breaking down. By becoming silent, you will experience soul consciousness and forget your body.

In this world, if there is anything superior to be achieved it is silence. You can reach a higher level of consciousness only when there is complete silence, when all conversation ends, like that silence where far away in the forest all is quiet, no sound of the birds, and no noise of leaves rustling in the wind. You will merge yourself in happiness in union with God. At that moment, you will experience that the soul is the ruler. At this time, the mind becomes charged because it feels that it has gained what it had to gain. You need to become neutral towards your thoughts.

Don't let wasteful thoughts go on in your mind. Whenever you find that wasteful thoughts are going on, then become silent and impartially go on observing them as if small pieces of clouds are floating in the sky. One thing which you will notice is that when you observe neutrally, the mind is engaged in talking but the soul is quietly standing still. In experiencing the state of neutrality, a time will come when your wasteful thoughts will cease. Only then will the birth of thought power and willpower take place. Thought power comes not by thinking, but by ending all wasteful thought.

That is why it is said, O devotees of success and divinity, take a new birth of silence. Bring silence into your being. There lies the supreme kingdom of peace. There flows the wave of happiness. This is the place where there is an unending source of divine power, and by going there all your tiredness and depression will end. Try to forget your relationship with your body and external objects. This silence is very auspicious. The more you go into the depths of silence, the more truthful will be your speech words. You will experience the fragrance of truth. You will also find that whilst talking, your silence is never broken. Once you go into deep silence, then your speech will give off a fragrance, mystery and depth. Initially thoughts arise internally and silence is exhibited externally. Now it will be the other way round, that is, silence will be within and thoughts will be outside. You need to experiment and then you will find that success comes your way. Your way will become your destiny.

True Success

2

True Success

Today's world is a world of science. On the one hand there is the culture and materialistic prosperity of society at its peak and on the other hand, man's character is deteriorating. Man is becoming confused in these new trends of success. Today, a common man measures success in terms of gaining an abundance of wealth, position and fame. Not only are new inventions emerging, but also new desires are becoming a never ending process. People are wandering around because of these unending desires. In order to find true peace and happiness, man becomes crazy and finally is becoming addicted to mental diseases. He is surrounded by depression, disappointment and mental tensions. In order to gain some temporary relief from this he starts to take medications, drugs, etc and in the process of attaining temporary happiness has destroyed his social and moral values. At this stage man has to reincarnate human values for a prosperous and happy society. We have to reflect deeply on this and, in order to attain success in ever changing circumstances one has to work very hard.

The Foundation of Achieving Success

Start using the stock of powers at every second and with every breath. Go on investing your thoughts, power, speech, actions, relationships, etc. in whichever field you wish to achieve success for yourself and for others. Do not let them go to waste. Then you will be experiencing the joy of success. To invest means to be successful in the present and to invest for the future.

Besides material prosperity, the most important is how to increase our mental, moral and spiritual prosperity. We cannot achieve success until our behavior and thoughts become divine in accordance with our pure and elevated goals.

There are obstacles on the path of achieving this success. The most valuable purpose of achievement is related to the development of the human character and the welfare of the world.

One aspect is to achieve success in life and the other is to live a successful life. These two are different aspects. It is not necessary that he who has achieved success in fulfilling mundane desires will be happy and content for ever, neither does it mean that he will be blissful or joyful throughout his life. Let us take an example, suppose a person sets a goal that he has to win a gold medal in the 100m Olympic athletics. He wins this gold medal, but can you tell whether he is full of joy and contented just because of winning this gold medal? Now suppose we assume that he achieves this gold medal at the age of 20, whereas, for in the past 10 years he is working physically hard and thinking that at some point in the future he will achieve success. Now hoping for this, he cannot live happily at that time. For the past ten years he has been postponing his life.

Another stage is that suppose he gets the gold medal, he may experience joy but for how long will this last? He has to maintain this joy until the next Olympic game. To maintain physical and mental fitness until the next Olympic game, with his time, practice and tension. The third stage would be if 1,000 people in the world spent ten years of their lives in attaining this goal, then how many of them will reach their goal? Surprisingly, only one person, the rest would feel deflated and disappointed.

This means of achieving success may be by wealth or position or fame. It is observed that qualities such as self confidence are losing their importance whereas ego is taking its place.

I personally do not think that one should not attain success in this way – life should not be analytical like mathematics, but rather should be filled with beautiful colors to create an artistic picture. It should contain divine music so that it can colour other people's lives and bring them joy.

What is success?

Western and Indian philosophers have given different explanations to the meaning of success.

Henry Ford said, "There is no mystery to success. It expects only excess hard work."

Mahatma Gandhi said, "The mystery of success lies in four means, i.e. intelligence, good character, strength and good behavior."

Swet Modein, "Those who possess hope and self confidence to attain success, only those people can reach the height of success by tolerating all opposition that crosses their path with a smile on their face."

Edison, "If you want to achieve success in your life then make patience your best friend. Experience it as your consultant, precaution as your elder brother and hope as your protector.

Earl Nightingale rightly said, "True success lies in continuous progress toward a set goal."

You can become happy by merely fulfilling all your desires, but this is not success in a real sense because this is related to life. Those who have earned wealth by unrighteous means cannot be called successful. Those who are pessimistic may succeed through wrong activities, they may experience temporary happiness but can never be labeled as successful people. A person cannot be called successful until his life is filled with spiritual values because in this universe the philosophy of karma is filled with justice. Success achieved through wrong means often destroys that person because the universal laws are such that whenever a person wants to achieve success through immoral means, the reward for that action becomes poison. To conclude, it so happens that the whole life of that person becomes poisonous. Whenever we carry out any action it is natural that its seed will first fall on our mind and that seed will also give rise to a banyan tree. We may be compelled to eat those fruits which are hanging on this tree because we ourselves are responsible for its creation.

People receive wealth from an inheritance or by other means. A person cannot be called successful until he strives hard to attain something or unless and until he donates divine and moral values to others.

One is to achieve happiness in life and the other is to live a successful life. These two concepts are different. Still, they have an inverse relationship.

Success has a multi-dimensional meaning. It is decorated with different colours and shapes. Wealth and contentment are its essential elements. In reality, the aim of life is not success, but is a brief pause during the journey of life. These pauses are in the form of achieving material objects and make a person attractive, entertaining, and blissful. There are different dimensions of success which means good wishes for mankind, a loving relationship between two souls, liveliness in life, complete health, positivity, mental strength and silence.

Success means good reward

Our reward should come through effort that creates bliss, happiness and prosperity, not only in ourselves, but also in society. Do such actions through which society receives divine inspiration. At the same time your personality should be full of morality as this gives rise to contentment and happiness. This is the new meaning of success.

Action-reward relationship is a law applicable in this universe. As you sow, so shall you reap. That is why happiness and sorrow depend largely on our actions, emotional action or thoughts. The philosophy of action has another subtle dimension. If you understand the subtle things of your physical and mental strengths and do your work, you will definitely be successful in achieving that set goal. The universal laws are the same for everyone. In spite of this, you will find that one climbs to the peak of the Himalayas and the other is incapable of walking along the road. Why are there thousands of successful people in history? These successful people have been listed because of continuous effort in right knowledge, right thought and right direction. If any person with a burning desire, a great interest and powerful concentration goes on trying, then there will definitely be success. The same laws apply to everyone to gain the power for success. It is not important whether your goal is superior or inferior. But by following the rules, you will definitely gain power.

If we have a spiritual attitude towards a successful life, then by putting in less effort you can achieve success easily. Because by respecting the universal laws we create harmony between ourselves and nature.

There is no alternative to spiritual power to live a successful life or to achieve success in one's life. For this spiritual laws have to be followed in life. First of all we have to understand that our original nature is purity and the source of endless strength. Our valuable consciousness consists of a wonderful balance and harmony between silence, bliss, love, strength and knowledge. The moment we start experiencing our original nature as divine and powerful, our dreams start to come true, because we ourselves are the kings of endless possibilities and unlimited powers.

Many people think that we are unsuccessful because:
- We have taken birth in a poor family
- We are physically unhealthy
- There are others who are more capable than us to complete difficult tasks
- We are handicapped
- Our place in society is not respected.

Those who are never defeated are the ones who become worthy. You are not unsuccessful because there is opposition or circumstances are not in your favour, but rather because your

True Success

Those who are not defeated by defeat, are
alone worthy of a garland

mind is negative which destroys your thought power, intuition, hope, trust and imagination. Let us wake up and take inspiration from those ideal and successful people from society. Sometimes problematic surroundings work as a challenge which strengthens one's powers. This is called the power of transformation. Every one of us has this power secured with them and at the time of need this power automatically arises. At that critical moment you can regain your powerful stage immediately.

Many great people on this earth were from poor families, for example:
1. Abraham Lincoln
2. Ishwarchand Vidya Sagar
3. Vinoba Bhave
4. Hitler

In the 1960s in the athletic competition of the Olympic Games one female who won five gold medals was lame in one leg from childhood. Another famous Indian dancer and film actress "Sudha Chaudran" has an artificial leg. You will be surprised to learn that she maintained her self confidence and received many dance awards from the Indian government.

You must have heard about "Joan of Arc". A simple girl from Gadrea changed the history of France by taking an army under her control. Besides this, the king of that place used to ask for her consent. History has many such wonderful examples.

On the other hand, the majority of people born with a golden spoon in their mouth have destroyed their entire life because of luxury and entertainment. What would you call such people? Lucky or unlucky? However, those people who were born into a poor family have had their names written on a golden page throughout history.

The first formula for success is to set a goal and make a plan of what one wishes to achieve. Secondly, devote the powers of the mind in that direction and you will become successful in achieving it. It can be a goal in the materialist world or spiritual world. Either way the steps would be the same. You have to see in which direction your mental strength is working. Does it want to create a spiritual image, for example, or does it wish to create some artistic painting. In this way, the direction of achieving success and many other things have to be kept in mind.

Soul Analysis

Essentials of a successful life

It is essential to be successful in life. Nutritional food, sleep and exercise are necessary to maintain good physical health. Similarly, self analysis, knowledge of the soul and the practice of meditation are essential for mental wellbeing. Analysis of the soul means that the soul becomes neutral and analytically observes actions of the mind and body. Intellectually most of us know that I am a soul, this is my body. This world is a stage of entertainment. I am immortal, truth and a point of light and this is my body. This knowledge becomes meaningless the moment I start taking the pleasure from the sense organs. At this point in time the true knowledge loses its importance. Now man gets trapped in a world of illusion due to attachment, ego, jealousy, etc. A person cannot correctly analyze himself until he possess a good intellect through true knowledge. Soul analysis is essential for success and progress. Through its process true knowledge, power, understanding, patience and intuition can be gained.

The inner powers are contained within the soul and not in the pleasure of luxuries. We either observe our "soul" or objects and people, or emotions and thoughts. The moment our connection with 'self' ends, we connect ourselves with some other thing outside ourselves, and thereafter we lose our identity of self and become attached to worldly things and subsequently different types of physical, mental and social problems begin to arise.

Today even scientists agree that the universe is not an element but rather an energy. This proves that whatever is visible in this materialistic world is all the outcome of the unseen world. This game of visibility and invisibility is a subtle law which works in favour of nature and human beings.

There is a unique love, unity and order between the energy of nature and a pure soul. The moment you understand this true inner law, you achieve success easily. Here the law which is applicable is to put in less effort. If you implement this law in your daily life your experience will bring your power of purity very close to your soul. We accumulate wealth and maintain relationships because we feel insecure.

While analyzing the soul we must also look to our place within the family and also society. It is possible that others may not correctly evaluate us, but we can evaluate ourselves. Having fewer expectations makes you, in a sense, superior to your family members as you stand in a better place in comparison to your near and dear ones and friends and neighbors, etc. Are you recognized as a polite person, a well-wisher or a good citizen in society? You have to give importance to achieving this image on the path to achieve success.

The Mystery of a Successful and Blissful Life

Accept the challenge

Life is a challenge. People live through old habits which are harmful and sometimes resist change. Progress means to go ahead. For this, the decision to change is most needed. Whenever problems arise in life, a lack of judgment may lead to an increase in the problem. And right judgment at the right time can solve the problem. Accept the challenge to change because it is due to this that all necessary qualities and powers come into one's personality which brings success, courage, self confidence, etc.

In today's cultured society, moral values, spiritual values and a positive attitude are once again gaining importance. Today many people are enjoying luxuries and comforts but are living with greed.

The greed to gain has made the youth of today lose patience and hope because they become unsuccessful in dealing with small problems. The need of the hour is to change our negative thought patterns. The purity of gold is achieved through heating it to a high temperature; to achieve anything one will be put through the furnace.

To be unsuccessful means that you have not used your powers in the right way. However, there is no need to be depressed about this. Obstacles may come on your path to success but you have to accept them as a challenge and draw upon your internal powers.

Failure is a Temporary Means to Analyze the Soul

Swami Vivekananda said, "Do not accept the tension of defeat. Defeat is the beauty of life. It is worthless to live without struggle as this is the poem of life. Do not be too concerned about past mistakes, but set your ideal goal and put in effort to move ahead towards that goal. If you are defeated a thousand times, still try once again."

History holds the names of all those successful people who had faced defeat in the initial stages and later on became successful. It would be unwise to assume defeat at the first attempt. Abraham Lincoln was unsuccessful many times but he did not lose hope. A person can be continuously disappointed, but he should not give up, but with courage and determination he has to keep on trying to achieve success. A stone may not break in the first attempt, but due to continuous hammering it ultimately breaks.

Saint Vishwamitra was defeated several times on his way to becoming a saint but in the end he succeeded. He accepted defeat as a challenge and learnt something from every defeat until he reached the height of success.

Only human beings have been given the boon to think and understand. Undoubtedly, there are other creatures that are physically stronger than human beings. We have to ask ourselves how much are we benefiting from this Godly gift? Very few people think first before they act and later on they repent for their actions. The other type of people are those who do not act until they have thought things through. Life is a mixture of external incidents, circumstances, fate and effort. We cannot postpone our fate and the impact of nature but we can create something like a potter works at his wheel. You cannot prevent famine, earthquakes, disease and accidents but it is not useful to be depressed about these natural disasters. We can at least save ourselves from bad deeds and bad habits.

Once upon a time, two friends were passing through a forest. They heard the roar of a tiger. One of them removed his walking shoes and put on running shoes. The other friend said strangely, "Do you think that you can run faster than a tiger?" The former said, "No, this is not possible but I can definitely run faster than you."

Many times we unnecessarily destroy our powers due to imagination but often our fears are like paper tigers. Today man is going through such tough competition that he needs to con-

We unnecessarily succumb to our imaginary fears and destroy our life powers. In reality they are paper tigers

trol his emotions with willpower. We should learn from every defeat that we have removed one obstacle on the path of success. Are there not thousands of people like Abraham Lincoln, Edison, etc. Did they run away from the defeat? No, they re-evaluated their defeat again and again and achieved success by keeping a positive attitude towards success.

As they became successful, why can't you? There are small obstacles on the path of success, so man takes immoral shortcuts and destroys his valuable life. Can this be called intelligence?

The melodious combination of reward and practice

Each person has an internal desire to successfully attain his goal. But life is a wonderful mixture of success and defeat. You will find defeat coming onto your path again and again but you must not lose your courage. Accept every obstacle as a challenge and entertainment. The measuring stick of success is struggle and practice and this depends upon one's state of mind how each person deals with the challenge.

Fear of defeat

Every moment the ghost of fear chases after us. There are different types of fear such as fear of defeat, fear of death, fear of insult, fear of discomfort, fear of loss in business, fear of insecurity, etc. What will happen then? It does not mean that you following unethical paths such as gambling, smuggling etc.

The attitude of escapism

It is observed that in order to attain our goal we start our work with enthusiasm and excitement but when the cyclone comes in the form of difficulties our courage and patience are overcome. In such a situation, a lack of willpower reduces our courage and patience and we abandon our work and run away.

Besides skill we need self-confidence and courage to become successful in adverse circumstances. Continuous practice and development of helps us to succeed rather than to escape. Maintaining hope alone is not sufficient as we also need firm practice and confidence full of Godly love to bring about success.

If the basis of willpower is moral and spiritual values, then the peak of a prosperous life will be reached. You must have self confidence, willpower, positive thoughts, happiness and constant effort towards your goal. This is the key to your success. Just stay away from negative thoughts and bad company. It is surprising that all of us want to achieve success but we maintain the attitude that if it doesn't happen then what? We don't trust our internal powers. When it becomes your habit or routine to experience happiness, then you can create heavenly bliss in a hell, whereas one who has a depressed mentality will turn heaven into hell. Defeat is nothing other than accepting that you have not put in full effort to achieve success. One who has the determined thought to try once again is guaranteed success. What is the problem in gaining success? Lack of effort and positive thought. So think deeply and you will find that the door of expectation is always open for you. A person should not always show off that he is always successful but after falling down he needs to develop the thought of being success. The goal of a person should be more on how to increase mental happiness rather than success. Because happiness helps in raising peace and concentration and this is essential to achieve success in life.

Keep a Distance from Negativity and Always Maintain Faith in God

"To have faith is to succeed." A person can become wealthy by confidence and courage. Scientific explanations are meaningless without dedication and devotion.

Sometimes on the path of attaining success difficulties may come in the way. Excess struggle is needed in order to remain stable. At that time, encouragement, faith in God and Godly direction is needed. In order to attain success, you have to believe yourself to be an instrument and to surrender your life to God. "Where there is faith, there lies your fortune."

In this universe, each human being and object is unique. You cannot compare yourself to anyone because on the stage of this world, each one of us plays a different part. Whether one is small or large, this attitude is not only imperfect but incorrect too. A person who has a set goal can succeed when he performs better in the present than what he did in the past. He has to keep faith in his dream and desire that he will definitely succeed because God is with us. You may think, "We are weak, but still that doesn't matter because God is our true companion who is almighty." It is definite that the boat of truth on which we are sailing will shake but will never sink. The boatman is God himself. Make sure that no-one defeats our friendship with God. Where there is God, there is definitely success.

Always have positive thoughts such as:
1. We are the sweet children of God.
2. We are the superior creation of the world and so we are great.

3. The form of God is a point of light
4. Elevated thoughts that everyone be happy
5. I am a sweet child of God. I am one of the luckiest people to experience such superior respect and bliss. So I have the right to attain all superior achievements.

God's remembrance can make impossible tasks possible. You will find some wonderful ability within you which makes you achieve success at critical times. Now all your wishes will be fulfilled and your life will be lived in abundance. You can achieve your goal by having strong faith and love in God. The result will be that you will be free from obstacles and problems. A person who has great goals will not only think about his own welfare, but also the welfare of others. People who have superior confidence and surrender themselves definitely receive the blessings of God. Besides this, all Godly powers make his life beautiful and light.

Elevated Work Capacity

"Today people are lazy, not only in terms of acting, but also in thinking. Such people are idle and passive and for them nothing is possible. For them everything is impossible like a fire spreading over a vast area cannot be extinguished by a drop of water. The need is to find out alternative ways to awaken their abilities.

According to Andrew Carnegie, an ordinary man uses 25% of his ability and potential. The world gives regard to those people who use 50% of their abilities and those who use 100% of their abilities become the most famous people.

Psychologists believe that a maximum of 20% of mental powers can be used by each person throughout his life. The reason this does not happen is a lack of knowledge and confidence in these powers. Now the question arises how to develop these powers? For this we have to pay attention to the following points:

1. Work capacity increases due to tolerance and peace of mind.

2. Work capacity increases by maintaining continuity in work. There should be no stress. Select an easy method of doing the work.
3. There is not only one path or one instrument by which you can attain your goal. There are many instruments and many ways. Select that path which is the easiest and this will bring a good results with less effort.
4. To attain the maximum result you have to set the right goal and focus your attention with neutrality.
5. Your result may have an adverse impact due to tiredness. That is why there should be balance between work and rest. You will get good results when you get rid of tiredness and at the same time enjoy the process.
6. Continuous practice becomes a habit or part of our subconscious. Once a habit is cultivated, then work becomes powerful and the result is easily achieved.
7. There must be a balance between physical and mental powers. Physically and mentally one must be fit. On a daily basis create harmony between your physical and mental surroundings so that your workspace is pleasant. If you want to succeed, then you have to learn this art. Don't spend your life expecting some miracle to happen.
8. You should ask one question to all those who have gained a lot from their life whether your work and goals are beneficial. If the answer is yes, then you must leave behind all those activities which pull you down. If you have any doubts then remember you can never attain success.

Success makes your life completely blissful, polite, sweet, tolerant, loveful, merciful and forgiving. Such people know the mystery of life so they put less effort and get good reward. If you want to decorate your future dream through the colour of success, then set yourself small. That day is not far when you will achieve great goals and make your life successful.

Reasons for Success

For any kind of success it is essential to see whether the work is done according to the plan in a proper order. Careful

planning is to be carried out as to what work is to be done first and what needs to be done later. This depends on individual choice as to what is to be given priority.
Tips before going to sleep and whether the order of work is correct or not:
1. Remove all doubt
2. Try to keep a distance from vicious thoughts which reduce courage, otherwise this will become an obstacle on your way to reaching your destination
3. The world neglects those people who are helpless and dependent on others. Successful people are talented and rich people have strong personalities. So if you take on board their qualities this will help you
4. Do not give credence to all those thoughts which you would not like to come true in your life
5. Lack of good judgment is an obstacle in achieving success. The attitude of "Not today, tomorrow we will do this work" does not bring success
6. Less effort in work and more reword should be implemented
7. Learn the art of doing work in a relaxed manner
8. Keep your willpower strong and be confident in fulfilling your goal
9. Keep faith in achieving success rather than having the aspiration
10. Try to fix your goal according to your mind
11. Fix your time within which you can achieve your goal.
12. Make plans to achieve your goal and make effort to make the dream come true
13. Allow a longer time to fulfill large goals and plan to fulfill small goals in a short time.

In order to achieve great goals and lead a superior life one has to give serious thought to the following points:
1. Do not let people with negative thoughts and negative emotions stay around you.
2. Keep a distance from those people who waste your valuable time.

3. Become an expert in the work which you are doing. Do your work so efficiently that no-one else can do it as well as you do.

Hard Work is the Key to Success

Hard work is one of the great religions. This is the direction towards good fortune. Tireless hard work and tolerance is the key to success.

It is through hard work in business that a persons' work proves to be successful. Just as a deer cannot enter into the mouth of a lion who is sleeping, similarly, if you want to climb the ladder of success, you must work hard. Knowledge and meditation cannot be attained without hard work. An ordinary person does not succeed because he tries to escape from hard work. That is why those who love sleep need to open their eyes and work hard. This way you will eliminate all types of poverty. Your hard work should not be aimless and without direction. Many people work hard but they are not successful because they lack the knowledge of how much and when to put the hard work in. Hard work includes 'continuous' work because the formula of success is continuity. Generally, people have the habit of postponing their work. When you postpone the work, you may have to bear a heavy loss. So remember, whatever work you wish to do, do it now.

Hard work

Success cannot be achieved by desire only because this is not a union of the river and the boat. History speaks about all those successful people who have done preparations well in advance. And those preparations include necessary practice, hard work, patience, discipline and surrender. Fate is a shadow of your hard work which stands behind a person with his hands tied. Thus, it can be concluded that hard work is the fastest means through which one can reach his goal.

"A candidate went to a firm for an interview. When the interviewer asked him whether he has any work experience, the candidate replied that he had two years' experience in one of the reputable firms of the city. The interviewer enquired about the correctness of the candidate's experience on the telephone. The employer of that firm said, "It is true that this candidate was with us for the last two months."

The fruit of hard work is sweet. It is always respected.

The fruit of hard work is always sweet. It always gives you respect from others.

Any hard work done with loyalty always gives birth to realization. Guru Nanak rightly said, "If you earn a dry chapatti by hard work, it is equivalent to milk but if you are disloyal and earn porridge, it is equivalent to blood." You will find many people in this world who are very talented but still they remain unlucky. On the contrary, you will find talented people from simple family, who by hard work can attain their fortune. The reason behind this is simply hard work.

Service and cooperation

Why do you feel ashamed about doing hard work? You should experience happiness and be proud of doing hard work in order to achieve your goal. Any hard work done with loyalty gives rise to respect and happiness.

Once upon a time a beautiful palace was being built. One saint was passing through the area. He asked a question to the first worker, "Brother, what are you doing?" The worker replied angrily, "Can't you see that I am breaking stone." The saint smiled and moved forward a few steps and, curiously, he approached the second worker. With a depressed voice he said, "Oh father, hard work is my destiny and for this I am earning my bread and butter." Now the saint walked a few more steps and asked the same question to the third young worker. The third youth had a feeling of happiness on his face and replied, "Oh Father, here a beautiful temple is being built, where every day, prayers and festivals will be celebrated. I hope this auspicious and great work will be completed soon. For this, I am contributing just a small share of my hard work towards this good deed."

Was not the third worker full of self confidence, happy and proud towards his work? Can we take some inspiration from his lifestyle? If so, then definitely you will attain success and divinity in life.

Understanding Behaviour

Good behavior, good wishes and elevated thinking is the highest in the art of living. It is wrong to say that understanding is a sixth sense. Besides academic knowledge, people with understanding have achieved much success by doing wonderful work. Whereas, on the other hand, in the absence of achieving good academic knowledge, they are usually defeated. That is why knowledge is not power in its own right. But much can be achieved through hard effort and experience. You can call those people intelligent who use knowledge in their daily life and become experienced. It is far better to live spiritually for one year rather than to impart spiritual knowledge throughout life. Because the real purpose of knowledge is to bring positive progress rather than to be just knowledgeful because knowledge gains importance only after experiencing it in practical life. In other words, it is just like digesting food. Your understanding increases due to eating the food of positive thoughts and its daily practice such as deep thinking, introspection, analytical thinking, etc.

One who achieves success is in a better position to understand their weaknesses. Unsuccessful people's concentration revolves around their weaknesses. Behavioral understanding means a person who has abundant information about the work, whether it is on physical level or mental level. Besides information he needs to have prior knowledge of the outcome of his work. The more behavioral knowledge a person possesses, the more quickly he can succeed in fulfilling his goal. A person can easily attain success if he possesses behavioral knowledge. If a person has knowledge of different behaviors such as how a person speaks, walks, makes decision, show patience in differing circumstances, how one experiences peace, etc, it becomes easy to achieve success. When a person starts making plans, his knowledge in various aspects enables him to make a proper choice. His intelligence and power of judgment work easily and brings success to that person. A person who possesses behavioral knowledge knows when to remain quiet and when to speak. He knows when to speak sweetly and when he has a right to speak. Similarly, he needs to be knowledgeable about food, such as, which food will benefit his health and which will be harmful. Otherwise, excess food and wrong food makes him fall sick and his valuable time is wasted in finding a cure. All of these routine things of behavioral understanding are essential for success.

Strong Will Power is also Essential in Life

If anyone wants to acquire material comforts, good character and might, then he must possess strong desires.

If any goal has to be accomplished, then it is necessary to have strong desire power. In order to achieve that, a person must be ambitious. However, degraded ambitions bring defeat. So we must have superior and auspicious desires (how desires are deemed good or bad will be explained in the next chapter). It is thoughts which are in the form of desires which emerge in this inner world. They enter into our subconscious mind and create an attitude known as interest. In other words, in order to fulfill that goal, we become engrossed and interested. Now this interest takes the form of action and unwillingly it emerges from the subconscious mind to the conscious mind. Every moment knowingly or unknowingly our subtle emotions, desires, thought power and sense organs of the body exhibit the power of work. But for success, the desire power merges into interest and does its work. This is one internal law of success, which is one of the universal elements of the material and spiritual world.

Desires which seem to be like breath

One youth started having a strong desire to attain God. He placed his wish in front of Saint Farid. It so happened that Saint Farid used to neglect his request with a smile. But he could not postpone the repeated requests made by the youth. So one fine day the Saint took him to Sarovar River to bathe. Both of them were bathing close to each other. After a few seconds, they went into deep water and suddenly the saint pushed him under the water. The youth found it difficult to breathe as he was trapped in the water by the saint. He tried his level best to come out of the water, but all his efforts were in vain. Then suddenly the youth kicked the saint and came out of the water. After breathing for a few seconds, the youth said, "Oh Saint, you seem to be a murderer. Today, it would have been my funeral. You wanted to destroy my goal of attaining God but I am surprised as to why you have done this? The Saint with a smiling face said, "Forget this topic."

First of all tell me which thought was going on in your mind when you were under the water. The youth said, "All my thoughts became passive. I had only one thought as to how I could gain my breath. And I gave my last bit of energy to try to come out of the water at any cost." The Saint said, "The day when you have the same determined thought to acquire God, that day you will succeed in achieving your goal. So implement this valuable formula in your life to achieve success. Now start increasing this thirst of attaining God."

A temperature of 100 degrees cannot create vapour to pull the engine of a train, it requires 212 degrees boiling water so that vapour is created out of the high temperature. Similarly if you want to achieve anything in life, you must have a strong, burning desire. Then let your goal be spiritual or scientific, but the rule applicable would be the same.

New Meaning of Success – Right Character

The strength of a tower depends upon its foundation. Similarly, the foundation of a successful life is good character. Character is a combination of power and good character. Just like a magnet, it attracts friends and relatives and shows a happy path to a successful life.

Rabindranath Tagore said, "The transformation of character is not due to excellence but due to Raj Yoga."

Agyat said, "Character is like a diamond which cuts different edges of a stone. A person having a good character always goes straight towards his goal."

A good society is formed because of good people and finally gives rise to a good culture. Now the question arises as to how we can create good people. Whereas in today's world we find that changes are rapidly taking place, we find human values and character are losing their importance. All of us desire to see good character in each individual, but still a good culture is missing. The politicians talk about many things but achieve little. The worst condition of our society and country as told by many thinkers is "lack of good character." Today we find material progress and wealth is necessary for man's luxurious lifestyle. And why shouldn't it be necessary? But a few great well wishers of the world are fearful thinking that this good culture may be destroyed due to the degraded character of man.

Today everywhere we find degraded cultures in the form of dishonesty, violence, corruption, crime, robbery, disloyalty, sex lust, greed, jealousy, etc. The concept of success has changed. Now a person wants to achieve success by different means. It can be for wealth, position, fame, etc. But its outcome is unlimited grief. In reality, man is in sorrow and does not have peace of mind. He was not so unhappy a few years ago. You will not find a single person who is free from stress. Man is full of anger, jealousy, ego and the day is not far off for the occurrence of the Third World War. Just think, if your culture is destroyed then what will be the use of your success?

Firmness alone is the key to success. The quality of leadership is contained within it.

You have achieved success but did you overcome your sorrow? Most of your answers would be 'no'.

The key to success is willpower. The quality of leadership is included in this.

Now the need of the hour is to substitute the old concept of success by a new concept. It is necessary to attain success in building a progressive and ideal character. The primary and utmost necessity is how to create good qualities in an individual. Behind every attainment, work and effort, there should be high spirituality and moral values and this should be a rule. If we set our goal for the creation of good character, and if we strive hard to succeed in achieving this goal, then definitely we will not only attain material prosperity, but also experience true happiness, bliss and peace.

Cultivate good character for success

Success is not possible without good character. Because without good character, the height of success is like that of a vulture who flies high in the sky but whose eyes are always on the flesh on the land.

After studying the biographies of all great people of the world, one quality which is common in all of them is self respect. In spite of opposition in life, they never lost their self respect. They accepted many inconveniences in life and lacked material happiness but never compromised their self respect. This is the reason why people respect their calm personality.

Generally, it has to be observed that many people reach the height of success by doing work dishonestly. But a time comes when they are destroyed. If success is a tower standing on the foundation of immorality and lack of character, then soon it will crash. If you have attained any great vision in your life, then there is no other option left other than self respect. So remember one thing, that if you ever aspire to achieve success then never compromise this quality.

Imshurn said, "Happiness is the fruit of man's good character."

Romon said, "Character is the only indicator of success or defeat. If the character is good, then life will move towards success. On the other side if the character is bad then success will slip away."

Mahatma Gandhi said, "The greatness of a man can be judged by his character and not by his clothes."

Ramkrishna Paramahamsa said, "If flowers are given a chance to blossom, then automatically honey bees are attracted towards them. Be of good character and the whole world will be attracted towards you."

Swami Vivekananda said, "Our foremost and utmost necessity is good character."

Abraham Lincoln said, "Character is a tree and fame is its shadow. Whatever we think about, that is our shadow because the reality is the tree."

What is an ideal character?

A person whose speech, mind, actions, relationships, etc are full of divinity and who is full of truth and self confidence, such an individual's behaviour reflects social service for the world and is known as a person of good character. On the basis of these values, whatever you attain is known as true success.

When you study the biography of all great people of the world, one quality that you will find in them is self respect. They had serious problems in their lives, but still they never lost their self respect. They had many problems such as poverty, lack of luxuries ad comforts, etc, but still they never compromised their self respect. This is the reason why today their names are taken with great respect and dignity.

It may so happen that you succeed in buying a car but at the same time it is important to use it. But it is more important to give attention to its maintenance. In the same way, in order to attain success in any way, one needs to be of good character. This can be compared with the maintenance of the car as character is just like gold which needs to be tested in times of

difficulties. The gold has to undergo intense heat in order to prove its purity. If it contains some alloy then it burns into ashes. In the same way, during difficult times your character becomes stronger. Otherwise, it would shatter into pieces. The qualities of good character are:
1. Purity
2. Patience
3. Tolerance
4. Simplicity
5. Merciful
6. Politeness
7. Truthfulness
8. Self Introspection, e.g. positive thoughts and self analysis
9. Self confidence

Self respect

Sabet Modern said, "If you reflect you will understand that successful people become great only due to good character."

A person who lacks good character in his personality can never attain success. All great thinkers of this world, especially Indians, have spoken about the importance of developing good character. Success does not mean just accumulating wealth or attaining a high position. It is a fact that without patience, hard work and willpower, attainment is impossible. But today, people of our society are attaining their vision by the wrong method like foul play. It is better not to inculcate these divine values rather than to compromise them on a low level game. The consequence of this type of attainment would be very dangerous. Do you think you would have contentment, true happiness or true peace of mind? Experience says that it is impossible. On the contrary, the realization of the offence will make you feel inferior from within. Your personality would become a dual one. You would lead an uncertain life between these two dual faces. Therefore, you must inculcate divine virtues so that your personality becomes a lighthouse to inspire others.

Courage and patience

Where the River Ganga originates from the River Gangotri, on its way it creates innumerable scenes and melodious music around it. Sometimes in the form of beautiful waterfalls music sounding murr .... Murr... kal kal... You do not find this on flat land. Whilst flowing it dashes against so many rocks and creates this beautiful scene. This truth is also applicable in our flow of life where we need patience and courage.

Courage means not to be disturbed by the ups and downs of life while completing a task. Many times the circumstances are so difficult that a person loses courage and leaves the work incomplete. Now he thinks that he cannot work hard any more. He starts doubting his abilities which makes him depressed. In such circumstances he leaves the work and runs away. He loses the capacity to head on and loses courage which makes him unsuccessful. One who does not accept defeat in spite of a thousand times being defeated; he is the one who has an abundance of self confidence. Success touches the feet of those who have full faith in their physical and mental abilities. Therefore, courage is the most important quality amongst all.

If you take the first step of courage, you receive full help from God.

Mahatma Gandhi said, "Courage and patience are such qualities which are very much needed at the time of difficult circumstances."

Ingar Sole said, "If you tolerate defeat without becoming depressed, it is the greatest examination on this earth."

Shakespeare said, "Taking revenge is not courageous, but tolerance is a courageous task."

Patience is essential for success

Until a person does not have devotion, faith and knowledge within him, he cannot attain patience and self control. And until he attains this self control he cannot attain spirituality in his life.

Once upon a time a saint wanted to test the patience and abstinence of a disciple, who was staying in Ashrama for a few years. One fine day the disciple was called by the Saint who gave him a closed box and gave the instruction to hand it over to the other person. On his way, the disciple could not keep control of himself and he opened the box to see what was inside. A small rabbit leapt came out of the box and ran away. On finding the box empty, the man said, "Oh disciple, I am sorry to say but you no longer have the chance for the last initiation. This is what happened when he came back the Saint with a smile said, "Oh disciple, go from here and do not return until you succeed completely in your self control." Deeds are in our hands but the fruit is created due to many opportunities. That is why different deeds produce different fruits at different times. Man has to wait with patience. Today is a world of science where the speed of every task is very fast. The result is also exceptionally good. But one wrong consequence of this is impatience and restlessness. If you want to increase the speed of work or enjoy the fruit, then you must have the quality of patience. When you are aware that in the corporeal world every action has its fruit, so it would be foolishness to lose patience and peace of mind to get easy fruit. Nature also teaches us the lesson of patience: It takes 3-4 months for green leafy vegetables to grow. It takes much longer for a mango tree or coconut tree to produce fruit, maybe a few years. So until then these trees have to be patiently taken care of. Even the medicines take some time to have their impact. After you eat your food, it takes some time to digest it to form blood and energy. In other words, to lose patience is to lose peace. And one who loses peace of mind destroys his whole life. So do not see your life like instant tea or coffee.

Let the fruit of your actions work with patience. Do not become impatient and eat the fruit unripe. The consequence would be stomach ache and pain. The medicine of every hurt is patience.

Sheikh Saddi said, "Patience is the gateway to your goal because without patience there is no other door."

Bhartuhari Nitishtak said, "One whose nature is patience does not become impatient at the time of a disaster."

Plots said, "If you inculcate patience at the time of a disaster then you have won half the battle."

Yog Vasishtha said, "Man cannot get rid of a disaster without patience."

Vanbhatt Kadambari said, "The only wealth of a gentleman is patience."

Benjamin Franklin said, "One who has the quality of patience can attain any desire he wants."

Obstacles to Success - Greed

Where desire has an important place in fulfilling a goal, greed arises and this destroys a person's life. If desires elevate one's life, then it is good.

Bhartri Hari rightly said, "The person in whom greed is already present, there is no need to have any other bad quality." A saying goes, "Greed is the father of all sin." Mahatma Buddha said, "One who is trapped in the net of greed does violence, gambling corruption, lies and motivates others to do the same. That is why greed is the root cause of all problems." According to Swami Vivekananda, "Greed destroys your intellect and then you feel ashamed. When you feel ashamed, your religion is destroyed and then your wealth and happiness are also destroyed."

Sheikh Saddi said, "A person becomes a fool due to greed. A greedy person may conquer the whole world but still may remain hungry. But a contented person may satisfy his hunger by eating one chapatti."

Ramcharit Upadhyay says, "The father of all sin is greed. There is no bad deed which is not carried out by a greedy person."

Today people's mentality is to become a millionaire overnight. Now this is impossible for a person possessing a good character. This will only be possible for those who live an immoral life performing actions such as stealing, corruption, gambling, black marketing and hoarding wealth, etc. The consequence of greed is very dangerous. Today whatever turmoil we see is a result of greed. You can fill your stomach but how much does a man need to survive?

How much land does a man need?

Once upon a time, a Saint stayed in a farmer's home overnight. During the conversation, he came to know that the farmer is a poor man. The Saint said, "Oh farmer, I am aware of a place where you can get a huge plain of land at a reasonable price. At the same time, the fertility of that land is also very good so you can sell your land and go there." The farmer thought for a while and placed his proposal in front of the villagers who said, "You give all your money and you can keep as much land as you want after sunrise and before sunset. The only condition is that the place from where you start walking, you have to reach that exact spot before sunset." Now the whole night he was making plans as to what area he would cover, the speed at which he would walk and so on.

The next day the villagers wished him good luck and he started on his journey. He thought for a while that if he walks he cannot cover a large area, so running would be a better option. He started to run and very soon it was 12 o'clock. He became totally exhausted through running and thought of returning. He became more greedy and thought that the area ahead of him is more pretty. He thought that he could cover more area and that it is only today that he has to work hard and tomorrow he would be able to take rest. He forgot his ability and due to greed started running faster than before. It was 2.00pm and he thought of returning but did not have the desire to do so. He was completely exhausted. Still he managed to run and gave up the idea of food and water thinking why should I waste my time eating. He thought that only today he would be hungry and the rest of his life his stomach would be full. The sun was about to set and he was becoming tired and nervous. Now he could hear the cheers of the villagers but unfortunately the farmer collapsed before reaching his destination. He struggled hard to get on his knees and just as he was about to reach his destination the sun had already set. He lost his promise completely. His last breath was in vain and due to the strain his heart failed. All the people of the village were making fun of him saying that there is no limit to the mad people on this earth.

Remember one thing, that no-one can become the owner of this land. This is the story of an ordinary man who keeps running from morning until night and runs throughout his whole life. Tomorrow we will live but today let us credit some money into our bank account. Let us own some more land. Tomorrow we will live and tomorrow never comes. Regardless of whether he is rich or poor all die because of unfulfilled desires. No-one leads a complete and full life. For this, one needs little rest, little peace of mind, little understanding and some realization that "I am a soul, I am a child of God and thus bliss, silence, etc are my true nature." The world can give me wealth, luxuries and comforts but not true happiness. Just think how much do you want?

Responsibility

The attitude of accepting responsibility builds good character. When a person sets a goal and endeavours to strengthen his willpower he has to face various difficulties in the form of unexpected challenges. The moment he accepts this challenge there arises an inner power which helps him to reach his goal easily. This is the internal realization which creates a picture of a responsible character. The realization of success builds self confidence in a human being. This inner quality helps him to achieve success in order to complete great tasks He becomes an ideal in front of the whole of humanity and feels blessed. This state of mind is the superior contentment, bliss and happiness.

One who fulfills his own responsibility without any excuses or without blaming others and accepts his work becomes great. In this context, the Prime Minister of Britain, Winston Churchill rightly said, "The price of greatness is responsibility".

John F. Kennedy said, "Our rights cannot be greater than our responsibilities. Our security of rights cannot be greater than the fulfillment of our responsibilities."

Albert Hobward said, "Responsibilities are attracted towards that person who can carry them on his shoulders."

We have to first understand our responsibilities and then implement them. Responsibility becomes our moral duty and should be:
- Towards society and the nation
- Towards office staff and business partners
- Towards the family
- Towards the environment and pollution
- Towards oneself

When we blame others for our mistakes our problems increase several times. When we start making the same mistakes, then comes the need to accept responsibility. Now comes the turn to change ourselves. In reality, the status of our deeds is higher than our rights. But today people have misused their rights and have failed to do divine deeds due to an egoistic nature. Sooner or later his rights will also be snatched away.

Due to a lack of responsibility the strong character of a person does not come in front of the world and he does not realize his inner capabilities. And finally this type of person spends his whole life in fulfilling the goals of others. By doing so, he ends his freedom of thought.

In Africa, while Mohandas Karamchand Gandhi was traveling, if British people had not insulted him, then he would not have been called the Nation's Father, Bapu. In spite of having first class ticket, he was forcefully thrown out of the first class compartment by the British. When he was thrown onto the platform this insult and injustice gave rise to an inner energy which he used to liberate Indians from the British. This strong challenge made him more responsible towards his work and attain his goal. That is why he has been designated the highest post and proudly called the Father of the Nation.

If you spend your life in doing trivial work you will be deprived of those wonderful powers and your incomplete life would be spent in an ordinary way. The moment you think of taking up work, the first thought that comes to your mind is how to complete this work. Right from the planning stage through to completion of the work our inner power shows us the path at every step. If you have a strong willpower such as "I have to do it", then you will receive guidance from your inner mind. Then, depending on the type of challenge, power will emerge. Every individual has some secured powers in him, which emerge automatically at the time of need. Let us take the example of a female monkey. In ordinary circumstances you can handle monkey with a small stick and succeed in making her run. But if it is a question of the young monkey's security then the mother may put her life at risk and try her best to keep her children safe.

This incident is a true story. When a small baby screamed, her mother ran towards her. She found the baby under a vehicle. When the mother saw the baby she lifted the vehicle up to save the baby. It was difficult for the mother to lift up the baby from the upturned vehicle. When a neighbour asked the mother how it was possible for her to lift the heavy vehicle, the mother replied, "I am totally ignorant of how this became possible." This was an inner strength which came out at a time of need. This strength is visible and contained in everyone and anyone can evoke it.

In this way, it can be either the parents towards their children or husband towards his wife or any other independent person towards another they become so responsible in these circumstances that even at the cost of their own life they give help. The sense of responsibility at that time gives rise to wonderful inner power. In this way, success gives rise to self confidence and self confidence builds courage to take up any responsible work and this courage helps in winning great challenges. And it is success which builds self confidence and this cycle goes on repeating in one's life. This way a person becomes successful in attaining his life's great purpose.

Throughout history we have many examples of such great

people who succeeded in overcoming many great hurdles. A few of them had a unique experience. According to these unique categories of people, it was not until everything was snatched away from them and when all doors of help closed upon them that they realized their inner powers. There were a few who became beggars but who once again realized the powers within themselves and once again became wealthy.

The crown of responsibility

Sometimes it is observed that when a person is given some responsibility, then the capability comes to him which was totally absent before. If at any point in your life you have to accept any responsibility then accept it without any hesitation. It may happen that you will have some bitter experience at the initial stage but if you fulfill the role successfully then definitely you will experience wonderful happiness and self confidence. So always be responsible towards your vision and you will find success is always yours.

Qualities of a responsible Person

The greatest quality of a responsible person is that he always admits or accepts his mistake. And he always tries to learn from it rather than rectify it. If any person becomes indifferent towards his mistakes or weaknesses, then throughout his life he will be making the same mistakes in different ways. These small mistakes may become a major problem in the future by wasting his time and energy.

A generous person accepts all his responsibility as challenges and accepts them as a divine task. The love which is gained from responsibility not only brings contentment and happiness, but also brings courage to bear the problems and dangers. A coward or weak and lazy person never takes up any kind of responsibility and keeps on waiting for a favourable atmosphere.

What is Self-Confidence

Sukti said, "If you want to complete any difficult work you must have a wonderful inner capacity and complete trust in your courage, for only then can it be called Self-Confidence. But one who has the capacity to complete the work in opposing circumstances is known as a confident person."

Ramdhari Singh Dinkar said, "Don't give importance to what others speak and think about you, but what you think and know about yourself is more important."

Aesop said, "If you equate self-confidence to mustard, then no work will be impossible for you."

You will find many people making such statements as 'if we had enough wealth or a particular quality or a strong family background, then even we would have done this work so beautifully that others would have admired it." Such people are not only lazy but also dependent on their fate. In reality, if you want to reach a goal you must possess the necessary qualities, powers and self-confidence. Self confidence is that magic which attracts all necessary objects towards itself. You will find many such confident people in history that had started their journey from poverty and became wealthy. You will definitely find many people in different areas whether it be education, art, music, spirituality or science or philosophy who had great powers of self confidence that the work which appeared to be impossible was made possible. When they had decided to start a task they completed it without giving a second thought to their mind. Though the atmosphere in which they were working was not conducive, still they did not give up. Because it is self confidence by which we can test our power of inspiration and find out how strong we are internally.

In this world you will come across many such people who have the capacity and ability to perform the work. It is not that they are incapable of doing the work, but rather that they lack confidence in themselves. On the other hand, there is another category of people who do not possess many qualities and capabilities but still they are able to complete the work. The only reason for this is self confidence which makes up for the lack of other qualities.

Man has a stock of unlimited powers, knowledge, superior qualities and character. Let us take the example of an iceberg which floats in the sea. You can only see 10% of it on the surface whilst 90% is merged in the water. Psychologists also believe that 10% of one's mind is conscious through which man thinks and carries out his work. The remaining 90% is the sub conscious mind. There are the powers present in our

If we move from doubt and lack of faith and work with self-confidence then success is certain.

subconscious mind which allow us to discover new things. Mind contains a stock of different powers. The need of the hour is to discover those essential qualities and passive powers so that you may become self confident. Guru Gobind Singh said, "One who can fight equivalent to one lakh can truly be called Gobind Singh."

Success is definite if you overcome your doubts and work with self confidence.

Let us look at the self confidence of that saint from Sabarmati who liberated India from slavery.

Wasn't Swami Vivekananda's devotion strong since he was full of self confidence? The same Kanyakumari which you visit to see Vivekananda Rock, Swami Vivekananda used to cross those high waves and meditate on that rock. If you go there you will find that this work would have been impossible without courage and self confidence.

Shivaji also destroyed the Mughul Empire on the basis of self confidence and established the Maratha Empire. Indian Nightingale Lata Mangeshkar had to struggle hard in the initial days of her singing. It was on the basis of self confidence that she reached the peak of success.

According to a report published in India Today, you will be surprised to learn of the self confidence of a handicapped female designer who had a broad smile on her face. She had two arms hanging from her shoulders. In spite of having this disability, she designed beautiful saris. It is none other than Ila who had set herself as an example in front of the world.

Amongst three children, Ila Bhavnagar, a 26 year old, was the eldest daughter of a farmer. She used to do all her routine work by her legs as taught by her parents from childhood. She was struggling hard right from her infancy and could only receive her education up to higher secondary level. In the meantime she became a genius in gaining the skill of designing from her mother and grandmother.

For the first ten years she was doing the work for fun. Later on she took this work seriously. It is difficult to narrate 26 years of her struggle in life.

It was possible for her to show her artistic talent with bed sheets, cushion covers, pillow cases, dress design and wall design. These were the areas in which she used to decorate. The talent which she had in her gave her a golden chance to visit foreign countries to attend art exhibitions. A few years ago, she received an award from our President. She received rewards from different areas too and became a source of inspiration in front of the whole world because of her dedica-

//True Success//

tion, self confidence, willpower and hard work.

People should learn the skill of discovering their inner powers. Success will be guaranteed if you discover those vast and great powers. For this, you have to become introvert. It is necessary to study the biography of those great and successful people who were full of self confidence. If they could reach their goal due to self confidence then why can't you? God has given the same gift of nature to everyone.

If you look at all the successful people in the world you will find that the one thing they all had in common was self confidence. Though the circumstances were not in their favour, still they accepted the challenge and set an example of bravery. Firstly they had great vision and secondly the circumstances were against them. You may not have entering into such opposing circumstances in your own life. If not, then why are you so depressed and disappointed? Forget disappointments and bad luck and work hard with willpower. Go through the biographies of a few great men who were successful, Prime Minister of England, Benjamin Disraeli, America's famous politician, Daniel Webster and famous artist, Michael Angelo.

Do you lack education? There is no need for tension. If you have a shortage of wealth, still it does not matter. You need not be disturbed if you are not famous. We find people who did not have any of these things, but still on the basis of self confidence they attained their goal. If you want to achieve your vision then you need to have a burning desire. You can make it possible by willpower, self confidence and patience. You will come to see the wonderful truth. Your inner and outer powers will unite with each other. All of your invisible powers will attract like a magnet to bring you success which will strengthen your effort. This is the help offered by God.

All those invisible things which could not be seen through these eyes will be seen clearly as and when we get in contact with invisible mental powers. People must come out of confusion and doubt and invest their time in building strong self confidence.

There is no limit to such type of people who are cowards as well as unsuccessful who give negative suggestions to other hardworking people. Very often you will find them saying, "Oh brother, this is not as per your talent. You lack capacity and ability which are present in successful people." Such people always blame God and their fate for no reason. They fail to evaluate the cause of defeat because the efforts which were needed were not there. A self confident person must reject all these weak suggestions boldly. A day will come when these people will be impressed by your confidence and abilities and will be inspired.

Napoleon has proven that if you have the power of self confidence then you can make a mountain appear like a mustard seed. He showed bravery by climbing on the peak of mountains though he had to tolerate snow and blizzards. If he would have listened to his weak advisor, then he could not have become so famous in this wonderful achievement. Remember whatever you do, looking at you, others will also follow. If you are full of self confidence, then the same atmosphere will be created around you because our thoughts and emotions automatically spread and enter into other people. That is why your self confidence becomes inspirational for others.

Self confidence means to have faith in inner powers. Swami Vivekananda said, "One who lacks self confidence, how can he keep faith in other things." This is the basis of our progress. When you find your friends are not helping you then meet your inner friend known as self confidence. You will get an answer, 'yes' every time. The flow of activeness towards work automatically turns towards a self confident person. A self confident person is always enlightened as he continually projects noble thoughts. Go on throwing out defeat and difficulties. Light is protected by glass in the form of positive thoughts so that the cyclone in the form of wasteful thoughts blows away. Your life will be full of enlightenment reflected in this glass.

Bal Gangadhar Tilak said, "Let people make fun of our

thoughts but if we have complete self confidence then we can make people feel ashamed. Until we have self confidence we cannot do anything in this world."

Just think, it has been more than 50 years to the day since this statement was made by him with self confidence. Today we find this dream coming true. We find people going into space. You are flying better than any bird, you are swimming at a depth of the ocean better than fish and you are climbing on the peak of the Himalayas. For this one needs to have self confidence. Today effort is being made to send and receive information by telepathy by sitting in space, because if there are technical faults there would be no communication with those who have gone to other planets.

Misuse of Powers on the Path of Success - Miracles

It depends upon yourself as to whether you would like to use your powers for receiving auspicious fruit or to fulfill your inferior desires. All successful people to date had a subtle attraction somewhere in the corner of their mind for either material or immaterial attainments. Those who have not understood the significance of inner divine powers or those who have lost moral and spiritual values for the sake of satisfying their ego have destroyed their life. Such people believe in magic and become jugglers in making their life miserable. Now this can be made clear from an illustration so that you can know the different dimensions of every accomplishment and become successful in attaining your vision.

Ways to attain magical powers

The truth behind attaining success in any work is its principle. The powers can be either materialistic or non-materialistic, body, wealth and mind may be related to science, but the basis of attaining all powers is only through concentration. This is largely known as mental powers or thought power. The only formula of devotion is concentration. In the past many sages of the Vedic Yuga had discovered formulas to attain mental powers by concentration so that a healthy mind or beautiful ideal society could be created. It is through this concentration that good character of a person is created. But due to the passage of time, this important formula went into the hands of a few selfish people. Such people started a new path away from social life. Even in Buddhism there was a separate path followed by lamas. These were collectively known as the hymn path, mantra path, fearful path, etc. We are not going to discuss all this in detail. Such people perform hymns or rituals to gain powers by concentration and later on misuse them for selfish means. This leads to a depressed life rather than a successful one.

Which is preferable, power or purification?

If a person gains power before purifying his inner mind, then people generally call it devilish power. Purity means purity of soul, sweetness and softness. After attaining these qualities, the power achieved by a person is known as divine power. In Jainism there are two types of meditation. One is irreligious meditation and the other is religious meditation which is also known as concentration of auspicious thoughts. Irreligious meditation means concentration on impure thoughts. If your inner mind is not pure then you are bound to misuse your powers.

Here is an illustration. Most of you must have heard of Rasputin from Russia who had a very strong mind. He had attracted Tsars as well as their wives completely. He had complete control of the kingdom of Tsar. Tsar had only one son who was always sick. Rasputin, with the help of thought power, cured this boy. He had attained all these powers through past meditations and from a Lama of Tibet by great devotion. But he lacked purity of the soul. The main reason for the downfall of Russia and Tsar was misuse of power and an impure mind. Another reason for success achieved by Lenin's revolution was because of misuse of power. It is said that after the revolution when he was sentenced to death he was made to drink poison which could take the lives of 500 people. But surprisingly, he did not even faint. He was shot with 20-22 bullets, but still he did not die. Afterwards he was tied to a stone and thrown in the Volga river. Surprisingly when his dead body was sent for investigation to a doctor, he had rescued his soul from the body. You can estimate how much power he had accumulated through concentration. But the tragedy is that he had not purified his mind. Such a powerful person was destroyed because of a lack of purity of mind.

It is meaningless to gain magical powers without purity of mind

It is important to have purity of mind before attaining magical powers. Inner purity is an important part of our devotion. That is why Buddha told his disciples to inculcate four qualities – mercy, friendship, sweetness, equality. Patanjali also highlights these qualities for purification of heart. Restraint, rules, asanas, pranayama, self denial. After that he discussed dharna, meditation and Samadhi. God has taught us Raj Yoga meditation. He has emphasized the importance of the purity of the soul, not magical powers. God has placed more emphasis on purification of attitude, food, mind and thoughts. If a devotee attains magical powers before purifying his soul, then what would be the consequences? This can be clear from the example given below. We asked one person if he attained such powers that all his wishes came true or he could become invisible, then what work would he do? He started smiling and said, "First of all I would bring money from the bank by becoming invisible. And secondly, I would put aside any man who would become an obstacle." I kept on listening and he went on relating this as he talked about the fulfillment of all his desires which were related to the vices such as lust, anger, attachment, greed and ego. Then I said, "Oh friend, you have not said that you would become invisible to heal people or offer water to thirsty people or give peace to a peaceless soul." He really felt ashamed. I reflected on this thinking, "How strange, you have an impure mind." Just think for a while, who has conquered all the vices that if one attains magical formulas then how much good and how much bad would he do.

The universal truth for man's upliftment is his positive thoughts and success in elevated actions. but we have to keep a distance from such magical powers. We must concentrate on the point of light and positive thoughts. The power of positive thinking which arises from concentration gives rise to peace and divinity. Man will attain the goal of deitism. Until these divine qualities and powers change our behaviour we must not be attracted by these magical powers.

It is through our actions that we should lead an elevated life so that in the near future in the golden world life will be complete. Just as a person whose life and thoughts are surrendered for the wellbeing of others, they attain these magical powers in the form of a gift from God. Then, like God, these souls use their powers for the benefit of others and do selfless service. Lack of inner purity along with magical powers brings happiness to a lesser degree but remembrance of God, Godly service, supreme knowledge, and divine virtues can bring unlimited immortal happiness. Why do they think about happiness in a limited way. At the end of Kaliyug it is a million times better to attain happiness derived from union with God.

Hope for Life

Sri Mannarayan said, "Let clouds spread over the sky, but the brightness of one light is enough to spread light everywhere. This is the light of hope on the world. Man is one of the beautiful creatures on this earth. This world is a garden and man is a fragrant flower who is beautiful and has a wonderful fragrance and with this sweet vibration always maintains hope. But it is our bad luck that, instead of life being a beautiful garden, it becomes a jungle of thorns, a jungle full of violent attitudes. And many times life becomes hell. You must have heard about people saying "What is the use of repenting after the birds have entered the plain." We become helpless and compelled to see our tragic life getting ended.

Positive thoughts are nectar for a passive life and hope is its heartbeat.

Your life is God's gift on this earth. Your life is not only valuable for yourself but for the universe also. So decorate this life with the light of a pure intellect. Become an inspiration by filling the colours of divine qualities and spread the fragrance of a divine and blissful life. Never lose hope in life, though you may get disappointments. Always sow seeds of divine qualities and positive thoughts on the fertile land of the mind, then you will find your life becoming valuable. So remember that the foremost inner quality and power for a successful life is complete faith in hope.

Become a tower of inspiration

Create an atmosphere of awareness and alertness. You are aware of this truth that, "whatever you give, you get several times more in return. " Only one who has a stock can donate. This stock can either be divine qualities or wealth. I strongly believe that on this earth the definition of a wealthy person would be one who has an abundant stock of positive thoughts, positive emotions, vitality and hope.

The pillar of success – hope

Agyat says, "A hopeful person always looks for solutions to every problem, whereas a depressed person finds a problem in every situation."

In spite of being defeated again and again the desire to strive hard to attain the desired goal is known as 'hope'. Happiness occupies a very important place in one's life. This happiness can be derived either from the senses or mental bliss or by experiencing the soul. People generalize happiness as a life filled with luxuries and comforts. Whenever a person finds some kind of obstacle on his path of achieving his goal, he finds that he is incapable of overcoming that obstacle with little effort, and feels that it is not in his capacity or thinks that others are more capable than himself or that his luck is not in his favour, etc. The conclusion is that this weak attitude shatters his hope and he becomes depressed thereafter.

Depression brings dangerous results in one's life. A depressed person is already dead before real death knocks at his door.

Depression pushes the person into a well of tension and destroys all beauty of his life by making his life full of ugliness. His willpower and determination get shattered into small pieces. All his vitality, awareness and cheerfulness fade away and before time his wonderful youth finishes.

Depression is a delusion

Mahatma Gandhi said, "Hope is important and devotion for it never goes to waste."

Overcome the attitude of depression from now on. This is the darkness of ignorance. Darkness does not have its own identity. Brightness has its own identity. Do you have to put in effort to destroy the darkness from a closed dark cave which has been closed for a thousand years? No. You simply have to light a candle to destroy the darkness as it has a unique place in one's life and has its own unique quality. You can take it anywhere with you. Still a lack of brightness is the result of darkness. Many times you see a rope at night time and believe it to be a snake and become fearful. Darkness not only creates fear but also destroys ability to see things clearly. This results in wrong judgment and leads to the wrong result in life. For instance, if you insert a straight stick into water it appears bent. If you take it out of the water it remains straight.

A person having hope definitely reaches his goal; let the sun of hope shine in your life and let no clouds of depression come in your way. For this you have to be ever aware.

"This will also change." Once upon a time there was a king of Bulk. He called a famous goldsmith in his kingdom and said, "Make a beautiful finger ring for me and write a beautiful sentence which will be helpful to me in any circumstance. But remember one thing that a ring should be inside a small box so that at any time it can be opened and read. In other words, the valuable statement would be closed within that small box.

The goldsmith returned to his home and thought deeply as to what was to be written on the ring. He could not find a solution to his problem. One fine day a Muslim saint came to his kingdom. On hearing the news of this Muslim saint, the goldsmith rushed towards him and presented his problem to the saint who whispered something in the king's ear and with great joy the goldsmith offered the finger ring to the king.

Unfortunately, some other king had conquered his kingdom. Besides defeat, Ibrahim had to run away from the war in order to save his life. But some soldiers of the enemy were chasing him. How was it possible for a depressed and tense king to save his life? This thought caused his horse and solders to hide behind a mountain. Suddenly he remembered the ring which he had received from the goldsmith. He opened the box and read the sentence written on it which read "He will also be transformed."

The king felt a ray of hope in his depressed state of mind. He realized that man must not lose hope at any cost. Then all the soldiers of the enemies who were chasing him went ahead. It seems that after some time the king once again got back his lost kingdom as well as his army.

It seems that while returning to his kingdom and celebrating, his attention fell on his ring. "He will also be transformed." Now the king started smiling. Now his state of mind was beyond hope and depression. That is, he knew by now the mystery of life, "How to be always happy."

Raghubeer Sharan Mitra said, "One who has hope may be disappointed a million times but still will never be defeated."

Ramdhari Singh Dinkar said, "A person who never accepts defeat receives many blessings."

Analysis: We must never become depressed at the changing scenes of this drama. Because here circumstances are changing every moment. If you wish to stop the sad circumstances, still you cannot. They too will change. There is no need to become worried and depressed.

Just become neutral towards the changing atmosphere. By doing some practice and Rajyoga meditation, your hopeful and joyful life can become sweet.

For a successful life a person needs to have a burning desire.

But before that let the quality of hope remain forever, the thought of hope, the candle of hope be enlightened forever. This light of hope will always give courage, dedication, positivity and success.

According to Premchand, "Hope is the mother of activeness. Hope consists of strength, power and life. Hope is the source of all power in this world."

Suppose you wish to become Henry Ford and if you do not strive hard to make your hope come true, then you can never expect the desired result. On the one hand you want to become rich and on the other hand you think that "I am poor, how will I earn money? I don't know." And suppose you would like to invest in a business in spite of tough competition, then you have thoughts such thoughts as, "Will I be able to succeed or not." "The money which I have instead I may lose, etc "This type of confusion, doubt, fear and foolish thoughts will definitely make you unsuccessful by making all your hopes shatter into pieces. See to it that such thoughts do not arise in your mind. Let anyone tell you that you do not have the capacity or ability to do this work but with full confidence and willpower prove that you will complete the work. We have to complete this work at any cost. A depressed person's thoughts destroy his power of positivity and creativity.

Remember: There is tremendous power in hope. One of the superior emotions on this earth is "Hope." If a person wants to reach his goal, he must always be hopeful.

Ramdarash Mishra said, "Hope is very powerful. If man wasn't hopeful then the species would have vanished."

Overcome suspicion, confusion, foolish thoughts and inculcate awareness otherwise your mental strength will be destroyed.

Whenever we have a desire to achieve a goal we maintain values in order to achieve that success, but many obstacles come our way. These destroy our hard effort again and again. And the conclusion is that we become depressed and lose hope. No...No. Wake up once again, put in effort and rein-

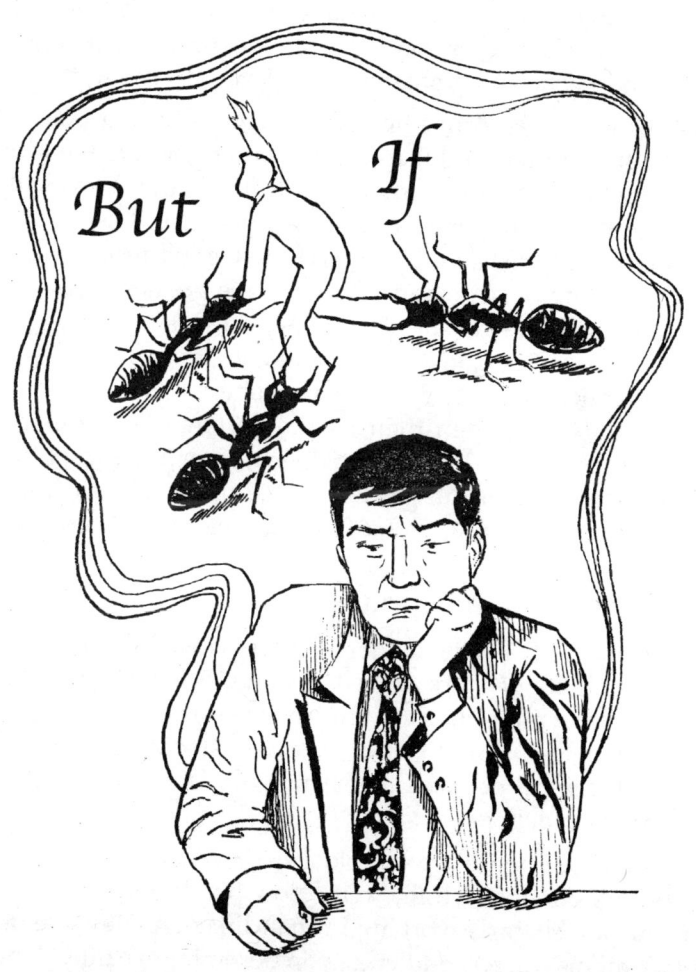

Come out of doubt, indecision and other foolish thoughts, and fill yourself with joy and enthusiasm, otherwise these will destroy your mental strength

carnate your thought. Now speak to your inner mind. Give ideas or suggestions to it. Success is our birthright. We are the children of the Supreme Soul. The blessings of Almighty God are always with us; his unlimited powers are with us also. Always experience the mercy and good wishes of the point of light, God. You have to visualize that all powers are coming from the Supreme Soul and making the mind free from tension, stress and depression. You must experience this as if your mind is becoming charged with joy and vivacity.

Practice: You have to imagine God in the form of a point of light for some time. And then feel the rays of light in the form of peace, bliss and love entering into the mind. Gradually visualize that your mind is becoming peaceful, blissful and loveful. If you practise this you will have good results.

- The feeling of depression is one of the greatest sins
- Depression destroys a man's inner powers
- A depressed person is like a walking corpse
- Depression gives birth to unfaithfulness

If your life is a garden then let the cyclone of depression come, but still never lose hope. Always spread the fragrance of divine virtues in the garden of the mind. For this, one needs positive thinking and a few minutes of meditation.

The Power of Concentration

If one wants to reach the ladder of success then it is necessary to have stability of body as well as mind. It is impossible for an unstable mind to invest all the inner power in completing a particular task if mind or body are unstable. It is natural that unsuccessful people either blame others for their fate or God for their actions.

For instance, suppose a person looks at a wealthy person and thinks of becoming rich like him. Now his desire power and thought power starts working in that direction. He starts investing all his interest and energy in becoming wealthy. Now on the second day he meets a body builder and thinks of becoming physically strong like him. On the third day, he comes across a book and thinks of becoming an author. Now you can think for a while, can he become successful? No, because he does not have that much time at his disposal. All of us have a life expectancy. You must have heard about a man who has one leg on one boat and the other leg on another boat, both heading in different directions. That is why a person can become successful only when he focuses all his con-

True Success

Success

- Accept challenge
- Must be laborious
- Wisdom ensures trumph
- Introspection
- Use sublime work-efficiency
- Be virtuous
- Enkindle hope
- Remember-Success resides in failure
- Self-confidence is necessary
- Misappropriating Mira culous power is obstruction
- Have faith in self and god Rama in minds heart
- Greed is hindrance
- Practical knowledge
- Renounce despodency
- Nourish tolerance
- Develop imaginative power
- Responsibility
- Sanctification earns propriety
- Develop a firm determination in worthy by direction
- Maintain self-respect
- Counterbalance is unavoidable
- Patience has utility for self-discipline
- Patience of greatest value for concentration
- Preserve self-respect
- Crowned with responsibility for this
- Meditation of destiny earns attainment

centration in completing a single task. Concentration means you are enjoying the work that you are doing. By focusing your attention in completing that work you are experiencing inner satisfaction.

Many times you will find that all of a sudden a sad situation arises which activates your consciousness due to which man becomes unstable and loses concentration. You must have heard how a poor man won the lottery and due to extreme happiness had a heart attack! Sometimes the moment a person gets up to give a speech he becomes speechless and forgets everything, his legs start trembling and he feels thirsty, etc. All these symptoms indicate that this person has lost his mental stability. Concentration power is directly related with success. In other words, the stronger the concentration the more easily he will achieve success. Now comes the question of practice. The best place is a Rajyoga Centre where the atmosphere is pure. Concentration means strong willpower and faith. Let obstacles come your way but face the problem with willpower and keep full faith that "I will always remain mentally stable." With willpower and faith everything will start to appear easy.

Stop all your thoughts for some time. Allow a pause in between thoughts and then practise increasing the length of the pause. And in this pause, experience the soul.

The other meaning of concentration is to focus your attention on one particular topic from all angles and stop the flow of thoughts. Whilst doing this it may happen that the flow of thoughts may be fast but thoughts or attention will not go anywhere other than upon the topic in the mind. The topic can be either an essay or a scientific invention or any artistic painting, but deeply engrossed and passive thoughts are called "Concentration."

3

Attitude

What is Attitude?

Information on a topic, object or person gives rise to a judgment and whatever judgment is arrived at through emotions and thoughts is called attitude. This is a subtle emotion based on thoughts.

The stronger your thoughts, the stronger will be your attitude. The more clarity of attitude towards any topic, object, person, thought or emotion, in that proportion will be a person's success. A person's success or defeat largely depends upon his attitude which is negative or positive. Attitudes are generally activated by thoughts. If attitudes are just in theory and not in practice, they remain as a thought only and do not become actions. But it is not always necessary that thoughts become actions. That is why, if attitudes change into behaviour, then they can be beneficial as well as detrimental.

An apple may look beautiful from the outside but it is not necessarily sweet, tasty and juicy from the inside. In this way, a nation, organization or company can become great and successful only when its workers have good character from the viewpoint of morality and spirituality. If today there is any rating scale for measuring success, then it would be an ideal good character. All that glitters cannot be gold. Success and divinity are impossible until you have positive attitudes towards hard work and good character. Man is more precious than all the precious commodities of the world. But today, unfortunately, man's attitude is such that he is giving importance to comforts, luxuries, wealth, etc, but not his character. The reality is that man himself is responsible for the creation as well as destruction of his wealth. This is also a truth that for attaining wealth, along with working efficiently, various seminars and workshops are organized. Here discussions on topics relating to increasing productivity take place. But if there is a lack of moral values positive attitude, then there is doubt as to whether there will be real success.

Today's atmosphere is full of immorality and evil, which are manifest in the form of bad habits. The outcome of such valueless thoughts is that life has changed and each one is blaming the other. At any cost success has to be achieved. For this, man is ready to break the norm of moral and spiritual values. Until positive attitudes become the norm on a practical level, there is no benefit at all.

The foundation of a tall building has to be dug deep into the earth, in the same way, if the building of life has to touch the heights of success, then it is necessary to build a strong attitude. Suppose you want to become an ideal administrator or an ideal businessman, or an ideal industrialist or shopkeeper, or home-maker, you must give utmost importance to your attitudes.

If a person wants to achieve success at any point in time, his attitude holds an important place. A man's all-round success largely depends upon this inner light. You can start your beautiful time by just bringing positive change in your attitude. The way a tall tree has to spread its roots deep into the soil, in the same way, if a person wants to reach to the height of success, he has to spread his deeply. On the way to achieving the set goal, the reasons for defeat have to be evaluated and, with the help of education, patience, interest and courage, once again a person may become successful through his positive attitude.

Is our Far-Sightedness Strong and Short-Sightedness Weak?

We often keep an attitude of indifference towards our faults and weaknesses and our attitude is strong towards other's weaknesses. No-one can escape through this magnifying glass. Such a person can find out, not only big mistakes, but also the smallest mistakes in one second. Today man has fallen into a trap of bad habits. About 90% of the solution to any problem is to remove the habit of finding mistakes in others. When a person points one finger at others' mistakes, three fingers are pointing towards himself. The habit of finding fault in others is so bad that if a person goes to heaven he will also find fault in them. Actually, whatever man tries to search for, he gets that somehow. You will always discover strengths and weaknesses in a person. Now this is important as it reflects whatever you would like to discover and it depends upon your own attitude whether it is positive or negative.

One day a person went to a psychiatrist and said, "Doctor, I am not feeling very well" So the doctor replied, "No problem. From now on you will start to feel well." So behind every defeat, there is an experience of success and it increases the inner capacity like it happened with Thomas Alva Edison. He became unsuccessful a thousand times and after every defeat he used to think positively that he had to end all mistakes. If a person with a negative attitude is unsuccessful at the first attempt he would lose confidence and lack energy believing that success is impossible.

How to Create Attitude

Attitudes are cultivated from childhood, from the family in which you are raised as well as from formal education. Whatever experience is gained in life, if that understanding is not sufficient, then it does not matter as you can still start a new life. For success in life, or a successful life, the foremost practice one needs to start with is a healthy attitude. This is possible and a new inner subtle light will start spreading in your new attitude. For this you must increase your information, knowledge, experience, concentration and analytical intellect.

You can gather information through various sources of media. You can gather as much information as you want to know or understand. You can form your attitude by gathering information from various areas such as social, political, religious and cultural. But today unfortunately we have learnt the art of earning our bread and butter but have lost the art of living happily. The speed at which we are moving towards temporary valueless attitudes, temporary happiness, material happiness, etc, is dangerous.

How to Inculcate a Good Attitude in Life

Always look at the beauty and fragrance of a flower and not its thorns. The universe is a mixture of a variety of wonderful experiences. On this huge stage of the universe, there is a unique and important place for every object and every individual. It seems as if an artist has used different colors in his wonderful work so as to make every part of his painting look unique and wonderful. Life is a stage on which pure and impure points intersect.

Whether there be any bad habits or bad character in others, do not allow tension in yourself. Go beyond finding faults in others and encourage his self respect and self confidence by highlighting his strengths for this is the way to develop a positive attitude.

We always expect the same attitude from others and in the same way, are we having the same attitude towards others? How good it would have been if we had a weak far sightedness and strong short sightedness so that we could overcome our own faults. Who in this world is free from weaknesses? That is why God has to come down on this earth to liberate man from all vices. If man had no evils in him, then there would be no point in God coming into this world. The habit of finding fault and weakness is so intense that we always discover one or other fault in every individual in any situation. Our attention does not fall in the right place. This does not mean that we cannot discuss or analyze anyone's faults or weaknesses.

There is a saying, "A stopped watch also gives correct time twice in 24 hours."

Whenever a social worker or a religious leader works towards a great goal, they have to face many difficulties, but their attitude is always busy in building a perfect personality so that a beautiful and happy society can be created.

The way a good sculptor cares not for the uncut stone and his attention is on the image contained within, in the same way, the attention of Buddha was on Valmiki and he did not care for Angulimal dacoit.

Negative Attitude is Universal

There is no limit to such people be it at home, in a shop or office, etc. who take great interest in finding weaknesses in others. People love to insult others. Insulting, blaming and finding fault in others has become a business for many people. This has made people lose interest, courage and patience. People put the blame on others for their own weaknesses while their attitude is generally negative towards the whole world.

Such people are like a contagious disease spread all over society and in the country. These people spread viruses in others in the form of inactiveness and hopelessness. Such people having a negative attitude can discover weaknesses even in a perfect person. The following are different types of attitudes:
1. The negative attitude of insult.
2. The attitude of postponing or cross checking
3. The attitude of neutrality towards life
4. Dual attitude
5. The attitude of thanksgiving
6. Selfish attitude towards explanation
7. Depressed attitude
8. The attitude of contentment

The negative attitude of insult – attitude is that mirror through which one's mental reflection is mirrored

We all are aware of the fact that finding fault in others makes us fall. This is very important for those who want to live happily and who want to reach the ladder of success. Thinking about others means either finding weaknesses or back-biting. It is observed that people take great interest in insulting others. But why? It may be that our inner attitude is not aware of drawbacks of insulting others. So let us neutrally look at the different dimensions of our understanding.

It is easy to discuss and prove negative angles such as bad habits and insults, but it is difficult to prove them from a positive angle.

Meaning of Insult – Negative Aspect

Insulting others develops a wrong notion that we are more talented and intellectual than others. That is why we start feeling great and maintaining our own reputation. Therefore, it is very difficult to prove any work from a positive angle. For example, if someone tries to prove the existence of God, it is the most difficult task. The person who tries to prove it will have to spend his life preaching four rules, i.e. purity of food, transformation of self by overcoming the vices, celibacy and meditation. Only then can he attain bliss, love and purity. And the moment a person experiences bliss, the moment this fact is proved that God is blissful. One needs a very divine mind to accept God. A very sensitive and warm heart is needed for this. On the other hand, some claim that God has no existence, or one wants to shatter the identity of God, then for this there is nothing to prove. All that is required is to possess the skill of debating. It is not a question of intelligence. A fool can also prove that God has no existence. Every individual feels that "I am in no way less than another. I am the greatest amongst all". He thinks that his ego should be praised and it will be very difficult to prove it because if each person starts proving that he is the greatest, then there would be a great war amongst all people. Amongst so many people no-one knows who will win, so it is certain that they have to accept defeat. Therefore, the mind is very clever and starts playing a new game that it is difficult to prove that I am the greatest of all, however it can be proved that no-one is greater than me. And due to this reason, people form the negative attitude of insulting others.

Insulting Others is a Visible Means to Praising Oneself

Whenever we point at a person and state that he is bad, it means that we are better than him and you have proved that you are truthful. In this world, you will find wicked people who are interested only in insulting others. Insulting has only one purpose – to hide our defects or wickedness. We must stop finding defects in others and become introvert because self introspection is a ladder to success. Today we find many pages of newspapers having this attitude of insulting others.

Yeah, every day in your life you will observe the news such as a certain saint has had a love affair or the arrest of an education minister due to corruption, or a neighbour's wife ran away. Such news is listened to with great interest. Suppose the reporter only gives a brief account of such news, the viewers say, "Oh brother, please tell us in detail, come and sit comfortably, drink tea and water." People go on asking for more and more details. Listeners become so engrossed and attentive that they forget the whole world. But why are they so interested in spreading such news? If a wealthy person falls from his self respect or if a minister, social worker, saint or any good person makes a small mistake, the news spreads quickly in a few hours, as if some major incident has taken place on this earth. See how this news spreads like wildfire in the forest. People discuss it to such an extent that they elaborate and exaggerate ten times more than the actual incident. Why? Because people expect you to get trapped and fall and insults begin. It is strange that people make small things into big things and continue to spread the negativity. At the same time people trust such people blindly.

Negative attitude

You will find that if someone relates that a particular person gives a wonderful lecture, other people disagree with this fact. They retort by saying, "Yes, we have seen many people who can render such beautiful knowledge but good people have often fallen down. There is a lot of difference between speaking and doing. You will see, if not today then tomorrow, his hidden habits will emerge." It means that by accepting all his good things, it seems that I myself am not as great. Then comes the process of insulting others. On the other hand, if someone tells us that one particular person is a thief and tomorrow he cheats someone, then immediately we accept this fact. And we assume that he must have done such an act. We take it for granted that we are an exception and all others are wicked. When the time comes we get to know everything. Our state of mind is such that the moment someone states that a person delivers a beautiful speech, we immediately disagree with it. We try to discover one or other fault stating that this person was showing anger towards someone. If the same person, who was delivering a good speech was showing anger, then if someone points and tells us that, see that person is showing anger, we don't say to them, see how beautifully he delivers the speech, how can he show anger? Now what is the problem in delivering knowledge. It is obvious that sometimes he may become angry. But we fail to think that this is due to a lack of positive attitude.

Some believe we are an exception and all others are wicked, or whosoever gives us help we accept immediately. When a person is defamed, people feel very relaxed and welcome the occasion to see a person becoming characterless. It is very difficult to create a good character or to achieve fame in society but it is easy to defame people By insulting others, the more you find fault, the more your ego of becoming nice develops. An insulting nature becomes stronger from within and creates an impression on our conscious mind. Life becomes passive and the charm of life comes to an end. This negative attitude slowly and gradually closes the doors of love and mercy. Life becomes full of hatred and gives rise to a very unhappy life.

Now this does not mean that we lead our life by closing our eyes. Truth can be related but we refer to it as criticism. Sometimes insulting others and debating takes place but there is a slight difference between the two. Positive criticism arises due to mercy and insulting others arises due to hatred. Positive criticism is the nectar of life whereas insulting becomes a means to destroy. Criticism means to investigate different angles of truth in life. This can be sometimes rigid too. But the original aim of criticism is to wash the dust from the diamond and make it pure so as to bring back its sparkle. Criticism is full of friendliness which brings about transformation in a person. The aim of insulting others is to shatter someone's ego or to hurt someone's soul. Try to understand in this way – when you attack thieves it is to insult them but when you attack stealing, it is called criticism. When we attack the criminal, it is to insult and when we attack the crime, it is to criticise.

If you want to save your life from the poison of insulting others, then invest all your positive thoughts in your life. Try to fill others with hope by your positive, divine thoughts. Invest your positive thoughts, speech and actions in the welfare of the world. Allow your life to become liberated from the poison of insulting others, for only then will your soul experience bliss. And then in every nook and corner of the world, you will find only success.

One who satisfies all souls becomes the benefactor of the world.

An instrument means one who remains egoless and can re-create the world.

Difference between Positive and Negative Attitudes

Positive Attitude	Negative Attitude
1. A person with a positive attitude is always a	1. A person with a negative attitude is always

problem solver rather than problematic.	problematic and not a problem solver.
2. A person with a positive attitude always tries to find various alternatives to achieve his goal.	2. A person with a negative attitude is neither interested in attaining any goal nor find any measures to achieve anything.
3. A person with a positive attitude converts difficult work into easy work. He converts a mountain-like situation into a mustard seed and converts a mustard see into cotton wool.	3. A person with a negative attitude creates problems in the easiest of tasks and converts a mustard seed into a mountain.
4. A person with a positive attitude easily accepts his own faults	4. A person with a negative attitude has an egoistic nature and thus does not accept his faults. Such people are very rigid and try to prove themselves to be great people.
5. A person with appositive attitude is creative and works with team spirit. He works in unity within a group.	5. A person with a negative attitude breaks the team spirit and isolates himself from everyone.
6. A person with a positive attitude is polite and does social work in which he gives a helping hand in the welfare of others.	6. A person with a negative attitude does not accept any work without obtaining fees. He

Attitude

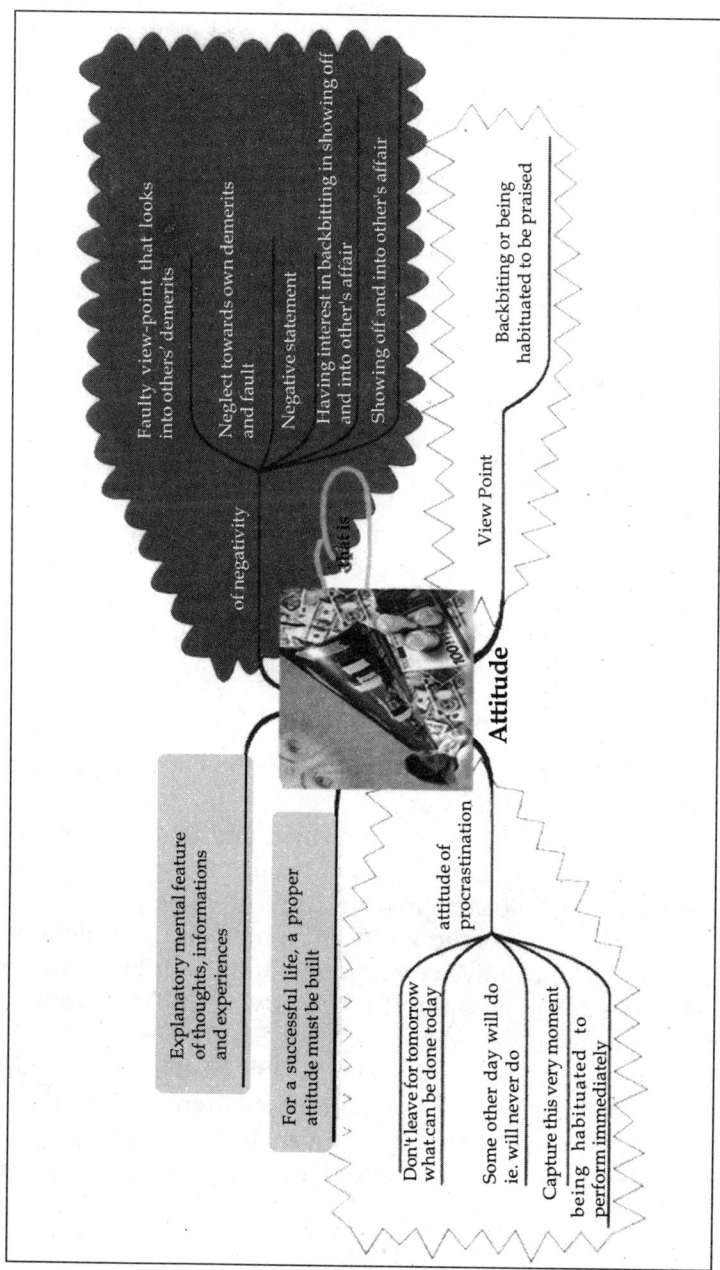

- Faulty view-point that looks into others' demerits
- Neglect towards own demerits and fault
- Negative statement
- Having interest in backbiting in showing off and into other's affair
- Showing off and into other's affair

of negativity

View Point
- Backbiting or being habituated to be praised

Attitude

- Explanatory mental feature of thoughts, informations and experiences
- For a successful life, a proper attitude must be built

attitude of procrastination
- Don't leave for tomorrow what can be done today
- Some other day will do ie. will never do
- Capture this very moment being habituated to perform immediately

	always gives priority to money before work.
7. A person with a positive attitude always remains hopeful towards the future.	7. A person with a negative attitude lives in the past and lives in a state of depression and tension.
8. A person with a positive attitude adapts himself according to changing situations	8. A person with negative attitude fails to adapt to present circumstances and ultimately becomes tense and nervous

The attitude of postponing or cross-checking

One of the greatest revolutionary formulas is "The work which is to be done tomorrow, do it today and that which has to be done today, do it now." It is through this that a person can easily go up the ladder of success. If a person has right understanding he can easily and quickly reach his goal.

Do tomorrow's work today

We must not postpone the thought of doing the work thinking "I will do it tomorrow".

If you observe people's lives, you will find that life is a long journey. A person's 20-25 years of his life are spent in education. He thinks that a day in the future will come when he will acquire formal education and will enter into a profession. Henceforth, he will live comfortably throughout his life. Now is the time for intense effort and study. Your 20-25 years of life are spent in preparation for your life. This way when he gets a post according to his choice, still he thinks of getting married and later on thinks about his children's bright future. And then he starts accumulating wealth for his children's future. His life comes to a standstill for the next 20-25 years. Now think for a moment that is around 40-50 years of life are spent in learning the art of living. About 50 years of life is spent by old methods which by then cultivate the habit of postponing in life. Now the question arises whether he is able to get rid of that old postponing habit? Can he experience a new type of bliss every moment?

Most of us have the tendency of putting a lot of pressure of work on ourselves by preaching. "Let us do the work tomorrow, forget today." Such people spend their life by just mentally postponing their life. The charm of life is in today and not in tomorrow. If today is joyful then your future will automatically be joyful. Make plans for the future but see to it that you enjoy every moment of the present happily.

See to it that you never repent thinking, "I could have done this work but I didn't do it. I wish I had done this work then I would have benefited enormously."

"If not now, then never." This is one of the greatest revolutionary formulas in the world of the mind and in the world of emotion, due to which a person can easily reach up the ladder of success. This has a unique importance in worldly attainments. But there is no question of the importance even in the world of spirituality. If we understand this matter then our hard efforts will increase by leaps and bounds. But why is this not possible in our daily life? Reflect on the reason for this and the solution.

The attitude of postponement

The world famous author Mark Twain wrote that when he was listening to a Godly lecture from a saint, he was very impressed. He thought, "I have $100 in my pocket. Why don't I use this in charity?" Mark Twain wrote, "After 10 minutes my mind changes and maybe $50 dollars would be the right amount." Now he was not listening to the lecture. Because of this $100, he became engrossed in his inner dialogue. After half and hour, his mind changed from $50 to $5. And at the end of the lecture, his mind came down to $1. When the time for charity came, instead of donating one dollar, he was busy thinking about the $1 and whether anyone would notice.

God Shiva says, "Oh children, the thought of doing work tomorrow must be overcome". Suppose you keep fresh fruit for a few days and then eat it, what will happen? It will either get spoiled or dry out or lose its vitamins. There is a lot of difference in eating a hot chapatti and eating a two-day old chapatti. In the same way, as soon as pure thoughts come into your mind, put them into practice immediately for good results. Do not postpone it until tomorrow. The reason is that the moment that thought gets power to make it practical the soul receives inspiration. If that thought has not become a deed, then it is possible that it will change or its power will be reduced. If any good or positive thought comes into our mind, then we often think "Let us do it tomorrow or let us start from early morning, etc." This attitude of postponing starts to emerge from within us.

The way a person thinks, hence his attitude, deeds and actions

Do today's work tomorrow

If anger comes, we start showing it at that moment. We don't postpone our anger. It should be that the thought of showing anger should be postponed until tomorrow and positive thoughts, good deeds, meditation, and charity, should be done now. It is observed that people think a lot in a positive way but do less in a practical way. But for anger or negative thoughts we think less and don't even postpone them. We do it instantly. The good thoughts of detachment do not enter into our lives, so for this we think, "Where is destruction? Where is the end? Where is death?" Now there is a long way to go in life, we will do it at the end." And in this way we keep postponing until the end. We remain ignorant until the end. Psychiatrists believe that suicide and murder take place only when thoughts become instant deeds. If such acts are postponed to a future date or if this mentality is stopped for some time, then this evil deed would not take place. In the same way, if any auspicious thing is postponed then its occurrence becomes impossible.

The way a person thinks, hence his attitude, deed and action.

This moment is in our hands

The nature of human beings is that he always thinks about the past and future. He never thinks about the present. But our experience teaches us that we have neither the past nor the future is in our hands. Only the present moment is in our hands as tomorrow is the shadow of the present. If you want to make your life full of awareness, then do it now. Who knows whether the next moment will come or not. We need to become soul conscious in this moment and fulfill our needs now. Just think for a while, who is stopping you from doing this? Why postpone this work until morning or until the evening? If you recollect in the morning, then it is morning and if you recollect in the evening, it is evening. You may recollect either in the office, or on the bus or at the dining table, but whenever such thoughts come, see God in your heart. Speak sweetly to God. To do this work, who becomes the obstacle in our life? If you wish, so you can do. Spend your time lovingly in hard work exactly in the same way as the sun's rays are collected in a lens and immediately fire is produced. Our life should not be haphazard like the sun rays spread everywhere. Every moment of our hard work should be as deep as the ocean and as high as Gauri Shankar. However, we live a life where there is neither depth nor height.

Cultivate the habit of instantly doing work

When good thoughts come into your mind, at that moment we are on the peak of doing good deeds, because at that moment God and nature's power is in our favour. There is nothing to think about, but rather something is to be done. The moment the thought of charity, sacrifice, meditation comes, that moment you must do it. It is not sure whether the next moment will come or not and it is not necessary that this powerful thought remains in your mind forever. Let us make a rule in our daily routine. Whenever good thoughts come, fulfill them immediately. Whenever negative thoughts come, postpone them indefinitely. That is why positive and good thoughts apply this formula of "Do tomorrow's work today" and for negative thoughts apply this formula, "Do today's work tomorrow." That day is not far away when you can develop the new habit of changing all your good thoughts instantly. If you want to do Godly service do it instantly. If you wish to remember God, do it instantly, but if you want to be angry, then do it later. Then whichever way you would like to put your efforts for attaining success, it will be possible. Such people will be happy for ever like a blossoming flower whose fragrance brings divine bliss to the soul.

Your attitude reflects your perception

There is a famous story. There were four blind men who were asked to describe an elephant. They were shown an elephant and had to answer the question by touching it. They were taken to the elephant one by one and all of them touched it. Then they were asked to give their experience. Let us see what interesting replies they gave. The first man said, "the elephant is something like a wall" because he had touched only the middle flat part of the elephant. The second man said, "The elephant is like a pillar." It was obvious that he had touched the legs of the elephant. The third man said, "The elephant is somewhat similar to the snake Ajgara." because he had touched its trunk. The fourth man said, "The elephant is like a huge fan". He related this because he had touched the elephant's ear which was exactly like a fan". This means that limited knowledge is an obstacle in building a good attitude and lessens the attainment of success.

The attitude of neutrality towards life

Lack of information gives rise to a distorted attitude exactly the way a blind man touches an object and identifies what the object is, e.g. what is its use, etc. In other words, such people gather information mostly through sound and touch. Their attitude on any topic depends largely upon limited information. Then how can one call it a complete attitude?

The manner in which we wear thought and emotional glasses, we see exactly in the same manner. If one is great and generous, then the whole world appears in the same way. The sages had a healthy attitude towards different classes and built a strong society. They classified them depending upon people's natural qualities and capacities, rather than on the basis of low or high class. For example, in the olden days the right of imparting education was given to Brahmins and the security of society was given to Kshatriya. Brahmins had an inborn quality of introspection whereas Kshatriyas had qualities of courage, bravery, extro version. A few selfish people changed this beautiful attitude into low level classes and succeeded in building a wrong attitude. The outcome is that we have not been able to rise from the dangerous consequences until now. This wrong attitude is still present in some sections of society and country such as in the case of the 'untouchables', Brahmins and Shudras, and on the other hand, Hindu - Muslim - Christian, and some are based on nationality such as, "I am an American, I am a German, I am British, Chinese, Indian, etc."

Today we find war, differences in opinion and terrorist activities are all due to this kind of attitude. The whole world is in the midst of the storm thinking that in gaining power and greed, we ourselves are not responsible for destroying our beautiful culture and civilization.

Our ancestors had given birth to a healthy attitude from their deep realization that "Nature is your family". "Vasudev Kutumbkam" means let all species be benefited, and this is how there was an inner attitude of well being.

Those who had experience of this had created such a beautiful attitude that Hindu, Muslim, Sikh, Christian are all brothers. They rose up beyond their class, society, and nation and found the immortal truth that, although we are in different bodies, we are a point of light, a soul. That is why we are brothers as our original form is light.

Then why not remember that unique light because light has its own unique quality.

Suppose two people are entering through two doors of a dark room with two lighted candles; can the light of two candles clash with each other? No, but two lights combine to generate more light.

Light is always pure. When it clashes with dirty things and reflects back, it does not carry the dirt with it, but maintains its complete purity.

Light is always weightless. By seeing this it seems as if man experiences this knowledge and implements it into his daily life, then all evils of the world will be destroyed. From this, one can conclude that the root cause of all sin is a body conscious attitude. If our soul conscious attitude emerges that we souls are a point of light, then within a short period of time, the whole world would shine with infinite goodness. It becomes possible to experience the point of light, the soul through the medium of knowledge and meditation. For this experience you may have to practise RajYoga meditation. For your kind of information, this is taught by the Brahma Kumaris World Spiritual University. Look, think and find a means to attain a healthy attitude.

Dual attitude

Some people have split personalities. They generally think well but often carry out bad deeds. Such people commit mistakes and you will find them asking for an apology. They think that they aren't angry people, but by mistake they speak of something indecent or have the habit of speaking in a loud voice. In reality they are not bad people. The conclusion is that such people do not realize their mistakes and assume themselves to be good and keep doing bad deeds, due to which it becomes impossible to change their personality. The realization of the truth that "I am bad", is always absent in them. The question of change and transformation arises only when they realize that they have certain weaknesses.

If such people wish to get rid of weaknesses, then they must once again evaluate all those mistakes which they did due to ignorance or which were habitual. It is rather difficult to overcome this bad habit but not impossible. Our habits are like that rope on which every day one knot is tied. In this way, the impact of attitude falls on success as well as on defeat.

Attitude brings colour from within

Attitudes are manifestations of our inner state of mind. That is why if our state of mind is prejudiced then our attitude becomes partial and wrong. Attitudes can be correct and pure and at the same time they can be impure, incorrect and imperfect. Positive attitudes are the materialistic angle and pure attitude is the spiritual angle. Complete success will be impossible to achieve if there is no harmony between positive and pure attitude.

Your attitude will not become generous, true and successful until your vision becomes pure from both a moral point of view and a soul conscious from a spiritual point of view.

The attitude of thanksgiving

We become tense over things which we do not possess but are we thankful for their existence? Do we exhibit our thanks to God saying, "Oh merciful One, if I surrender my whole life in your service, still I cannot repay your compassion." Always remember "No-one else can perform your work better than yourself." There is one rule for the mind. It always runs towards inefficiency or even lower. If we give importance to whatever we possess, then we will be full of contentment and happiness. We think about things which we lack and we devalue our whole life.

Right valuation of 'self'

Human nature is unique and is in one's own hands but he does not give importance to it. Whatever a person possesses, he is not happy with it and that which he does not possess, he always cries for it. No one cares for his own luxuries and comforts but keeps an eye on others. No-one looks at the grief of others but looks at their own. In this cycle the peace of life is destroyed and discontentment occupies the space in a dissatisfied mind. And this is the cause of all unhappiness. One who attains peace of mind and bliss is one who really lives. He is the winner of the contest of life, though he may or may not have a car or wealth. If a person does not have peace of mind then in spite of having wealth, luxuries and comforts, he will still remain discontented and dissatisfied. All religions, knowledge and moral scriptures were different ways of discovering inner peace. One who attains peace of mind is knowledgeful and is a true devotee.

- Anant Gopal Shevde

One day Ramesh was going to take part in a small programme. His slippers were old. While leaving his home, his slipper broke. He thought of wearing shoes but his socks were torn. He started walking barefoot but with disappointment. He was on his way when he found a lame person who was walking with the help of a stick. He became silent for a while and looked at the sky with tears in his eyes. He thanked God and uttered to himself, "Oh God, I was tense for no reason and had no shoes or socks, but this man has no legs. If I was in his place then who would I have blamed? In which court and against who would I have filed a complaint? Thank you,

Attitude

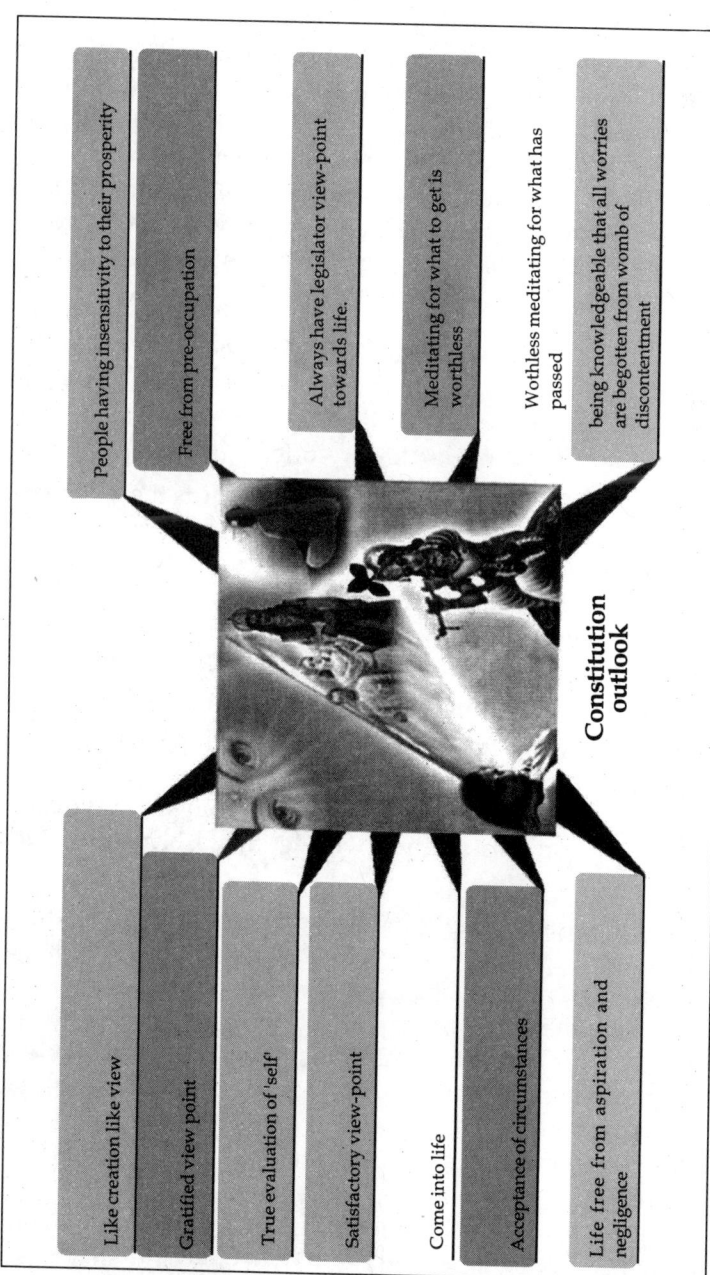

- People having insensitivity to their prosperity
- Free from pre-occupation
- Always have legislator view-point towards life.
- Meditating for what to get is worthless
- Wothless meditating for what has passed
- being knowledgeable that all worries are begotten from womb of discontentment
- Like creation like view
- Gratified view point
- True evaluation of 'self'
- Satisfactory view-point
- Come into life
- Acceptance of circumstances
- Life free from aspiration and negligence

Constitution outlook

God, I am so lucky." Now Ramesh thought, let me go to that lame man and show sympathy. Ramesh went to that man and showed his sympathy. The lame man was delighted to meet Ramesh and said, "thank you for your sympathy but I am one of the happiest people in the world. My wife is very polite, loving, sweet spoken and efficient in the household. I also have a florist business and by God's grace everything is going well. I always think of helping others." This is a thanksgiving attitude towards life.

Preparation of last offering towards god

Do you offer any inferior thing to God? Or do you complain to God? No. In our day to day life we never offer such things, and then at the end of our life we offer ourselves to God.

Saint Kabir had a very beautiful attitude towards the last phase of his life that "God had given the life to us to use in whatever way we wish." Your self-confidence will give your sympathy from God. Let us decorate our life with morality and spirituality. Let us colour our life with the canvas of divine virtues so that we can offer the best gift to God. And you can make both your spiritual and material life successful.

If in a family or society while interacting with people, you are not only clever, polite, sweet spoken but also thankful and without expectation, whatever you get from them, you remain happy and this attitude will definitely bring you success.

Generally people do not pay attention to the fact that they possess many things:
1. A few parts of our body can be taken out but a few cannot. In spite of this, suppose someone tells you to give one of your hands to him. If he promises to give you two lakh rupees for your hand would you do this?
2. Suppose someone asks you, "Give me two legs and I will give you 10 lakh rupees. Are you ready to accept this bargain?
3. Will you accept this argument if someone asks you to donate two eyes and is ready to pay you any price?

4. Suppose he asks you to donate one kidney, are you ready for this?

(Note that if this question is put in front of an educated youth, then it is natural that the answer will be 'No'.)

If you observe your thoughts you will often find that we are not having an attitude of thankfulness towards our self respect. It is a different aspect to put in extra effort in order to gain more than what we possess.

This example does not mean that you evaluate yourself by commodities or money. This example is being cited because your value cannot be measured in terms of money. You are invaluable. Try to respect it. Whatever you are, you are great, so love yourself. You must remember one thing, that you are very precious.

If you compare the strength of all species of the universe, you will find that man is the weakest. Still, why is man called superior, great and strong? What is the reason behind this? The reason is that man possesses mental strength, a superior mind and a good intellect. Man needs only to change his attitude to show thankfulness towards God. This does not mean that whatever you lack you need not put effort in to fulfill it and inculcate contentment. Contentment is a different thing. Contentment means enough and not any more. The meaning of happiness is to compromise oneself and live in such a manner that if we do not possess anything, it does not matter. It may be that we have this much only in our fate.

What we demand

One famous lady visited a poor artist to paint her picture. After a few days when she returned to the artist she was delighted and said, "Oh such pretty picture. What a unique combination of colour and brush strokes." She was so happy that she continually praised the picture. Afterwards, the lady asked the poor artist to quote the price at which he would sell the painting. The poor artist was so happy that his heartbeat started beating faster. He was thinking about how much he could charge. How much can a poor mind full of desires and expectations ask? So the poor artist thought, "Maybe she will not pay very much. Should I ask for £100, should I take £100, £300 £500". Then he thought, "I hope she cannot pay that much ". Later on he decided that it would be better if he did not take any money from the lady. The lady had a purse with her and gave it to the artist saying, "Keep this purse, it is very valuable." The poor artist was so disappointed. He thought, "Undoubtedly, the purse is valuable but what will I do with it. It would have been better to charge £100 instead of this purse." The lady said, "Whatever you wish". The lady opened the purse which contained £1,000 and removed £100 pounds and gave it to that artist. She took back her purse and left. Now the artist started crying and weeping saying, "Oh God, I was so unlucky that I lost one golden chance to make my fortune."

Attitude

Today people are almost in this situation. One's demands and desires are not only simple but also degraded. Are we so helpless that we think of destroying our poverty by £100. The donor is giving in lakhs, crores and millions, but our demands are like a huge empire.

Whatever God has given to us is locked away. The invaluable property of our life such as knowledge, peace, bliss and love which is given to us by God is locked away and we never open that purse to see inside. What God has given us is several times more than what we are demanding. But we are so crazy in demanding that we fail to see that unlimited property. We ask God to fulfill selfish desires such as a bank balance, lovely car, a bungalow, etc. We must not ask for all these since they are all degraded demands. Just open your eyes to see your surroundings, you will find that without demanding from that ocean of love, God, you are experiencing purity, holiness, bliss and love. When you gain all these then all your demands are fulfilled forever. Our mind becomes transformed from an impoverished state into a carefree emperor. A saying goes, "When you don't beg you receive pearls, and when you beg you receive nothing."

Then that begging may be for wealth or fame or position. If you really want to beg then go for continuous remembrance of God and establish all types of relationship with God. In this way the valuable properties of this world will become your slaves. If you want to attain everything, the key is remembrance of God. If you want to demand anything then ask for the key.

Selfish attitude towards explanation

Illustration

This incident is of that time when Swami Vivekananda's fame was at its peak in America because of his intelligence and good character. It was natural that a few priests became jealous of him. They joined together to make a plan to spoil his good character. One night at 10pm Vivekananda was returning home after finishing his lecture at the Vedanta

Centre and had to pass through a quiet road. On his way, he felt the touch of a soft hand. He looked back to see this young female and saw a very affectionate attitude in her eyes. He paused for a moment and looked with motherly love at the female saying, "Aaha, what a pleasant moment has come today in my life. You have made me remember mother Shardamani. Mother Shardamani used to touch me with the same affection. Tell me mother, for my sake, cry loudly without any hesitation. Now the female felt insulted and with a guilty feeling said, "I came to spoil your character, but your greatness and compassion has elevated me. Looking at this, I am full of insult and guilt. Oh great man, forgive me". After a few days, Swami Vivekananda came to know about the plot of the priests.

- Can we not build an elevated attitude which can go on inspiring values in human beings?
- Can we destroy negative attitudes and build spiritual attitudes and soul conscious attitudes so that we can save our values which are deteriorating?

Depressed attitude

Depressed people habitually think in a negative way. They only look at other's weaknesses and not at their strengths, because then he gets a false feeling that "I am better than he because these weaknesses are not within me".

They spend their life filled with doubt. They always keep thinking that, "If something happens like this, or if it happens like that."

Consequences of suspicious attitude

One day a tired man sat to rest in the shade of a huge tree. He was feeling thirsty and thought, "I wish I could get some cold water to quench my thirst." The moment he had the thought a jug of chilled water appeared in front of him. He satisfied his thirst by drinking the water. After some time he was feeling hungry, so he thought, "I wish I had some food to eat." Surprisingly, the minute he thought this, plates full of different types of tasty food appeared in front of him. He had a stomach filled with tasty food. Now it was natural for him to feel tired and the moment he thought this, a small golden palace with a comfortable bed and maid servants all emerged before his very eyes. Now he had a suspicion in his mind that someone may come to destroy all his luxuries and

happiness. And truly, a devil emerged. The man thought that this devil may eat him. The moment he thought this, the devil came and ate him after killing him. Now that tree was not a simple tree, but rather The Genealogical Tree (Kalpa Vriksh).

The Genealogical tree is a symbol of our inner powers. The greatest powers of this world are thoughts, desires and emotions. It is through these inner capabilities that whatever we want to get, we can attain. A depressed thought is like that devilish thought which destroys all our inner powers.

- People generally remain engrossed in past painful thoughts and thus become depressed.
- Some people are such that they always look at others and think that this disease may not come to them and sometimes they are affected by these diseases which they always think about.

A person with a positive attitude always thinks the opposite to this. They keep themselves busy with happy and healthy thoughts. Their attitude towards daily life such as doing, thinking, looking and talking is always the best.

The attitude of contentment

Contentment enables a person to become like a stress free king. If any millionaire is not content then he is not a millionaire but a beggar of desires. Desires means stressful desires which can never make you a better person. That is why one should be content with whatever one possesses.

In this world where there are unlimited desires which keep coming into our minds, how can one expect the happiness of contentment? The shadow of intense unhappiness is spread everywhere. Man is surrounded by unlimited desires and thus feels as if he is in a trap like unquenched thirst. It so happens that before his dream comes true, new desires arise which are not necessary. A series of thoughts like, "I want this also, I want that..." makes his mind dissatisfied and unhappy. Today there is tough competition in this materialistic world where advertisement is giving due weight to unnecessary goods. In this situation, is it possible to remain far away from these unnecessary goods and experience happiness and contentment with fewer necessities? Our protest is not for essential goods but for unnecessary goods. Let us first understand what this contentment really means?

What is contentment?

A saying goes that 'contentment is a precious stone and no-one can measure this in terms of wealth." The basis of contentment is completeness. Completeness means a life full of Godly knowledge, divine virtues and goodwill. And this contentment gives rise to happiness. Such contented souls remain free from questions and on their face spreads the fragrance of happiness. A contented soul becomes a source of inspiration for other souls because of their vibration and the sparkle on their face. Therefore, ultimately all souls experience happiness through him.

If any old, helpless or poor man fails to achieve success then he tries to make himself feel happy. But this is not contentment but consolation. Contentment is a subtle inner power which is a divine virtue and a positive energy. Contentment means "I am having several times more than what I need," "Whatever I wanted to get, I achieved." This is a way of giving thanks to God. Contentment is not a state of losing the emotions of the soul. But rather it is a state of victory where the soul destroys all vices and becomes wealthy through spiritual property. Contentment means victory over all weaknesses and useless habits. One who attains this quality of contentment becomes stress free forever. A contented soul has a cheerful face that allows everyone to experience bliss and silence.

How to become content?

Our life is as precious as a diamond, so let us not lose this happiness by becoming confused in useless questions. Let us not waste this valuable life by wasting time in gaining wealth, fame, position, ego, etc. If life is a celebration, then if we do not accumulate a stock of contentment, then our tears will not become pearls. Our desires don't allow us to improve. Desires are like that colourful rainbow which seems to be very close to us but when we reach out to touch it, it disappears. Desires are always difficult to fulfill. The desire to attain material goods is always unfulfilled, whereas the basis of contentment is completeness.

Contentment is that precious stone which can be bought on the basis of not keeping any desires within. Go on throwing out unnecessary desires from the purse of your mind. And go on filling it with precious stones.

From experience one thing that we have learnt is that whatever happiness we expected from desires by trying to fulfill them, did we attain happiness? No. Other desires take the place of happiness. Our history has the names of many kings and wealthy people who had all material goods but in spite of this, at the end of their life, they were discontented and felt something was missing. It is through the attainment of God that the soul can experience bliss, happiness and complete relaxation. One psychiatrist says, "Today those who are millionaires ask why life looks meaningless? Life is full of sorrow. All types of tension are due to unhappiness. If our hopes and desires are not fulfilled then this gives rise to unhappiness."

Discontentment means to be a beggar and contentment means to be an emperor

Contentment means to become a king in a palace where there is no sorrow. This is the qualification for a person who wants to achieve success. One who has such a contented attitude remains content in all circumstances. He has a positive attitude and good wishes towards life. A contented person always gives compliments to one who criticizes or shows anger. And if someone is wrong in doing so, he shows mercy and forgiveness. But a contented person can never be made to become angry whatever the circumstances. Behind every unhappy dark cloud there is a silver lining. A person with a contented mind finds a tender ray of light even in deep darkness. He accepts all situations where there is no expectation or desire. In this way, he always shines like a diamond. This is also a true fact that such contented people may be full of Godly knowledge and divine virtues but at the same time may not lack materialistic goods. If you impart Godly knowledge, Godly love, bliss, etc for welfare of others, then these will increase day by day. It never declines but goes on increasing.

Such people having a contented attitude are always busy in making others happy. Even God gives a Gold Medal of blessings to such contented souls who are busy in Godly service. They automatically get a gold medal of self respect, people's regard and God's regard. That is why if we want to spend a happy life then we have to remove the poison of hatred and grief from our hearts and become a river of contentment for the welfare of the world. Only in the garden of the heart, the golden flower of contentment will blossom and a happy smile of a deity empire will emerge.

Equilibrium in Life

4

Balance in Life

Passive Emotions

Do you spoil your work by becoming angry over silly things? Or do others assume you to be an angry person and show indifference? If you don't achieve the desired result, do you make any mistake because of the agitation? Do you become jealous because of other people's success or do you experience jealousy from within? Do you become disappointed in life due to stress and mental deficiency? Those who are well-known in society or are famous also become angry and make great mistakes.

You will find such angry people, not only in jails, juvenile homes, but also in mental hospitals. Such people lose their temper for a moment and murder someone, for which they lose their freedom and throughout life repent for it. Just because they lack patience, they reach very close to their goal but because of this anger they destroy everything. It is due to an expectation of respect and regard and false fame that he feeds a small pretty doll-like daughter and when she grows up, she starts to love a man and this makes the father kill his loving daughter. The consequence is a feeling of guilt, hatred for society and imprisonment for life. Anger is that enemy which destroys one's life. Anger is like a black storm which covers our character in darkness. It is compared to a devil called Bhasmasus, which converts one's life into ashes. Human wealth makes an impact in one's life in an invisible form, but anger makes an impact on human beings in a visible way. Many times differences of opinion are found due to lack of love and cooperation within the family, and it seems to be a place of war rather than a loving or restful place. At home also there is often the sound of bullets and guns. Many times, due to anger people speak as if foam is coming out of their mouth. In this situation, his whole body shakes due to anger. It takes a few days for him to become normal again. Such people spend a long time in a sate of jealousy, guilt, insult, stress and mental sickness. A mind which is filled with jealousy makes for a strange personality because it destroys a positive attitude, creativity, imagination, power, divine intellect and memory power.

Recognize the Powers of the Soul

If you wish to get rid of this dangerous state, then awaken that strong power of desire within, so that you can destroy the darkness of ignorance with knowledge. By doing so, you can fill yourself with love, mercy and bliss. There is no need to become concerned about previous defeats. Once again, start reorganizing all your shattered mental power. You possess unlimited mental power like an ocean and as vast as the sky. The only need of the hour is to develop them once again. After a few days, you will find that if you use these powers in the right direction then you will definitely succeed in a surprising way. For this it is necessary to possess the art of balance in life.

Powers are always impartial. If you use them then definitely they will bring a result. You can either become angry, or slap a person with your hand, or you can show mercy or love a person by touching the cheek. The result will be towards either happiness or sorrow. For this, one has to develop the power of one's intellect. There are many mental powers or qualities which have to be developed otherwise a person cannot achieve his goal. For instance, it is necessary for a person to have self respect or to be proud, but not egotistic. Similarly, a person can be economical but not a miser. He can have strong willpower but not rigid and inflexible. He can possess patience and peace of mind without being passive and lazy.

Balance – The Foundation of a Beautiful Life

A Balanced life is a lute which produces music of bliss and peace from its strings

In our daily life our internal and external circumstances keep on changing at a very fast pace. For example, on the one hand it is essential to possess the art of harmony in fulfilling responsibilities towards family relationships, and on the other hand, to fulfill responsibilities as assigned in an office and in society. And by fulfilling all of these responsibilities, there has to be a balance between these personalities, and so the power of balance is most essential. In all these centres in any given circumstance if you become unbalanced then in that proportion you will either be successful or be defeated as a result. The art of balance is a lifetime of practice. If it comes into one's life then a person experiences unexpected happiness, bliss and a unique kind of pleasure. The art of balance is a strong foundation which makes one's life successful. Regarding this there is a famous story – Mahatma Buddha had a disciple named Shrone. Before becoming a disciple he was a prince. The moment he accepted initiation, he engrossed himself in deep meditation. He forgot his wordly comforts while in deep meditation. The consequence was that he became a skeleton as only his bones could be seen. One day, all of a sudden, Buddha's attention fell on Shrone. Buddha called him and said, "When you were a prince you used to play the lute very well. Today play music for me." Buddha brought a lute from one of the disciples and made all the strings of the lute loose. He gave the lute to Shrone and asked him to play. Shrone said, "Sir, its strings are very loose. They need to be tightened." Buddha took back the lute and made the strings so tight that if someone put his finger on the strings they would break. Now Buddha said, "Now play on, Shrone." Shrone said, "Sir, it is still not set to play music". Then he added, "When you tighten these strings in such a manner that they are neither loose nor tight, only then will music be produced."

Buddha gave a mysterious smile and said, "Shrone, this life is also like the strings of a lute because if you want to produce melodious music, then you have to set those strings in the centre, not too tight and not too loose. In the same way, if you want to listen to the music of bliss, happiness, silence and love from life then balance is the key. In other words, you will only have success when you maintain balance in all aspects of your life. In this context Kabir presented a very beautiful saying that, "This body is like that flute; if you don't use it in the right way, you lose your goal half way."

What is Balancing? – How Much is Required?

The meaning of balance is not to be equal but how much is actually required. For example, suppose you are preparing a dish called Khichdi (a mixture of rice and pulses). Will you put all ingredients in equal proportion? In other words, if the quantity of rice is say 1 kg, obviously you would not put the same proportion, 1 kilo of pulses, 1 litre of water and 1 kg of salt. The way in which the ingredients are blended and cooked in preparing a dish is balanced. In the same way, in attaining a goal there should be a balance in positive thoughts, actions and varying circumstances, obstacles etc. When there is this balance, only then can success be achieved. You will find this in the lives of many successful industrialists or scientists or artists and writers and politicians. They had the correct balance between inner qualities and powers bringing them success in that particular field. Let us take an example of the Father of the Nation, Mahatma Gandhi. He had only one goal for which he fought – India's freedom, and his life was fully balanced since he had decided to succeed in his goal. He was a man with strong willpower, hardworking, self confident, a sweet nature, full of moral and human values, divine qualities, creative, thought power, desire power, idealism and between all these things he had a wonderful balance which could be seen from his life. He had a positive and strong desire, strong devotion, faith, strong self confidence, strong willpower, hopeful thoughts and continuous effortless practice. These are the important elements for success. If you are moving ahead towards your goal with these qualities, then no obstacle can spoil your balance of life even though you may not possess material things.

Suppose a person is showing anger towards you and using bad language. The need of the hour is to control yourself. At this moment, the power to discriminate and the power of judgment is most essential. You need to become like an ocean and inculcate patience and sweetly count from one to ten. If you can do this, then you will be well-liked by people and considered a person of good character. Many people became famous politicians just because they had a balanced amount of sweetness in their speech. In this way, if you use your inner qualities, powers and pure intellect, then you will definitely achieve success even though circumstances are not in your favour.

Many times it happens that people become so active that they use their strong willpower, hard work, invest full time, overcome laziness but by becoming unsuccessful fail to evaluate the loopholes or fail to discover the reason for failure and thus lose patience. Before completing the work he runs away. That is why a successful person can be said to be the one who maintains a balance between all necessary capabilities and effort. If there is one bad quality it makes a persons' character unbalanced.

Balance is an Internal State which Comes By Practice

Suppose a person is learning to drive a car, he is given all the information about the clutch, brakes, gears, steering wheel etc, yet in the initial stages of learning he does not maintain proper coordination between these. His mind is filled with stress and the fear of having an accident is always there. Gradually, when be starts to learn he becomes confident that "Now I can drive the car smoothly." While driving he keeps a balance in talking, while listening to music and driving he keeps also the balance of the clutch, brakes, gears and steering. Similarly, if you want to reach your goal you have to keep a balance in your mental powers, physical powers and different circumstances so that the art of balance develops in you. This becomes neutral in the same way as an infant grows into a youth. The same infant who was unable to stand on his tiny feet now learns to stand on his own feet by balancing because of support and help. Later on he becomes one of the greatest body builders who you cannot push over, why? Because balance came by inner practice and this gave the power to succeed.

Be the Ruler of Your Mind

Understand that your mind is the property of God and always light a candle of positive thoughts within it. This will make the state of the mind so stable that no circumstances can shake or melt it.

The foundation of all materialistic and spiritual attainment is mental power. Man has to keep this in his authority. One who has control over his mind can attain whatever he wishes. Work which may be impossible for others will be possible for a man who is the ruler of his mind. A weak-minded person can never attain his goal, so the foremost thing is to become the king of your mind. The second thing is to make your mind strong and pure. If our mind is strong, only then can we complete difficult work. But our state of mind is just the opposite. We are less a ruler of the mind and more under its domination. Today, one has to experience that there is a different authority that uses the power of the mind. Only after knowing that authority, will we be able to build a prosperous and complete ideal character. That authority is none other than the 'soul' which is the rule of the body and the mind. The soul is a child of Almighty God Father. The soul cannot experience ruling authority until it breaks the subtle connection from the body and the mind.

Positive thoughts, emotions and intuition can never be achieved until man realizes the central authority, i.e. the soul. To some extent or some proportion, this works but we cannot say that full success in controlling is achieved. That is why you will find that complete happiness does not come into the life of a man. Life is full of music but it is like the Ganga river in which the poison of depression, stress, fear and peacelessness pollutes it. We know that alcohol is a poison, and yet it is still drunk. We very well know that this is harmful to one's health and sometimes one strongly decides to overcome this bad habit but still carries on drinking it. Because this has become a part of the subconscious mind or habit one is compelled to do so. Suppose our willpower is so strong that we decide not to drink, only then can we succeed. Then the same question arises as to how to inculcate willpower. Experience says that repeated promises also break down in front of the habit.

Today man possesses many weaknesses and bad qualities which are like habits. It is difficult to overcome these through knowledge or formal education. Yes, one thing is possible, that he can take a bold step to overcome these habits through understanding. To maintain continued effortless practice, activeness and clarity, he has to manage his time and at the same time, he needs to have knowledge also. For this, he has one unique and important role in his life. But to overcome weaknesses and to inculcate good virtues in life, he has to put in conscious effort.

The solution or medicine to this problem lies only with scientists or saints of the spiritual world. Generally, people fail to understand that you are a soul which contains the mind, intellect and resolves. Suppose you go to visit any patient you will show your sympathy by asking about his health or you will console him by telling him, "Your body is unwell, it does not matter. You will get well soon." The patient will definitely experience your feeling of sympathy. Now he will think that you had told him that your body is unwell, so he thinks that the body is different from the soul. But suppose you tell him, "Your mind or brain is unhealthy," immediately he will show his anger, why? Because people consider their mind and brain to be so united that they fail to understand that they are a soul, separate from the mind. This realization that mind is one of the powers of the soul brings a turning point in one's life. This is not only our experience but other's too. For this, one must understand the creation of the mind.

Creation of the Mind and its Understanding is Necessary for Success

For transformation and development of creativity, one needs to remain in silence. By understanding the mind one can enter into deep silence and introspection. If we evaluate our past life then we will find that most of our life has become mechanical. Our attitudes and emotions repeat themselves through the senses, due to which most of our life is spent in wasteful habits and we are compelled to continue in this pattern. In order to break the sleep of laziness, we must have willpower to get to the root cause of these habits.

The meaning of a mechanical life is that those habits which are manifest through our actions and thoughts repeat themselves against our conscious will. In other words, we lead a life of a servant. For example, an incident takes place in the mind but its impact falls on the senses. In this way any work done unwillingly is shown through one of the sense organs and this habit has its source in the mind. Therefore, try to understand this mechanism of the mind.

Importance of the mind

In general, our mind is a point which consists of salvation and slavery. The gateway to hell and heaven is through the mind. Proper use of the mind takes a man to the ocean of bliss and improper use takes him to the lake of sorrow. If you observe keenly, you will find that the mind is neither a friend nor a foe. It is merely an instrument. If you want to make it your instrument, object, vehicle or servant, then this can become your path to reach that par excellence.

All types of ideas, options, efforts and rules have been brought about in order to solve the problem of how to be free from thought. How to use the mind in a proper way? Suppose one person is sitting in an asylum and another one is meditating and experiencing bliss. Both of them have used their minds, or let us say that the mind has used one person, the one who is sitting in the asylum. By using the mind in the correct way one becomes stable and free of thoughts and the soul remains as a king. You may tell others that the soul has used the mind and by misuse of the mind a person becomes sick and that the soul who is the ruler remains passive, i.e. the mind has used the soul.

The identity of the mind

If there are no desires it does not mean that the identity of the soul has vanished. It means that the mind becomes a servant and so whenever there is a need, just like a king, you can use it. In other words, it remains passive in a state where there is no action. That is why when a yogi is in a soul conscious state, his mind remains passive and thus remains cool. Ordinary people have many expectations and desires which make their minds peaceless and thus the soul remains passive or inactive or absent.

Balance in Life

'Self' means experience of the soul which liberates man from various bondages and sets him on the seat of a king. It is through this experience that man can control his subtle sense such as the mind, intellect and resolves.

Perfect use of soul

Now a question arises as to how to use our mind in a perfect manner and go beyond it? It is our habits of previous births that have caused us to misuse our mind and thus we experience depression. In other words, mind becomes the king and we, the one who is speaking out is the soul, who becomes the servant. At the end, the soul becomes the servant and like a shadow, follows the mind. When the soul tells the mind to wait, still it does not obey its orders. Mind is busy with memories of the past and future or, we can say, it gives orders to the soul to follow like a shadow. Mind was an instrument which was to be like a servant but has become the king of the soul. Our hands, legs and other parts of our body function as per our instructions. If we tell our legs to stop and our legs keep walking or if they don't obey the instructions, then there will be a great disturbance in the body. In the same way, if our life is peaceless then it is because of the mind which has spread mismanagement as we have given it the right of freedom over the soul for a long time. If you give an order to your mind, then there will be a great struggle in your life. But a yogi uses his mind just as he uses a part of the body, for instance his leg, In other words, he uses it like a sense organ because the mind is a subtle organ of the soul which is imperishable.

Mind is an instrument or a subtle organ

Mind means memory. If the king soul wants to converse with someone or impart knowledge through speech, it needs to memorise it i.e. the need for the mind arises. But it uses it just like an instrument and later on leaves it. This mind remains like a mirror. But an ordinary person's mind is like a photo film. Suppose someone comes in front of you and then after his departure your mind thinks of that person's conversation and an image leaves an impact on your mind. It is imprinted in your memory. But the minds of great people are like a mirror. If any person or any conversation comes its way, let it come, or if it goes away, let it go. This is what happens with such great souls. That is why the mind is a subtle organ of the soul and has to be a servant of the soul, for only then can man achieve success. The mind has to end its kingship and, like an instrument, has to become a servant. This is the reason why one has to understand the creation of the mind in the correct way.

Nowadays, a psychiatrist uses a new expression 'Mind Body'. In other words, the mind is connected with the body or it can be said that the mind is a subtle authority which is located between the soul and the body. That is why the impact of the mind falls on the body and the body's impact falls on the mind. We need to have the power to rule over our mind and for this we will analyze many points. But here we will explain different means by which the goal can be achieved. This is the knowledge of the creation of the mind.

Use the mind like a vehicle

This does not mean that the mind is a part of our awareness, no. However, awareness flows through the mind. It is not part of the mind itself. The mind is like a bulb and awareness is the electricity. If the bulb breaks, it does not mean that the electricity is broken. But the flow of electricity ceases. Mind is just like a vehicle, an instrument and an object. Awareness flows through it. When two souls connect with each other through conversation, the mind becomes a channel through which these two souls interact. If we are driving a car or flying an airplane, it does not prove that we are the car or the airplane. These are vehicles. In the same way, the mind is also a vehicle. But we never use this fully. Its complete use is the outcome of true knowledge.

We use the mind in the same manner as a pilot uses an airplane. The fans of the airplane can be removed and it can be run on the road like a bus. But our intellect will not agree to it. In the same way, the way we use a bus, we use our mind also for fulfilling our desires, expectations and dreams. But if we use our mind as per true knowledge, then this mind will become an airplane which will enable the soul to lead a beautiful life. Remember one thing it is the soul that is the king and this has been proven. The soul uses this mind as a vehicle. The meaning of experience of the soul is to stop using the mind on one level and to just experience the liveliness of the soul – sometimes bliss, sometimes love and sometimes silence.

In this blissful moment, the soul can use the mind like a vehicle. Mind can be used for suggestions, analysis and different types of competitions. The soul becomes the king and gets the work done through its mind.

Body and mind are both servants, it is a vehicle but the soul who is thinking is hidden behind it. But we have forgotten this and have taught ourselves to be a vehicle. The only way to break the similarity of the vehicle and king is through the practice of meditation, silence and neutrality. Any soul, after attaining a complete state, remains in a body to do service. Mind is not destroyed. But the practice of neutrality breaks the similarity of the mind and body. Now the soul starts to understand "I am a soul and this is my mind." The middle bridge breaks down. Just while using one part of a machine, the person keeps an eye on the full machine but he cannot become the machine. In the same manner, much of the work of the body and mind is centred around the soul. We can lead two types of life. Firstly, we consider ourselves as an instrument. For example, consider yourself to be of any name or position, such as female, male, beautiful, officer, doctor, engineer etc. This is known as body consciousness. This is called the structure of the instrument. Or consider yourself as a structure which is depressed and peaceless. This is the bondage of life. The other way of doing work is to become aware and to become soul conscious so that if there is any problem in this instrument it can be rectified. But there is no margin of becoming tense or depressed. If the instrument stops functioning completely, then there is nothing to worry about because you will get a new instrument and new life after death. That is why you need to lead a neutral life with full awareness, attention and care. For this the best method is through silence.

You will transform yourself and attain all divine qualities through meditation, devotion and attention and a stress free life. I have experienced this so you too can experience it now.

Unconscious Habits

Today we find that all great people of the world are famous because of some special qualities or traits that they possess. Everyone thinks that he already possesses all those qualities which are essential for an ideal character. But to achieve this high goal, these values have their unique place.

When a person breaks this predetermining measuring rod, then he experiences insult, depression and an inferiority complex. Now he starts developing bad habits and a faulty character such as drug addiction, degraded behaviour and criminal behaviour. It is not only today's youth but also others who also start thinking that he cannot overcome bad habits. These bad habits will go along with us to the grave. In this way, they fall in a well of inferiority complex and depression.

What is habit?

Habit is something that is repeated again and again in the form of attitudes or emotions or unconsciously through the senses. Because of this, many wasteful habits have occupied their place in life. And many times, man spends his life forcefully in a vicious circle of waste. If a person wants to break this habit of laziness or unconsciousness, then he must be a person of strong willpower. The meaning of a mechanical life is to repeat those thoughts or actions against one's will. In other words, to live a life of a servant, just as when a person becomes angry over something. Now this anger comes to mind but is exhibited through the sense organs.

When any work is done with a purpose, then you automatically attain the readiness to do the work. This work goes into the conscious mind of the person. Now he does not require any conscious effort to do the work as it gets done in a very natural way which is known as habit which can be either good or bad. The outcome of bad habits is always dangerous or stressful, whereas the outcome of good habits is always positive and happy.

Habits are mechanical

Today man's life has become more or less mechanical. His every action shows his mechanicalness. Just as a machine works when its buttons are switched on, in the same way, 90% of work is done because of habit or inner inspiration. Just like an efficient motor car driver drives well and no longer needs to use his inner power because he has practised. But when we become angry due to habit, at that time it harms us. Today man's life is full of negative mechanics. Just like actions are compared with farming, in the same way habits are also like farming. Our character is influenced by our habits. The way our habits are created, our character will reflect them exactly. Just as one evil gives birth to many evils, in the same way, one habit gives birth to many habits. The habits which are created by practice, that habit may be tested in difficult circumstances. If a person does not have the practice of patience, courage and self confidence at the time of disaster, then he becomes tense and nervous and therefore destroys everything. One peg of alcohol starts with pleasure and passion. When the second peg of alcohol is consumed, it increases the pleasure and passion. In this way, every few pegs become a necessity and after some time it becomes his helplessness. Some drugs are such that while taking them for the first time, it becomes a person's habit unconsciously. Heroine is such a drug whose first use creates a habit and after the second time a person becomes addicted to it by which time it is too late. Alcohol too becomes a habit of that person.

"A peg of alcohol or any drug may reduce your depression for today but this will make tomorrow more dangerous than today. So try to overcome this bad habit of reducing depression."

In this way, man's life has become mechanical. Now the management of his life is no longer in his own hands, but in the hands of habits which are none other than the switch. That is why habits prove to have more impact than knowledge and advice. Many things start out as pleasure and passion but sooner or later that stability turns into bad habits. Just like wasteful speech and excess talking gives rise to a habit. Due to the habit of talking, he thinks waste and negative which not only makes his valuable time go to waste, but also puts the dirt of waste on others' minds. When you speak something wasteful or when you tell a lie or speak harshly, at that moment you are also listening to the same things again and again. The consequence is that repeatedly these things enter into the depths of your subconscious mind. Now these become a habit and create conditioning in our life.

Once upon a time two friends were standing near the bank of a river and were talking of the pleasure of watching the floods coming from the river. The current of the flow was so high that they saw a blanket was floating in the centre of the river. Both friends decided to bring the blanket from the river. Due to their curiosity one of them jumped into the river and swam close to the blanket. The friend who was standing at the bank saw that, instead of bringing the blanket, his friend was drifting away. His friend was concerned because, together with the blanket, his friend was drowning in the river. The other friend standing on the bank of the river started shouting, "Oh friend, leave the blanket and come back. Don't put your life in danger." The friend who was drowning shouted from the river, "Oh friend, this is not a carpet but a bear which is drowning in the flood. Now this bear has caught hold of me and is not letting go. So please come and help me."

Due to curiosity people put a cigarette in their mouth to take the pleasure. After some time the cigarette sticks in his mouth and in this way he becomes addicted to it. In the beginning he feels as if he is taking pleasure by smoking the cigarette, but after coming in contact with these drugs, his whole life becomes ruined.

We ourselves are the creators of all habits

It is impossible to be free of all habits because we are the creators of bad habits. That is why we are responsible for the creation of the right type of habits and we ourselves can destroy bad habits.

Does any bird like to be in a cage? Let the cage be made of diamonds, but no bird will like to be in that cage. Will your mind not become happy when you see birds stretching their wings and flying in the blue sky? Who doesn't wish to get rid of these problems of the universe and become a bird that can fly happily high in the sky. But to enjoy this freedom, only your desire is not enough but one has to put in hard effort.

Today man is in the state of that parrot that has strong wings to fly but due to cleverness of the hunter he gets trapped in a net because of his foolishness and fear.

You may be aware of what will be the idea or plan of the hunter while catching the parrot. The hunter ties a thin rope between two bamboo trees. He puts the bamboo's thin leaves in the rope and adds some red chillies with the leaves. The moment the parrot sits on the thin leaves of the bamboo to eat the chillies, he falls down because of his weight and takes the support of the leaves with its beak in order to save himself from falling. The parrot hangs upside down and, due to fear, cries te... te... he forgets his ability to fly and is easily trapped by the hunter.

We too get trapped in bad habits which are created by ourselves and thus we become depressed. We forget our inner capacity and become a servant of our habits.

Generally, man is dominated by his habits. Man is surrounded by bad habits and wants to get rid of them. There are many habits such as drugs, over-eating, excess sleep and many other habits of excess. A saying goes, "Anything in excess is always harmful."

The Foundation of all Expectation – The Soul as the Advisor

Every individual has the scope of developing divine powers within himself. Now scientists have also proved this truth that man has a stock of abundant inner powers. It is unfortunate for that person who spends his life in poverty in spite of sitting in a field of diamonds. Our inner state is also something like this. If someone tells us about diamonds, still we will not make a bold effort to dig out the diamonds from the field.

It is through the medium of advice of the soul that a person can create a relationship with the inner powers so that he can succeed in difficult situations. The best medicine to destroy bad thoughts, emotions and habits is to take the advice of the soul.

But those who think in this negative way should throw out these thoughts. It is not that you cannot overcome these habits and lead a new life. You will not find a single person in the world who is completely perfect. Then why are you thinking in this way? Forget your inferiority complex, insult and guilty consciousness and focus your attention once again on the measures to be taken towards a new life. You will definitely achieve success over these habits. Always go into the depth of these thoughts. You will surely succeed in attaining your pre-determined goal.

Tips for transformation of habits

The solution to the riddle of life lies in self respect. Self respect means soul consciousness. When you are in a state of soul consciousness, then good thoughts and good wishes automatically come from within for others. The first lesson to be soul conscious is "Who Am I". The answer to this question contains complete knowledge and the hidden solution to all problems. This one word answer is the key to the stock of knowledge, virtues, powers, wealth, etc. This puzzle is easily solved for intelligent people.

Go on repeating this statement that you are a child of the

Almighty God and a point of light. Your father is the Supreme Soul, so you have a birthright to attain all divine powers. You can definitely attain all powers from God and succeed in overcoming all bad habits. Connect yourself with the Supreme Soul by establishing all relationships with Him such as mother, father, friend, bride, bridegroom, etc. Become soul conscious and full of pure emotions and talk to God. Now you will experience bliss, vitality and courage to do something creative. And you will definitely experience positive vibrations of divine powers so that you bring about the necessary changes.

The habits which you wish to re-establish, first of all create a beautiful picture of it and try to visualize this picture repeatedly in your mind. Because it is our unconscious mind where our deep habits are present, and it accepts visual images more than words.

Go on implementing this process every day 4 to 5 times at least for 40 to 50 days.

Your unconscious mind is like a ghost who is closed inside a box. If you wish to awaken it and give it advice you have to bring your mind into an elevated stage. Only then will it accept your advice and act on it.

Alpha, Beta, Theta and Delta are four types of mental waves which indicate the state of the mind of each individual.
- Alpha waves produce 8 to 12 Hz or a maximum of 15Hz vibrations per second.
- Beta waves produce 15 to 50 Hz times or more vibrations per second.
- Theta waves produce 4 to 8 Hz vibrations per second.
- Delta waves produce 0 to 4 Hz vibrations per second.

This is produced when the person is in a deep sleep.

The experience of the soul and the Supreme Soul is possible only through Raj Yoga meditation. It is through this meditation that a person can develop two important powers, firstly, to receive power from the Supreme Soul and secondly to send those vibrations to other souls.

Raj-Yoga can give many powers to mind

For this, the best time for experiencing is early morning at 4.00 am when the mind is free from activity. At this time, you should sit in a quiet place and remember God and take your mind into silence and bliss. And when your mind is in a stage of complete rest, then give clear instructions to your subconscious about the habits or character which you would like to build.

We have to always keep in mind that as far as possible we have to remember these instructions while working throughout the day. It may be possible that in the beginning your subconscious mind may reject this new instruction. But don't lose patience; carry on giving advice to your mind. You will definitely succeed in achieving success.

You have to integrate this into your character with conscious effort, willpower and self confidence. At the same time, follow the instruction and practice Raj Yoga meditation.

We will discuss different ways of practising meditation in the coming chapters. Let us take one type of commentary to be given to your mind. You are a point of light residing in the centre of the forehead. The Supreme Soul is like the sun residing above the sky. Its bright, silent rays are falling on your soul and you are experiencing that the dirt of bad habits is being erased from your soul.

It is easy to become addicted to bad habits which bring only temporary happiness to a person, but it will be difficult to live with the consequences which will not only be dangerous but also harmful at the same time. If it is difficult to overcome these bad habits, then is it easy to live with these? If you cannot overcome them, then prove that you can live happily with them.

It becomes impossible for people to continuously fight against defamation, hatred and indifference in life. Nature also creates different types of mental defects in that person and destroys his whole character. It can be concluded that an ideal person must overcome bad habits as soon as possible. It becomes easy for him to live with good habits because this makes your life happy, active and contented. It is a little difficult to inculcate good habits but not impossible.

Just as good and bad are quantified differently by society, nation, there is a norm which is the same for everyone. It will be better if you judge for yourself with a broad and open mind.

Self Control Means Decency of Self Discipline

It is so simple to split a thin thread. But a rope made up of these threads can tether a huge elephant. It is possible to extinguish a small fire with the help of a handful of water, but if the same fire becomes a conflagration, then it is impossible to extinguish even with the help of the fire brigade.

The fire brigade of 340 men failed to extinguish the fire which took place in the World Trade Centre Tower in America where an airplane hit the towers.

A person needs strong self discipline to build a good character and impressive personality. Success will be difficult if we do not have control of our inner excitement and feelings. Self control means that a person will be positive even in negative circumstances. If a person wishes to see success in his life, firstly he has to be stable in opposing circumstances and secondly, he needs to exercise self control.

A successful life means the flow of divine and pure Ganges of action against the banks of imperishable love. But in this corporeal world of action, only those people succeed who have control over their senses and who have developed their intellect for self control, and who wish to succeed in attaining the great goals of their life. They must know how to gain control over their senses.

The beauty of human life is in self control and Godly rules. Control of the mind and intellect gives rise to self control in a natural way. The remembrance of the self brings all work under control. The actions which I carry out whilst in remembrance, others will be inspired to do the same. This thought will encourage us to do work with full control.

The atmosphere which we are going through is covered by the illusion of bad habits. If you wish to break these old habits then you have to think intellectually and sit quietly in a room and experiment in this practice.

Resolves Become the Second Nature of a Human Being

Let us start with a small incident. There was a married couple who used to perform a stage show in a drama company. The husband used to make his wife stand in front of a rotating throne and shoot an arrow at her. He was such a genius in shooting arrows that they looked as if they were going to touch her body but ultimately would strike the throne. Her

Balance in Life

husband was so expert in this field that not a single arrow could touch his wife's body. He had been playing this game on the stage for several years. After some time there was a small dispute between the husband the wife and sometimes he used to become angry. Once he thought of ending the dispute by killing his wife on the stage whilst performing the game. One day his anger went out of control and he decided to shoot the arrow into her chest as he wanted to end the dispute. When the wife was standing on the stage he gave a glance and closed his eyes to shoot the arrow. Because he was already an expert in shooting with his eyes open when he pointed his arrow towards his wife's chest and shot his arrow everyone sitting in the hall started clapping hands and the whole hall was filled with the echoing of the clapping. He opened his eyes to see what had happened to the arrow and found that it was almost touching the body but had struck the throne instead. He had shot around 40 to 50 arrows, but surprisingly not even a single arrow had touched his wife's body. Just like the other days, his performance was exactly the same.

Why did this happen? Several years' practice was deeply rooted in his habit. Though he wished to shoot his wife he failed. Because the practice of aiming or shooting became a subconscious habit, even though he wished otherwise, still he was unable to shoot at his wife's chest. The same thing happens in most people's lives. That person's practice of shooting arrows was over many years, but our habits are not formed over several years, but rather over several births. The attraction of the senses is so strong that if even if we wish we fail to shoot at the target. Just as a scientist understands nature and attains success, in the same way we should become introvert and understand the senses of our inner nature. It is knowledge that can enable us to become the controller of the senses.

Self control does not mean suppression

Self control means wakefulness, wisdom and good memory. Suppression is like the lid of a can which is closed and the water is boiling inside. When the vapour rises then definitely it will burst. Man either suppresses anger or keeps expressing a little, but one day this suppressed power breaks all the safety valves. And this blast creates a huge loss. This power of anger can change its form either to mercy or spiritual excitement. Sex lust can change into love and celibacy. But if a person continues becoming angry and hates others little by little, then his inner powers will leak and from where will he bring forth the power of mercy? Pleasure is just like a bucket with a thousand holes. Even though you take out plenty of water from the well, when you bring the full bucket of water up from the well, it is almost empty. The power of the soul flows through a thousand holes due to sex lust, anger, greed, attachment, etc and the water of unlimited achievements is emptied from the bucket of life. There are two types of risk due to the senses in life. Firstly, the risk of pleasure which is equivalent to a bucket with a thousand holes and secondly, the risk of suppression is just like a can filled with boiling water. Self control means to be aware of the attraction of the senses. This understanding or knowledge makes us successful. Self control means to succeed in controlling the senses. But a person who knows the mystery of all the senses and understands their inner nature can succeed in controlling his senses.

Be watchful and alert towards inner excitement

Whenever excess anger arises in a person, he generally does not pay attention to it. He meditates and at the same time if there is urgent work to do he focuses his attention on that. This is most necessary. But the second angle is that even when you become angry, pay attention also to the anger. It has been observed that we think a lot but pay less or no attention. Whenever we become angry, we are taken away by those thoughts of anger and establish a good rapport with these thoughts of anger. Then it never happens that the anger boils inside and one becomes distant and simply observes it. The foundation of science is experimentation and observation. In the same way, in spiritual life observation and attention is required to bring about changes in values of life. You will not come to know the senses until you observe with neutrality and at a distance. Our senses keep on doing their work and we create a false impression that we have done or are doing something. If you feel hungry see to it whether you are feeling hungry or your stomach is feeling hungry? Try to find out the centre of the sensation of hunger. If you keenly observe you will find that the centre of the sensation is the stomach. One is to feel hungry and the other is to know. The senses of the stomach are an instrument which only gives the signal to put food into it. Otherwise this instrument will stop functioning

Food for the soul is important for success

The food of our divine intellect is pure thoughts.

Those who wish to attain supreme silence and bliss, must pay attention to the food of the soul. Food means to gather good from the outside and put it inside. We consume this food through the five senses. That is why it is necessary to gain control over the food we ingest. We must consume only food which is helpful for the soul to walk on the path of silence and that which does not make the soul become peaceless. The food should be such that it increases concentration and remembrance of God and which creates supreme, auspicious and creative thoughts. It is not only depression that affects the mind but also the pleasure of the senses which activates the mind. How will a mind be peaceful when it is running behind the vices and pleasures? When a person drinks alcohol, you can see how the mind becomes active and nimble. The food which stimulates a person, such as alcohol, meat, etc should not be accepted. It is not only alcohol but also lustful vision with which we look at others that makes our mind unstable. If a person watches films of sex, violence, etc for three hours, he is also consuming the wrong type of food through his eyes. Then, the whole day those thoughts will come to his mind and stimulate his desire will activate his mind and then at night he will dream of this. Similarly, when you are listening to the radio, then the waves are carried to the brain through the ears. This is also food. Suppose someone asks you what you are listening to. Many times your reply is, "I have nothing to do and so I am listening to the radio." But you are not sitting idle, because in fact you are consuming the wrong type of waves in the form of dirt. While walking along the road people also have the habit of looking at everything. People read advertisements about films and such like. It is surprising to know that what people are labouring for? Are they paid for reading these advertisements? If they open a newspaper, they read it from cover to cover, but do not realize the kind of food they are taking in through the sense of sight. Just as people do not eat grass and stones, then why are they putting dirt into the brain.

Vain thoughts are also dirt for the soul. So it is necessary to get rid of these as they are harmful in different ways. That is why the thoughts need to be checked by the power of the intellect for only then will time and energy be saved.

Remember that the food which you are putting in your stomach will not be harmful but consuming subtle food such as wasteful thoughts will definitely be harmful. If you get mucus in your stomach there are medicines to cure it. But if you get mucus in your brain then there is no medicine for this. Yes, the medicine is available from spiritual people and the medicine is self control. Self control means that a person has to keep an intellectual watchman at the gate of all the sense organs so that he could only eat those foods which keep the mind healthy and strong, due to which the mind becomes stable and experiences complete bliss and silence. Suppose a person is having complete control over his diet and does those activities which take the soul on the path of peace through the senses, then he will quickly reach the peak of divinity in his life.

Only those refined people succeed in self control who understand the hidden workings of the senses and who pay attention to the food which he is consuming. In this way a self controlled person walks easily on the secret path to attain his aim.

Importance of Volition, Concept Force and Action Force in Fate Formation

5

The Power of Desire, Thoughts and Actions in Building Fate

> Shakespeare said, "Our life is a mixture of good and bad experiences."

We are generally ignorant about the mystery of the laws of action between fate and effort. But the laws of action are unchanging and are fixed within the drama. Our fate and our effort intersect at some point. But it is very difficult to see this mysterious point. One thing is clear to see and that is that great people have come close to this mysterious point. It is happiness and a stress free attitude towards the reward of action that is important. Let us throw some light on these topics by putting forth suggestions so that we too can come to know this mystery and enjoy a successful life.

It is possible that man carries out his actions in the knowledge of the laws of action which are elevated, loving and full of justice. Various obstacles come on the way to success. A person can definitely attain success and the reward if he keeps in mind the laws of action in building his fate, understands the great power of action and the mystery of the interrelation between hard effort and reward. Before implementing the best way to carry out the actions to attain success, try to understand the great rules of the law of action. For this, it will be better to write something about the philosophy of action.

Action

Human beings perform three types of actions, namely:
1. Future Action
2. Present Action
3. Past Action

Future action

In this, both good fruit as well as bad fruit comes. This fruit can be of the previous birth or the current birth also. But it is always the result of past actions. Sometimes man is surrounded by such circumstances that he is unable to rescue himself from the situation. He has to suffer the consequences of the actions in previous births. But this does not mean that we assume this and become depressed and start thinking, "Whatever is written is my fate, I will get only that much," or "No-one can postpone their destiny." No, it is not like this. Fate includes both types of actions. There is a weight on both sides of the scales. By putting in some effort the balance of depression on the scales can be made lighter. Action has three powerful forms in building fate. The power of thought, the power of desire and the most important power is that of action. You can reduce your debts by receiving power through God by meditating and then using these powers in the right direction. This will be discussed in detail in the coming chapters.

Present action

There are those actions which are done by us at the present time. Some of our actions of the present moment are our destiny which end as soon as we complete the work and some are accumulated for the future.

Past action

Debts come at the end of our destiny or in the form of fate in our next birth or in the current birth.

Every individual, either knowing or unknowingly, builds his fate with the pen of action. Happiness, grief, profit, loss, success, defeat, etc happen due to the actions of previous births.

This law of action works in all circumstances of life. Now it depends upon you how deeply you understand this mystery and work towards creating your own success.

Rules for Action

Action means work. This work arises from desire and then comes the thought of completing it. Afterwards comes the power of action which comes after desire, thought and action. Our every action is the corporeal form of our desires and thoughts.

When each action is completed, at that time new desires and thoughts arise. In this way, the law of action is the law of change in the power of action.

The law of action works in a natural way. This is called the natural law. In this law, there is no external power.

For instance, a person may murder a person and can be saved from the court hearing but can never be saved from the law of such an action.

According to scientific law or natural law, if a person puts his hand in the fire it will get burnt. In this same way, along with the law of action and natural law, a person pays attention to the laws of the subtle world and the subtle powers and then does his work. The result may come immediately or may take some time. This is clearer for spiritual people as one of the major components is connected with the spiritual world.

There are three important powers in building fate:
1. The Power of Thought: which builds the character of man
2. The Power of Desire: which offers a chance to man to attract things towards himself
3. The Power of Action: which builds an atmosphere of closeness

The power of thought

The power of thought occupies an important place in the success of life and in building one's fate. It is through thoughts that the character of a person is built. Vinoba Bhave have said, "Behaviour becomes blind if the light of thought is extinguished."

Shakespeare said, "There is nothing good or bad, it is only our thoughts that make it good or bad."

The Upanishads say, "Evil thoughts take a person to a path of evil action."

Thought – a wonderful place to build character: That is why the power of thought has an important place in building fate. Thoughts are subtle action power. The moment we start thinking about any object, person or quality, or bad habits or strengths or weaknesses, etc, at that moment the vibration starts spreading throughout the world of thought. This vibration is in accordance with the object or person about whom we are thinking. When a vibration starts due to a special type of emotion or thought, then its repetition becomes easier. If you go on repeating any thought then accordingly that vibration starts spreading very quickly. After some time, this vibration automatically starts creating the thoughts. Against your wish, those thoughts go on repeating. In this way, it becomes our habit to continue thinking the same thoughts. The result is that bad habits develop and the qualities relating to these habits create one's character.

Thoughts which build fate and vibration: The good qualities or bad qualities are built due to these laws. If you wish to develop those moral and spiritual qualities, then you have to start thinking seriously again and again to patiently implement them in your practical life. You will find within a few days that those qualities are developing at a fast pace. Any negligent or lazy person can never develop any quality without this process of thought. If a person wants to get rid of these bad qualities, then it is possible only by following these laws. These are the qualities which gradually enter into the depths of the inner mind to build permanent, new habits. And it is according to these permanent habits that a person's character is formed. This character becomes an important element in attaining success or defeat or fortune or misfortune. Vibrations are created by continuously thinking about qualities and powers and this vibration creates the habits and thereby the nature of that particular person. These good qualities become the foundation of his happy and peaceful life. The accumulated habits of his previous births become the natural habits in this current birth. These natural habits are nothing but his character which is exhibited. These habits are an important part of action, due to which fate is built.

The power of desire

Desire power means thought power. Thought power is one of the superior root powers. The fastest communication is the language of thought. A person may be far away where there may not be any instrument for communication but through the language of thought, messages can be transmitted. People cannot be transformed by speech or any other instrument but can be transformed easily by the power of thought.

Attraction towards any object is desire. Whenever we desire to possess any object, person or emotion a magnetic relationship develops. Our strong desire of attraction compels us towards them or we attract them towards ourselves. This is called the power of desire. This desire power compels that soul to achieve that object and inspires him to put in hard effort to attain it. Many obstacles may come on the path to attaining the desired fruit, but he hardly cares about these obstacles and strives hard to achieve the goal. Finally, he gets the object either in this birth or the next, but he definitely gets it.

It is our subtle mind which works behind nature and along the way he will start to understand the mystery of nature at a deeper level and success will easily be achieved. However, a relationship has to be established between your mind and nature. For this, the foremost aspect is to stop useless thoughts entering into your mind. You will find that your mind will start producing strong creative thoughts which will not only activate nature but also creative mind of man to offer him the desired results.

You will find that there are two immovable or fixed energies present everywhere, which are known as wealth and debt. This is called the energy circuit. Like a magnet, the energy keeps moving between these two fixed assets. You will find that on the one hand, one fixed energy is always moving, changing and vibrating. On the other hand, the other fixed energy is always stable, strong, unchanging and not vibrating. Man also needs powerful thought power and controlled speed of the mind. The moment there is an establishment of harmony of relationship between the mind and nature, at that time unlimited doors of success and creativity open. The need of the hour is that you create powerful thoughts so that the flow of your creativity will be continuous.

The power of action

It is through action that our corporeal body and its surrounding atmosphere are built. Let us understand this in a clear way.

Suppose two people are donating two lakhs to society to build a pond. The first person donates two lakhs for charity without having any selfish attitude. The second person also donates two lakhs, but he has a subtle desire that people regard him as a social worker and consider him a pure soul. He feels that people will vote for him in the coming election for the post of Sarpanch (Head of the village). Let us see what will be the difference .

In the next birth, both of them will get equal wealth, a bungalow, money, etc because both of them had donated two lakhs. Beside this, both of them will get an equal proportion of happiness through varying ways such as friends, relatives, etc. But the greatest difference in the action will be that the first person will take birth with all divine qualities or good character such as good nature, merciful unselfish, etc. And the second person will take birth with weaknesses such as selfishness, miserliness, etc. The former person will use his wealth towards himself, friends, relatives and society and will get blessings from others. His life will be filled with happiness and he will receive unlimited love from everyone. Whereas the second person will be a miser and thus he will not utilize his wealth towards himself and family but due to greed he will invest his wealth in the hope of getting more interest. He will neither get any blessings nor any happiness in his current life. In fact, he will receive curses from everyone. The consequence will be that he will have to face serious problems in the later part of life. Even if he desires to do that in the next birth he will do this great work like others but still the current circumstances would be so extreme that he would be helpless in performing his work. And his life will go to waste in tears.

Whatever actions we perform in our lives we receive the fruit exactly according to that action. Whatever you give, you get the same in return. If you make someone depressed, then you will get that in return. This is the third law of action.

Impact of Thoughts

I strongly feel that on the basis of my experience I would like to clarify in the coming chapters how the subtle power of our thoughts works from the mental world or the subtle world into the corporeal world. I am familiar with those great souls who go beyond this body and corporeal world to the subtle world through divine vision. Their experience is unique. These great souls, by just thinking, see the vision of this corporeal world in that subtle world. They see things which are not only beautiful, but such unique objects that are of a higher order which are impossible to find in this corporeal world.

Today scientists have proven that the world appears to be physical but in reality it is a form of energy. In other words, if anyone could see the subtle atoms such as electrons, protons or neutrons with an instrument, then he can see that the whole world is seen as a mass of light and nothing else. At that moment you will feel as if this world is a dream. This world is created by some sort of light but the subtle world is created by even more subtle waves of light. That is why the power of action which is required in creating any object in this materialistic world is a larger energy of the natural world. The nature of the subtle world is so subtle that everything is created only by thought power. One mind gets affected by the subtle elements or subtle waves. In this way, if any person after going to the subtle world uses his thought power in the corporeal world, then that impact will be very powerful. But that mental power can be developed only here.

Extensive impact of thought power

Now let us analyze the extensive impact of our thought power. The vibrations that are created on the human mind create an impact and change our consciousness and this is called thought. The nature of the subtle world has different forms in which different types of impact are manifest. The way desires, emotions and expectations arise create different types of mental waves, in the same way the human body is a medium through which thoughts are expressed.

Hazrat Suleman said, "The way a person thinks in his heart, he is like that."

Mahatma Buddha said, "Whatever man is today is due to his thoughts."

Vivekananda said, "Thoughts are important inspirational powers."

Mahatma Gandhi said, "Man is made up of his thoughts because whatever he thinks, he becomes like that."

There are basically two impacts of thoughts in our life:
1. **Visible Impact:** Man has less knowledge in respect of thought in this field. Thoughts are the power of action. If it is not expressed in speech or action, still then its impact will be much more in the form of waves.
2. **Invisible Impact:** All of us know that the basis of completing any task is the power of thought. The way electricity is required to run a motor, in the same way the electricity of thought is required to run the motor of action.

The impact of thought can be broadly classified into two parts:

1. **The impact on the person who is thinking:**
    i. **Habit:** The impact of different thoughts and its forms are different. Its colours are also different as the vibrations per second or the length of the vibration depends upon the type of thought. Just like some thoughts of attachment are such that once the vibration starts, then without any effort its repetition starts and that person becomes trapped in the thought form which is difficult to get out of.
    ii. **Creation of qualities:** Our repetitive habits create a vibration in our unconscious mind for that object due to which that person's character is built. In this way, it is thoughts that build habits and qualities and this is the fruit of thought power.
2. **Impact created due to thought waves:**
    i. **The impact is in the form of vibrations in the external world:** Vibrations are like an unlimited sky and a subtle element which is more subtle than light. It is also known as the mind element. The moment a person thinks, at that moment the thought spreads into the whole universe. Just as you throw a stone in a lake, the ripples that it creates are more in the centre and gradually vanish, in the same way the vibration starts in the mind. In this way the vibration of thoughts spreads in the atmosphere and create an impact and this is like a contagious disease which enters into others' minds. The way rays of light and sound waves spread in the corporeal world, exactly in the same way these vibrations also spread throughout the mental world and the emotional world due to which many people are affected.

    People may have either one thought or a combination of thoughts. Generally, the impact of the combination of many emotions and thoughts affect different parts of the mind. The waves which are produced due to elevated thinking makes the power of the mind not only sharp but also divine. Whereas the impact of

simple and confused thoughts affects our mind which consists of low and simple emotions and a mind full of desire. Whether the thoughts are high, medium or low level, accordingly they create an impact on others.

The thought waves carry with them the emotions but do not carry any influence of objects. For instance, suppose a person has full faith in the Goddess Gayatri and prays. Another person who is a devotee of Shri Krishna will not increase his worship for the Goddess Gayatri, but he will worship Shri Krishna even more because he has picked up the emotion. The topic is not Krishna but the waves which are created for that thought start to spread far and wide and will create a different impact of its own. If these waves touch the mental stage of a person who does not have any devotion for worship, then it can produce elevated thoughts in that person. In the same way, if the negative vibrations of anger, jealousy or selfishness spreads in the atmosphere without making anyone a target, then this negative wave will enter into the minds of all people. It may be possible that the impact of these waves may increase unexpectedly and it may increase the waves of anger in a third person for his simple mistake and may kill him. We very often come across such cases in history in court in which the criminal accepts his crime with the guilt that, "I did not want to kill but I do not know what happened to me that I carried out this bad deed." This type of thought wave creates an impact in both directions, i.e. positive and negative. In this way the hidden man who has not murdered but became an inspiring force to put negative waves in the murderer also becomes in some proportion responsible for the fruit of that negative action.

ii. **In the form of an image:** The second impact of thought waves in the atmosphere is that it is from this that an image or figure is created. The type of thoughts we create whether knowingly or unknowingly or the moment it creates an emotion in our mind, at that time this state of mind for a period of time creates an image accordingly in nature. This image consists of liveliness which has the power to perform action as per our thoughts or emotions. For instance, suppose you are sitting in America and you have a feeling of hatred or evil, then an image of a person will be created from you who will search for that person and will do harm to him as per your thought or state of mind. Just opposite to this will be that you are loving towards someone and immediately your angelic image will reach that person and benefit him. Just like a mother has a bond of love towards her child and this image reaches the child and saves him. Such type of work was done even in the olden days when the sages used to either give blessings or curses. The angelic stage is the quickest way of doing mental service. In this form, there is no realization of happiness or grief. This image is for thoughts and state of mind which are affected by beauty or ugliness. The thought and the image remain for a short time, a few months or even years.

Its form, type, colour and time are affected by the following:
1. Implementation of good qualities along with its colour. (Good qualities mean pure and divine thoughts and bad qualities mean degraded thoughts.)
2. Its shape depends on whether it is good or bad
3. The more clarity in the thoughts and emotions, the clearer its perimeter.
4. Its time is related to strength and sharpness.

If something vibrates from 0 to 50 times per second then it produces sound.

If this vibration is increased one level then it produces ultrasound.

If this vibration is increased to an even higher level, then electricity is produced.

If this vibration is increased to an ultra high level, then it changes into electric light.

If this vibration is increased yet even higher, then the light cannot be seen through these eyes, such as x-rays and infrared rays. If it is made even more subtle then the result is that we have colour.

What is the quality of our thoughts? It is from thoughts that colours are created. For instance, the feeling of tremendous love produces shining pink and a feeling of devotion produces yellow. In other words, your qualities which depend upon the type of thoughts create a shape which can be either beautiful colours or ugly colours.

Suppose you have produced thoughts related to greed, then that shape which is formed will be like a bent nail or the shape will be snatched away. Suppose these thoughts are pure and clear emotions, they will be tall and beautiful and sky blue and red in colour.

The more pure, clear and divine your emotions and thoughts, the more clear would be your image or form. If your thoughts are simple, wasteful and illogical, then your image will reflect that and then become shattered.

Different Aspects of Thoughts

Suppose a person thinks of love, peace, anger, hatred for another person, then the initial impact will be in the form of a vibration. The second stage is that these thoughts will form an aura around that person. If he is sitting idle then it will enter into his aura and create the vibration accordingly. If that person is sitting with a particular thought or emotion then the speed of the vibration and its intensity will increase rapidly. Now that person's action will start according to the vibrations in the form of thoughts, desires and actions. Suppose a person is busy working, then the thought will be in his aura until he becomes free from his work. Good thoughts take the form of an angel and bring benefit to that person. However, evil thoughts harm the other person severely. In this way, thoughts either good or evil have an impact on someone only when his aura matches. Suppose a severely depressed person is sending such thoughts to a pure and great soul who has a very pure aura around him. Then the result will be that the negative thoughts will not match with his pure aura and will return to the sender. And it is likely that the sender of such thoughts will suffer serious losses.

Suppose one has a thought to fulfill one's own selfish attitude, then the aura will be revolving around him. And when he sits idle, at that time the vibration will enter his aura. This is why it is said, "Every individual is either a friend or enemy to himself". And "An idle mind is the devil's workshop." In this way each individual is surrounded by his own vibration of thoughts and emotions. Yes, a Rajyogi can liberate himself from the impact of evil as well as good. He can experience salvation by remaining neutral and becoming soul conscious.

In short, we have explained this scientifically so that while achieving your goal without any obstacles you don't fall into the trap of joy and sorrow. You can achieve a happy life along with success. If you keep in mind all our efforts on the road to success then you will find that self confidence gradually grows and you achieve your goal without any obstacles.

Desire and the Power of Desire

Generally, everyone desires to have peace, happiness and prosperity in life. The most important desire is wealth and fame and one tries one's best to attain these. Behind every action there is an inner aspiration. All great people believe that this universe is inspired by desires and expectations. The nature of a human being is to desire. But in order to achieve the desired fruit he must never think or carry out any action in an unethical or immoral way. Our desires must not be so strong that they destroy our intellect and we become impatient to achieve it at any cost. This is called greed. A greedy man can never lead a happy and contented life. An honest person can be judged by testing his greed.

Jaabidan-e-Khirad said, "If you remove greed from your heart then the noose will be removed from around your neck".

Ayodhya Singh Upadayay said, "One who always thinks of harming others can never achieve happiness in life because his greed will always degrade him."

In this way, due to immoral desires, a man becomes addicted to anger, sex-lust, jealousy and ego. It is difficult to overcome desire completely but it should not increase to such an extent that it kills our intellectual power and compel us to do unethical actions. This state would be comparable to an animal. Such desires must be overcome.

Desire has a very important role to play in man's progress or failure. On the one hand good desires lead to prosperity and on the other hand degraded desires lead to destruction. Any kind of lack creates a feeling of failure and due to this a craving arises and manifests as desire. Because of these unlimited

The Power of Desire, Thoughts and Actions in Building Fate

desires man continues to wander around and thereby shatters his inner consciousness by becoming peaceless. It is said, "Unending desires will never make a man good. The root cause of all evils is desire."

Maharshi Vishwamitra said, "As soon as one's desires are fulfilled, then another desire emerges like an arrow which is constantly aimed at its target." The desire for pleasure is never ending and sparks like a fire when oil is poured over it. One who always desires pleasure can never be happy in life."

Mahatma Buddha said, "Depression comes from desire, fear comes from desire, and to liberate oneself from desire is to neither know depression nor fear."

Desire power

Emerson said, "The one aim of life makes desire power strong. It is always a golden opportunity for a man having strong will power."

When a person's energy is used for fulfilling a goal, this is called determination or desire power. Desire power means to direct all one's energy in one direction. Desire alone cannot bring results but it is determination which is equally as important. A Chinese saying goes, "Great souls possess desire power and weak souls possess only desires." Man can create miracles with desire power.

How desires can change into desire power

Let us imagine that you have a gun in your hand and a bird is sitting on a tree in front of you. Now a desire comes into your mind to hunt the bird. If you want to get this bird you first have the desire. But by merely having the desire the bird will not come and fall into your lap from the branch. If the desire continues, this will have no impact on the bird. Indeed it will be singing its song with pleasure. The desire should change into desire power and for this you must focus your whole energy. All your concentration power must be focused on your eyes and on your finger on the gun. Now it is possible that the bullet could go towards the bird but you can still withdraw. But once the bullet is shot then it can never come back. This determination power can be experimented with in any situation. Suppose you become angry and want to harm someone, you still are able to withdraw. Your emotions have not taken the form of a bullet and no-one has been hurt. If the bullet of the emotions had been shot it is still possible to apologise so that the outcome will not be so bad. Whenever a person tries to achieve his greatest goal through determined effort, such a person is known as a strong desirous person. It is a blessing to have good determination for achieving success. A person's success remains hidden behind his thought power.

Rajendra Sharma said, "Thought is actually the ladder to success. If anyone wishes to do some routine work, he also needs to think first. Suppose your soul has the thought of appearing for an examination, then in order to be successful you have to learn. If one wishes to fulfill his greatest thought then he has to surrender his life to it. The faster the thoughts, the faster would be the fulfillment of auspicious thoughts.

Formula for Desire and Purpose

There is a strong inter-relationship between nature and human beings. On the one hand destiny has a great role to play and on the other hand there is a continuous flow of information, energy and the wonderful direction of the drama which is seen through this vast universe. When, where, what and how does it happen? From where does the drama come and who is the director? In every element of unlimited nature there is information. The human brain has the capacity to accept this energy of nature and utilise it in a wonderful say. Let us understand this in detail. Today science has also agreed that the universe is not an element but an energy. In other words, its form is subtle and invisible. This invisible energy then exhibits itself as an element and in this way the universe is a hide and seek play of visible and invisible elements. The form of nature is constantly changing and the form of energy is also ever changing.

If we look at the five elements we can see that there are many common things between us and plants, trees and other species. Our actions are very similar. And the same goes for the elements, but the subtle forms of energy and emotions which we possess are more superior because we possess a brain as well as mind and intellect which stores information and act as a memory. It is through the brain that you not only feel the subtle sensations of the body but also bring changes as per your desires by giving orders and directions. This unique capacity of ours can impact the information of the subtle world to bring about the desired fruit. With the power of the mind nature serves us and it is through might and purity that a person can make his mind holy and this is the most ethical path.

Rajyoga

Rajyoga means to experience a different authority separate from the body and to connect with the Supreme Soul to take power. Meditation is a platform which is conducive to creating an atmosphere in which all desires are fulfilled. The union of the soul and the Supreme Soul connects us to nature. Just as there are crores of cells in your body which understand your subtle emotions and work in a harmonious way, you may also be aware that each is constantly receiving messages.

If a person works in harmony with nature and spiritual laws, then definitely all his desires and expectations will automatically be fulfilled. Meditation opens the channel of energy within and ambition gives form to that energy by giving it some direction. It is ambition which changes the invisible into the visible without any effort when spiritual laws are followed.

Today man is surrounded by confusion and dilemma. Even though life is limited and uncertain, desires are unlimited. In the past it was possible to fulfill limited desires and attain limited fruit. But the question arose as to how anyone can possibly live in this vast empire of greed and endless desires. Can anyone live contentedly in this situation?

Swami Ramtirth said, "The moment you rise above your desires, at that time the object of your desire start to hunt you."

Swami Ramtirth also said, "On acquiring any object the greed which arises in the heart tells us clearly that the desire is a degraded wordly desire."

Acharya Chatursen said, "The root cause of all grief is greed. Greed does not mean using the practical world for necessities. It is when the desire for obtaining more than one needs that it is called desire. This gives rise to the vices and is the root cause of all misfortune. When one becomes greedy, at that time he enjoys it, but eventually this greed kills him and his life is destroyed.

Lack of Soul Awareness in Life

Man expects happiness in return for fulfilling every desire. The question arises, is it possible to become happy without fulfilling desires?

The senses are drawn to experience pleasure. Man is tempted towards the fulfillment of the vices because he identifies with the body and senses. He has accepted himself as the body and has created a false identity with it. Today every experience of pleasure has become an unconscious habit and he is dominated by these habits. If this consciousness breaks, then he will realize that he is a soul quite separate from the body. In this state his nature is peaceful and blissful. Man should not become addicted to his weak desires by becoming trapped in greed and must never carry out any unethical actions. Instead he should feed himself by pure thoughts and be mentally healthy so that he can experience love, purity and bliss. We are not the body, but a soul and the original nature of the soul is power, peace, knowledge and bliss. The root cause of all problems in the world is that we have assumed ourselves to be the body.

The moment a person liberates himself from the choice of desires or vices, he starts to experience eternal bliss from the soul. Anyone can be free from stress by controlling his desires through the practice of Rajyoga meditation. This is the best tool recommended by scientists too.

The Desires of the Mind Can Never be Fulfilled

It has been observed that man always becomes addicted to degraded desires and thereby fails to create a happy life. Once upon a time a beggar stood at the doorstep of an emperor and said, "O king, please fill my begging bowl." The king thought, if I have to fill this begging bowl then why not fill it with gold rather than rice. The king ordered his secretary to fill his bowl with gold coins. However, the king was shocked to see that although the gold coins were put into the bowl, still it remained empty. Now the king was concerned about his reputation and ordered his secretary to fill up the bowl. As his stock of gold coins were placed in the bowl, he was running out of coins and yet the bowl remained empty. The king's secretary lost his temper and said, "O king, this beggar seems to be some kind of wicked magician as his begging bowl does not look like an ordinary bowl." Now the beggar replied, "O king, I am an ordinary person, but the begging bowl is like a human heart." The king fell at the feet of the beggar and said, "Now throw this begging bowl away. Neither your bowl has been filled nor mine. We have wasted much time in trying to fill it. You have opened my eyes."

It can be concluded that desires can never be fulfilled. But our habit of begging has continued from birth. All negative results are due to desire. Some desires are divine in nature and some are filled with greed. The former brings happiness and the latter brings grief. Can anyone fill their desires by wealth, fame, respect, position, etc? Never, therefore, it is God who says, "Hey human beings, you become desireless because you are not a beggar but a wealthy emperor, you are a king and a child of God. Therefore liberate yourself from desires and stay in remembrance of Me."

The root cause of all grief – desire

There are basically two types of lives, either as a king or a beggar. To be a beggar means to expect happiness from others.

Begging for money also means to beg for happiness. There is also an assumption in the world that happiness can only be derived from others. Firstly from a wife or husband and then father or son or indeed from any other relationship, and secondly from wealth, property, position, fame and other material goods. The objects from which a person derives satisfaction naturally create attachment. He always wishes that his belongings should stay with him and if anyone interferes with them, this causes hatred which is expressed as anger. Attachment means expecting happiness from others and hatred means to experience sorrow from another person. When a friend turns into an enemy, then we think about finding another friend and with this hope at least we may find happiness from this new friend. But later on when this new friend becomes an enemy, we think of finding a third friend. The truth is that no individual can bring us happiness. God says, "No human being can gives us complete happiness. We may enjoy temporary happiness. The day you realize that happiness does not come from others but by soul consciousness, that day you will attain bliss, peace and love from God. In this way, neither happiness nor grief comes from others because there is no attachment. The more we expect from others, the more the chances of receiving sorrow. The closer the relationship, the more expectation and grief; this is the true philosophy of life."

Hatred and jealousy is the root

Experience says that the great people of this world cannot bear to see anyone who is rising up before him. Many people are at peace if they see you are facing difficulties or that someone has spoiled your reputation, or if your condition has become miserable due to poverty. You will receive sympathetic statements from others, but beyond this you will not get anything more. The moment you start progressing you will find that, without any reason, people who have no relationship in your life become your enemy. You will find these people waiting for a chance to attack you, even though you have never harmed them. The more you try to gain a position, the more they will be filled with anger and jealousy. Indeed they will not relax until you have been completely destroyed. There is no other reason for this than jealousy. Rather than be depressed at their own failure, they are depressed on seeing your success. You may have observed that a person may not feel so depressed when his distant relatives interact badly, but feels more depressed when his near and dear ones behave badly. Many people say, if others tell us something bad it does not matter but when you tell me, my heart breaks into pieces." That is why the soul which is progressing towards a great goal must not expect anything from anyone. Expectation means to desire happiness. One who has understood this mystery has destroyed all seeds of sorrow from his life. God says, "O my sweet children, do not even beg from Me. You have to end this habit of begging. You have to be soul conscious, be in My remembrance and go on doing good deeds". Yes, the happiness that you have derived from God can spread so that your life is filled with unlimited happiness."

Equality in knowledge and behaviour

If knowledge or morality is not reflected in our character and behaviour, or if it does not transform our lifestyle, then it gradually creates tension. Suppose you have over-eaten, if it has not been digested then instead of making us healthy it will make us sick. In the same way, if knowledge has been imbibed and manifests through our behaviour, it means we have digested it well. Now this knowledge has become your property and part of your experience. You have become strong in the true sense. To digest the knowledge means to use the sense organs properly while interacting with the world. Good behaviour means to act according to the knowledge. The knowledge needs to become natural in your way of living. Whatever positive thoughts you possess, you have to use them in your practical life so that you get the sweet fruit. If you postpone such positive thoughts then you can never expect good results because positive thoughts come very rarely and when they do come they vanish quickly.

Good behaviour means to be like a holy swan and many great souls have been compared to a swan. One can decorate life with divine qualities and overcome waste thought. A swan has two qualities. Firstly, it can differentiate between something wasteful and something of quality. Secondly, it can swim on the water, fly in the sky and walk on land. All noble people should be flexible and capable like a swan. To fly in the sky means to become like a spacecraft and spread positive vibrations to all souls. To swim in the water means to swin in the ocean of problems but save others from drowning. To walk on land, the land of the senses, is to inculcate good habits and to do divine actions.

The moment a person starts to liberate himself from negative thoughts, attachment and hate he will begin to experience peace at every second. As his expectations start to decrease his self introspection, knowledge and purity brings bliss and light. We need to purify our attitude with strong determination. You have to destroy all thoughts which give rise to attachment and hate and be in touch with the immortal nature of the soul. Here there is nothing which cannot be put into practice. But for this one needs good determination and complete faith in God. Then you will find divine bliss arising within you. And one thing is certain, you can be liberated from wasteful desires.

Don't Allow Desires to become a Need

George Barnard Shaw said, "The necessities of human beings can be fulfilled but not his desires. This is the Godly law."

It is necessary to earn money to fulfill our basic needs but greed in earning more wealth is man's downfall. Hence, if you reduce your desires all your problems will vanish automatically. If you wish to remain very happy you have to sacrifice your desire to be praised.

First of all man has to understand what the difference is between desire and necessity. Constant practice of being free from desire is the foundation to attain liberation. The question arises as to whether one can attain this state by overcoming degraded desires. Let us discuss this in more detail.

Try to understand this clearly. Desires are connected to the mind and necessities are connected to the body. We are neither the body nor the mind but a soul. The body has its own necessities and the soul too. Desires arise from the mind which is contained within the soul. The basic needs of the body are food, clothing and shelter. The needs of the soul are spirituality, love, bliss, etc. A man may not be in need of anything but still may create a necessity to possess something. Although it was not a necessity, the desire arose like a dream which has no roots. Necessities can be fulfilled, but desires cannot.

A saying goes, "The stomach can be filled but not a suitcase." For instance, when we feel hungry we eat, but stop when we feel full because the stomach says, "enough". But our mind says, "A little more... How delicious is this food." This is desire. Whenever we feel thirsty we satisfy our thirst and are freed from the thirst. We don't drink more than is required. However we may drink a little more when someone offers Limca, Thumbs-Up, Pepsi or other soft drinks. This is a desire of the mind.

One thing to bear in mind is where do necessities end and where does desire originate. If this concept is clear in our minds then we can understand that we have attained the formula to liberate ourselves from desire. There are some people who reduce their necessities and increase their desires. Just like those who are greedy for fame. People leave their necessities in order to fulfill their desires and sacrifice their physical as well as mental rest for fame.

Necessities can either be fulfilled or suppressed but desires cannot. A person can suppress his hunger by fasting. The only thing that he cannot do is to suppress his desires. Fulfillment is not its nature. Desires are just like dreams which can be destroyed through right understanding. If we wish to become famous, this is a dream, a desire. Voltaire has written a biography in which he says, "When I was not famous, at that time every moment I used to pray to God saying, "O God, make me famous, make me something so that I have a reputation." One day he reached the peak of fame. He has since written in his book, "I became very famous but it became difficult for me to walk along the road." In those days people in France had blind faith that if you at least wear a locket or torn clothes of a famous person, it was considered fortunate. Voltaire used to find his clothes had been removed after having been shopping. Later on, he had to take the help of the police to return home from leaving the office. He prayed to God saying, "O God, my life has become miserable, please make my life as it was before."

In light of the above, can fame fulfill any of our necessities? A person becomes handicapped because of fame. There is no place for such wasteful things for a human body. His needs are very simple such as food, water, clothes and shelter to be protected from the rain and cold, etc. But today man has been carried away from this beautiful path. It is not due to his basic needs but rather to his desires. Man is so immature that he cannot live without newspapers, cigarettes or cinema. His mind becomes very rigid like Hitler's. Actually, there is no need for fame, position and honour for a simple and easy life. Let us ask a question, "Can fame fulfill the basic needs of our body?" Do we become peaceful after becoming famous? Do we become happier? No. Our mind says that we want modern furniture or the latest fashionable dress, but if you observe you will find that modern furniture is not comfortable. People are becoming crazy to buy unwanted things in the name of fashion.

The basic needs of the body are simple, so they should not be suppressed. If they are suppressed then our body will become unhealthy. You should not care for irrelevant desires of the mind. But do not kill your basic needs. One who eliminates all irrelevant desires from his mind feels lighter and free and reaches his goal quickly. Now it is in your own hands to decide how much and when desire power is useful on the path to inner happiness and success in life.

6

The Basis of Happiness is Unselfish Charity

What is Happiness?

Happiness is a blissful experience which comes about through right choice. It is not related to a relationship, wealth, society or fame.

Who on this earth would not wish for happiness? Who would not wish to have the crown of success on his head and a diamond as a reward? This hunger is as old as human beings. Generally, people strive hard to remain happy for ever in life. Even psychiatrists believe that amongst the many desires of man, the most essential desire is the desire to live. And none of us wish to live in depression. Every one of us wishes to live happily. Man feels satisfied when he attains his desired result. The feeling of satisfaction creates a wave which brings blissful vibrations into the body and inner consciousness.

Happiness is an indication of achievement. A person can be happy if he always thinks positively and does good deeds, which bring contentment to both oneself and others. Where there is contentment, there are blessings from everyone. Contentment means happiness. The biggest treasure is the treasure of happiness and where there is no happiness there is no life. Your breath may cease but never give up your happiness. If the foundation of happiness is praise, then such happiness would only be temporary.

Forget the Past and Look Towards the Future

It is better to remember the lesson from past experience rather than merely thinking about the past. Do you see the difference in this statement?

The past is dust and it is foolish to keep it in safe custody. Human beings are bound to commit mistakes but it is not wise to feed it in one's memory. If you continue to feel guilty about the past and remember the pain you will lose your charm. It would be better to bury the ashes and move on. Only remember what is necessary and useful. It is better to make a firm decision not to repeat past mistakes in order to progress rather than to feel guilty. Make good use of every moment of your life.

It has been observed that remembering the past destroys mental power more than physical power. If you wish to make your life vibrant, talented and active, then do not let negative thoughts dominate you. God has given today as your most fortunate moment. Make the present moment a celebration. Do not look at the past in such a way that you fail to enjoy the present. Put away all thoughts of the past and enter into your blissful and peaceful home which is full of new, fresh energy and you will attain a new confidence, new inspirations and new courage for the future. Make your home like a generator which will create happiness so that it will liberate you from tiredness and bring in freshness.

Cultivate the Habit of Remaining Happy – A Healthy Attitude

If you want to make a list of the necessities of life then give priority to happiness. It all depends on you how you bring happiness into your actions. It largely depends upon yourself whether you choose happiness in all situations and how well it becomes your companion.

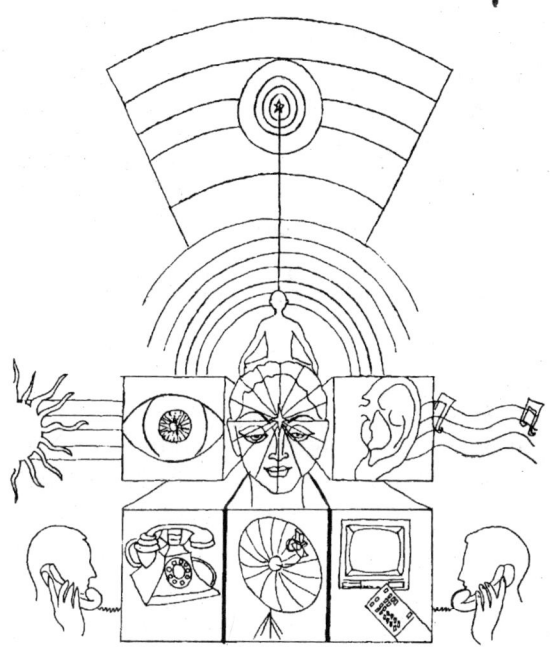

Three great laughers

There were three saints in Tibet who used to visit many places, but wherever they went they would make others laugh. The way in which sickness can weaken a person, in the same way laughter can open the heart. These three saints used to laugh loudly in a crowd and people would look at them with surprise and would also laugh on seeing them. They wouldn't even notice at what point they would start to laugh. As soon as a huge crowd had gathered and started to laugh the saints would stop laughing and ask them why they are all laughing. No-one could answer the question. One of the saints said, "A person can remain happy without any particular reason because happiness is the true nature of the soul."

We can remain happy simply by making happiness a habit. However we are too attached to our past negative thoughts. If anyone wishes to become happy, he can do so by cultivating the habit of being happy.

Is it Possible to Remain Happy For Ever?

Mahatma Buddha said, "Desires destroy us and the very nature of desire is to be unfulfilled. Human desires are as unending as the waves of the ocean."

Swami Ramtirth said, "Human necessities can be fulfilled but not desires because this is Godly law."

George Bernard Shaw said, "Fear and stress are the result of human desires. Sadhu Vaswani said, "Desires and tears are twin sisters."

Man always lives his life in scarcity. Whatever he possesses he is unable to enjoy because he continues to desire whatever he does not yet possess. Desires can be for wealth or fame or position, but they are always dependent on others. How can a person be happy in a state of stress and doubt where happiness seems to be far away.

Can Happiness be Achieved Through Knowledge and Meditation?

A few spiritual thinkers and meditators believe that it is possible to become happy through Godly knowledge and meditation. If man follows the spiritual laws in his life then he can remain happy. It has already been discussed earlier that happiness is a blissful vibration. It is through spiritual knowledge that one can realize that the soul and body are two different entities. The soul is a subtle point of light. It has an impact on the body through thoughts, emotions, desires, etc and performs actions through the body. If a person sincerely practises this meditation for a few days continuously then he will definitely experience the positive vibration of happiness. The more you start to become introvert, gradually your thoughts will become passive. By remembering the Supreme Soul, light rays start to spread within you. In this moment your connection breaks from your body and you connect with the soul. This positive vibration of happiness seems to be possible without any desired reward or material object. The union of the soul and the Supreme Soul produces a wonderful energy or vibration which fills the mind and body with bliss. It gives an experience of a dusty mind which has taken bath in cool water. Life is a play of the vibration of happiness and sorrow, so learn the art of producing the vibration of happiness.

Unselfish Service is the Key to Happiness

If you wish to experience the Godly virtues then you have to remember that God is the ocean of bliss and you have to become charitable without having any selfish attitudes so that you can liberate depressed people from poverty. Unselfish service is the key to happiness. Your small contribution to charity can bring happiness into your life. Man progresses towards betterment only by charity.

Keyl Sai said, "The telephone number of God is being without ego".

Stevenson said, "It is better to meet a happy person rather than receiving a hundred rupee note. Such a person is a centre for spreading good wishes and if he enters a room it is as if a light has been lit."

One of the most important treasures from God is happiness. If there is any gateway through which a person can successfully come out of a difficult situation, it is a mind filled with happiness regardless of the circumstances.

You will come across such cheerful people who always remain happy and full of amusement. Now whosoever comes in direct contact with them are attracted by their positive energy. Happiness becomes a habit for such people whether they come across depression or pleasure. It is due to a lack of self confidence that the brightness of happiness fades from their face. When you smile the whole world smiles with you, but when you cry you have to weep alone. That is why happiness gives inner power and brings courage at the time of need.

One who has honestly taken up the responsibility to perform work and remain neutral in all aspects of life, such as insult or praise, defeat or success, if such a person cannot remain happy then who can? It is not as important to be happy as it is to care for the welfare of the world. Those who care for others by thinking of how they can remove their sorrow and do this in a practical way remain happy for ever.

One who does selfless service to humanity and wishes for their well-being maintains a positive attitude towards others and gives moral support by wiping their tears and empowering them with courage. Such great people become a source of happiness for others and their heart naturally blossoms the flower of happiness.

Do you not experience contentment and happiness by giving a helping hand to a falling man, or helping needy and poor people, or admitting someone to hospital, or feeding a hungry man? They are all pure and healthy actions, inspired by truth. Such people whose hearts are filled with charity, all their problems finish. Just as flowers do not blossom for themselves, or the tree does not expect fruit for itself, in the same way a well wisher shares his happiness with others by making them happy too. The result of this is that he remains happy not only in this world but also in the incorporeal world. A man can rightly be called a human being only when he possesses an attitude of good wishes for others.

Such social workers who are always happy achieve success and thus they are cordially invited by all centres to inaugurate, say, an office or shop or any other association. For this one has to overcome the habit of finding weaknesses in others. One has to promise oneself not to find weakness in others, but rather discover strengths and good qualities. Human beings are the greatest creation of God, therefore, it can never happen that one fails to find a single strength in another person. God has definitely given some precious qualities to man which may be hidden. Now it depends on you whether you discover that hidden quality. We should also use sweet and inspiring words when communicating with others and look at them with a smiling face and a cheerful attitude. You will soon find that your life will be surprisingly blissful and happy.

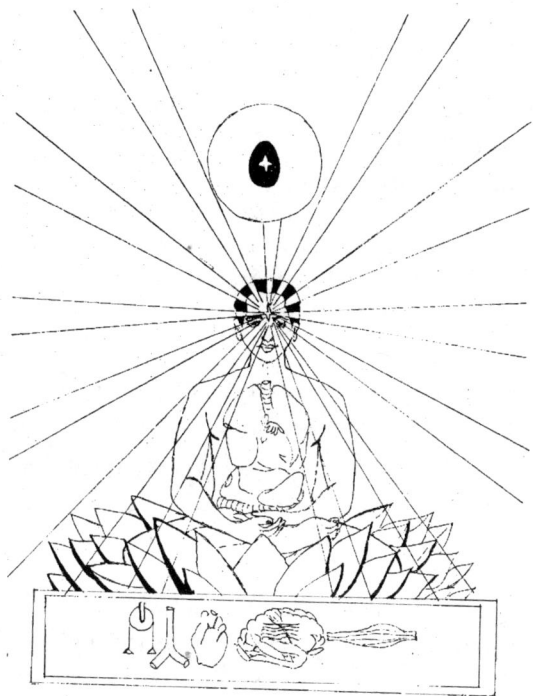

By easy Raj Yoga, Health and happiness are possible

Impact of Happiness on the Body

Edison Holly Burton said, "The best medicine for a healthy body is happiness. The friend of the mind and body is happiness and its opposite is depression which is a disease."

A happy person can perform more work without becoming exhausted in comparison to an ordinary person, even if they are doing the same work. Because of happiness, the mental and physical strength is increased. It is like oil which lubricates a machine, however, if you have an angry, agitated, depressed and revengeful attitude towards life, then make sure that your capacity to love is not being destroyed as the consequences would be dangerous, just like a machine running without oil. If you look back throughout history you will find that the attitude of all successful people was filled with joy and excitement. Their faces reflected love, hope, mercy and self confidence.

It is possible to attain complete health and happiness through easy rajyoga meditation

A happy vibration affects the glands and also different parts of the body, such as the digestive system, respiratory system, endocrine, etc. The Thorasic Society International Conference in America has done much research in which they concluded that by having a hopeful attitude you can improve your health.

Cheerfulness in Life is Just as Important as Breathing

In human life cheerfulness has an important role to play. Life is impossible without cooperation. Cheerfulness is most important in relationships and the process of giving and receiving.

- Cheerfulness is like a flower that spreads its fragrance everywhere. It sometimes makes a permanent memory with its temporary impact of fragrance.
- All, whether he is poor or rich, have affection towards it.
- The smile is divine juice for withered lips as the sun for desperately awaited morning.
- Its impact is of utmost importance in life. It creates good wishes in business, family and increases friends in society. It is wonderful. It can neither be grown in a farm nor be sold in the market. It can neither be borrowed nor can anyone steal it.
- This is that divine virtue which has come from the Godly world and the more you give the more you receive. This is a combination of satisfaction, bliss and happiness which is like a blossom that spreads everywhere.

Share your smile with others because people need it badly

Today where there is depression spread in every nook and cranny of the world the need of the hour is to find out ways to make their lives happy. This great work can only be done by one who is himself full of happiness. A man with a cheerful personality has no interest in wealth, luxuries, beauty and position and they speak very softly and sweetly.

Would you not wish to spend your life with such happy people. We have to protect ourselves from the company of those who insult others and are busy in criticism. The moment we find that a thought is interfering with our happiness we must immediately withdraw such thoughts. Remember that negative thoughts and useless people can destroy your happiness and distract your attention.

The greatest qualities of a happy man is that he always remains calm, patient, tolerant, courteous, introvert, sweet spoken and honest. That is why their impact on others is well known.

The Outcome of Charity is Happiness

Wherever there is an experience of happiness and bliss there is definitely charity standing behind it. When happiness is shared it multiplies several times and if you share sorrow it reduces by half whether it is seen or not. That is why happiness can be shared because the other person is ready to take it but sorrow cannot be divided because no-one is ready to share it. Bliss is an internal flow and happiness is manifest on the face. It is written in the Bible that God loves those who remain happy. The greatest quality of God is charity. Go out and do service to others and you will find that they will rescue you from yourself and you will regain your happiness.

Swami Vivekanda said, "The greatest and highest charity is spiritual charity."

Thiruvalluwar said, "More than generous charity is sweet speech, love and and an affectionate attitude."

Maharshi Raman said, "Whatever we give others, in reality we are giving it to ourselves. If this concept is clear in our minds then who on this earth will not give happiness to others."

Thiruvalluwar said, "But charity does not mean that we offer everything we have. Whatever wealth you possess, accordingly make a charitable donation."

One of the greatest deeds on this earth is charity. The essence of spiritual thought is charity. One philosophy of action is "giving is taking". In other words, the emotion with which we donate or whatever we give, we receive the same in return. If we give love to others we get love in return. Similarly, the same rule applies for hatred, animosity, etc. Charity means whatever you give; you receive the same in return. This formula contains the mystery of success in life. This is the ladder of success by which a person can attain the virtue of generosity.

Rules of charity

To live a successful and happy life self-surrender creates a magical and blissful impact which is an eternal principle. Whoever takes a courageous step to practise this, its magical results will definitely emerge.

In this vast universe everything has the capacity to change. Multi dimensional flow and frequency are its perpetual law and original nature. This is its religion also. If we wish to progress then go with the flow. If we try to stop the flow the well will dry up. A well which is used every day brings forth fresh water, but if you do not take out the water then the flow of new water will cease and the old water will stagnate.

Our sages believe that the human body is governed by the energy of the soul. Our body, mind of indestructible drama, and soul bring harmony into life.

In this harmonious principle of give and take an interruption would be like stopping the flow of blood in the body. Rupees means currency. Currency comes from the word "current" which means to flow. If you do not make use of wealth and lock it away then its flow will stop. It is necessary to allow wealth to flow for a prosperous and happy life and this is a universal principle.

Just as you sow a good quality seed on fertile land and it has the proper amount of water, sunlight and air, you will definitely get good quality fruit, in the same way, whatever we donate, where we donate and in whatever manner, such will be the reward. Without donation how would the world be transformed into a golden world. And let all souls benefit for only then will the fruit of charity be received.

Charity means the capacity to donate

Whenever the question of charity arises people generally think this means the donation of money. But wealth is a broad term which has many forms. It can be in the form of knowledge, experience, happiness, cheerfulness, divine virtues, good habits, love, sympathy, physical stamina. You have to use this stock of wealth for the welfare of others. If you at least have a feeling of giving to others, then let this positive emotion be spread into the atmosphere as this is great charity and Godly service.

How to use these different forms of wealth

Few people think that they do not possess money or material things. So how will a person make use of this golden formula to make his life prosperous? To donate one needs to have the emotion rather than the means. Whatever you can surrender as charity to others, do it. To inspire others by uplifting them and having good wishes or by giving cooperation and investing time in relationships are all ways to surrender oneself to Godly service. By doing so you will receive God's blessings and your life will progress.

Make a firm decision in your mind that every day you will donate to all people to whom you come into contact. Always remember that you should give at least something as charity to whosoever you meet. Your loving smile, sweet speech, good wishes and silent prayer will make you a philanthropist for ever. If you sow the seeds of high thoughts you will automatically receive the fruit. So make one thing firm, that no-one should go away empty handed. Start this process from now and wait to see the result. The secret of a successful life likes in this formula.

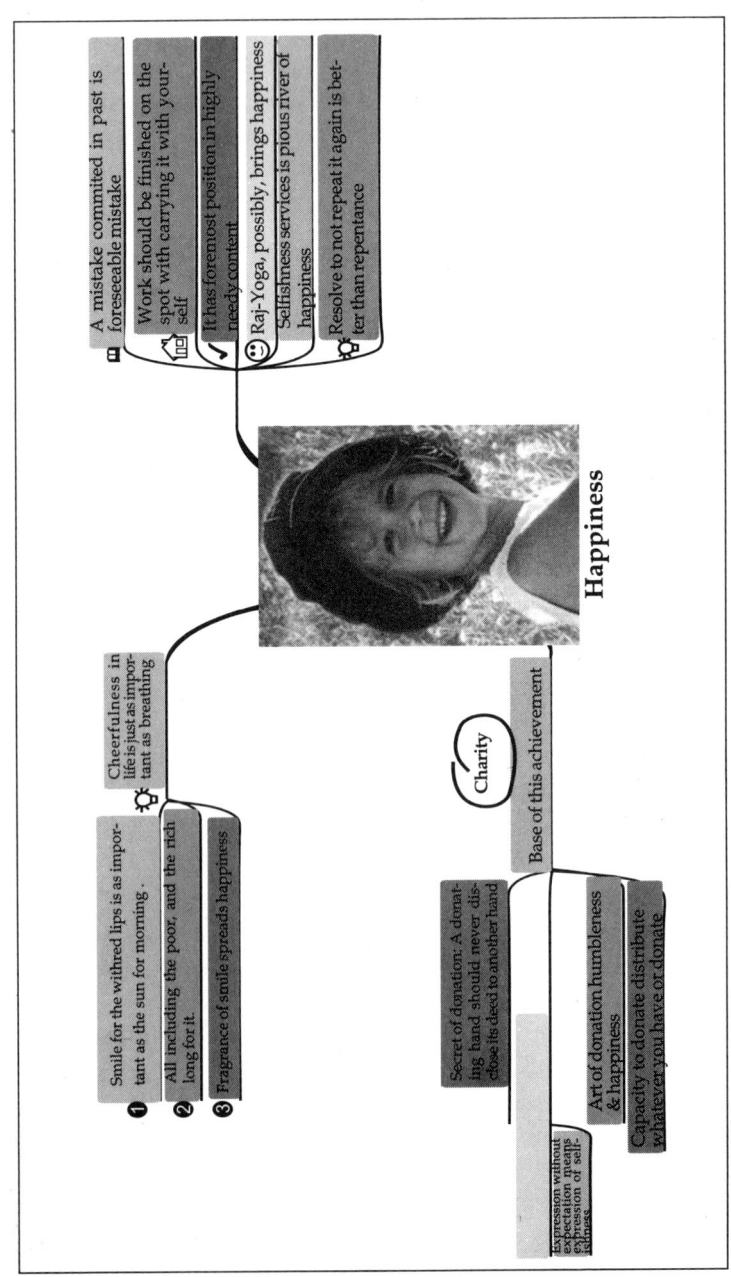

Whatever We Give We Get the Same in Return

To what extent the following news is true is not known. But it was reported on the internet that a terrorist from Iraq named Kherhanajot had sent a letter bomb in the post and forgot to put the postage stamp on the packet. Hence it was returned to him. Now he completely forgot that he had placed a bomb in this letter and opened the envelope and the bomb went off. It is said that those who dig a pit for others fall into it themselves.

–Taken from 'Punjab Kesri' newspaper

There is no-one in this world who has nothing to donate or offer as God's Prasad. If your thoughts are full of good wishes for any soul or you perform charitable acts, then your life will be auspicious regardless of whether others are benefited or not. This seed of thought will fall on the land of the mind and the right to own the fruit will be none other than yourself. This action and reaction of life applies from both angles e.g. when giving happiness as well as sorrow. If you think positively or express good wishes towards others both create a positive impact and likewise negative thinking and bad wishes create a debt. Just as when you throw a stone into a lake the ripples reach to the other side, in the same way thoughts and the waves of action reach the other side of the world. Our good wishes either knowingly or unknowingly come back to us in the form of blessings from various souls of the world. This world is a huge arena in which thoughts and deeds come back to you. Suppose you say 'mine mine', then the whole world will also say 'mine mine' and if you say 'yours yours', then the whole world will say 'yours yours'. In this way the more you donate or do service, the more you will experience happiness several times more powerful. If you start to donate from your stock of charity, then the attainment of this will be revealed in your life. Charity means that whatever I possess belongs to everyone. This does not mean that if a person donates everything he will be left with nothing. It is one's attitude which says 'Nothing is mine'. One's perception of life changes.

Happiness Also Depends on the Way You Give

Indian history includes the names of many great philanthropists such as King Harish Chandra, Sage Dadhichi, King Shibi, Karna, etc. Charity has been one of India's greatest traditions. You may not have been aware that in India charity and fee have been a tradition since the beginning. Fee means a tendency to give. The donor and the receiver used to play a vital role. The doner used to give a gift to the receiver. To offer a fee means thanksgiving. Secondly, when the donor used to give something as charity, he used to give a choice to the receiver to accept accordingly. This was also a kind of offering where the receiver used to experience happiness and contentment after making his selection without having an inferiority complex. Whatever you wish to offer do it with love, politely and egolessly, because this is one of the best ways of donating. Your donation will not bring good results if your mind is full of ego, selfishness, jealousy, helplessness or greed for fame. Sometimes it becomes poisonous fruit instead of sweet fruit. For instance, suppose you share your ideas or experiences with others then sometimes it so becomes that you discuss your high moral values in such a manner that the receiver either becomes depressed or becomes angry. They become so tired of listening that they start to say 'O Brother, it is very difficult to live a life like that of yours. Or else he may say, 'Are you the only intelligent person on this earth? You are great and the rest of us are nothing, etc'. So the giver has to be very humble and egoless while donating. This is the best way of donating. When someone offers you something, then it is natural that you will also have good wishes and also offer him at least something. It not only brings you the equivalent of what you offer, but you receive several times more according to the law of unselfish and merciful charity. Just like a tiny seed turns into a vast Banyan tree and this tree contains unlimited seeds, the capacity of the seed to grow into a tree has been made possible because of the fertile soil and sunlight. But is it possible for you to convert this tiny seed into a vast tree without this invisible cooperation?

No. This is the law of surrender. But if you offer to someone due to helplessness or selfishness, then it would seem as if you are making fun of this law. You are not getting anything for this charity. In reciprocation both parties experience pride while donating. The joy of giving will always create positive and creative energy which is an important element for success. Just like the breath acts as a bridge between body and soul, in the same manner energy which is present in this universe works as a bridge between the human mind and body.

Unselfish charity, no expectation

Once upon a time, a gardener called a few workers to work in the garden. Some of them had been working since the morning, some came in the afternoon and others came in the evening, but the gardener paid the same wages to all workers at the end of each day. Consequently those who came in the morning objected. The gardener replied, 'Did you all receive the wages you deserve or not?' So they nodded their heads and said 'We received but ...' The gardener replied, 'Whatever each one of you deserves I have paid but I had sufficient money, that's why I paid everyone equally because giving is my subject of happiness'.

Whatever happiness is attained from sharing with others can never be attained by any other means. We never give with the expectation of the other person thanking us. We have an abundance within us and do not expect even a small compliment from the other person.

If you wish to be without competitors in any field of life and expect success always then you must donate something without expecting anything in return each day. In other words, always donate a little more in the form of charity. There are names of great people throughout history who have donated everything for the welfare of others. If you do something for the good of others then you receive something good in return. If you show respect, love, honesty, confidence, cooperation and loyalty, then this proves that you have an abundance of these qualities within yourself. Just as eight hours of manual work is required to earn five thousand rupees, and if you work for around 8 ½ - 9 hours, it would mean earning a little more. A person who is full of divine property will always thank the receiver whenever he does charity. It is because that person has been given a golden chance to do Godly service. The receiver has opened the door of happiness to the giver by accepting his charity. But whenever a person donates with a selfish attitude, he will definitely expect thanks from the receiver. Few people believe that there is no religion superior to charity. But I strongly believe that until your life is full of divine virtues accurate charity is impossible. There can be no genuine charity without the inculcation of divine virtues.

The foundation of charity is love

The meaning of love is, all are for me and I am for all. That is why if anyone on this earth is sad, then it is my responsibility to find a way to wipe his tears away. Always remember that all are mine and all are connected with me. Let us look around us to see nature which does so many things for us and if it is polluted then it is our responsibility to purify it by our positive thoughts and vibrations. Today science has proved that nature also has an impact on human thought. Thus, love is a universal phenomenon which cannot be divided. It is love which teaches that all souls of this world are children of God. Love is that emotion which opens the auspicious door due to which a man rises above the nation, religion, caste, language etc and reaches beyond the peak of the Himalayas of generosity to a state of unselfish charity. The only language in which pure love speaks is, 'Donate whatever you possess with a smiling face'. He never steals anything from others but donates everything that he possesses. There are no words to express the bliss which is derived by loving charity.

It is essential to understand the foundation of charity before donating, for instance, love. When charity is done after keeping the above-mentioned points in mind, then the day is not far when you will reach the goal of happiness. You need to become a cloud of achievement so that you satisfy the thirst of peace and prosperity of all souls and the infertile soil of those souls become evergreen. By so doing, happiness will come into their lives. Now their minds will start dancing like a peacock. Now your loving charity will multiply the happiness in their lives. This is the easiest mystery of attaining happiness while donating.

James Allen said, "Sympathy is one of the widely accepted languages which are understood by all species."

Agyat said, "One who shows sympathy towards others creates sympathy for himself and one who fails to create sympathy has no right to receive it."

Sympathy means to feel others' pain and difficulties. Mercy and kindness liberate the person from pain. To receive sympathy from others there are two important view points:

Past experience

Past experience is to see someone based on past experience whereby one recalls a bad incident or some negative feeling from the past. Whenever the past is remembered the same negative feelings arise in the mind and all sympathy ends.
Dislike, disinterest, jealousy and anger are some of the bad emotions which kill sympathy towards others. As mentioned above, both these viewpoints are inaccurate because it is ones past experiences which create the thought that the other person is bad. It could be that the very same person has since become a holy soul. It could also be that your perception of the other person is inaccurate. Remember, if you are still thinking about the sins of others he will continue to be trapped in that. The same applies to negative emotions. Remove both of these and allow others to enter into the vast world of sympathy.

7

Forgiveness and Sympathy

How to Enter Into the World of Sympathy

Einstein said, "I experience every day that in building my inner and outer life there have been numerous hands of hard workers and this inspires my inner mind to do at least something for the welfare of the world which so far I have been accepting only."

The above statement of Einstein emphasizes his true brotherly love and sympathy towards all human beings. Can there be any worship superior to love and sympathy? What is devotion or worship? There is no other auspicious deed other than unselfish service and there is no love other than compassion. One whose hand is dedicated to the welfare of others, whose eyes are full of brotherly love and sympathy, whose speech is melodious, none other than he can be so divine, loveful ad sympathetic. There is no religion superior to sympathy and bliss. Just as a person is full of bliss he can charge others with his love, mercy and sympathy, because the very nature of bliss is expand and spread everywhere whereas the nature of sorrow is to contract causing misery. A person can learn from others' grief and become sympathetic toward others so that he becomes a well wisher and do good deeds. That is why one who shows mercy towards another becomes an instrument to receive sympathy in return.

Agyat rightly said, "One who is not having the practice of showing mercy has no right to receive sympathy from others."

Thousands of People are Searching for Sympathy

Lakhs of people today are depressed and are below the poverty line. They wish to liberate themselves from crime, sin, drug addiction, etc. In such situations the need of the hour is that sympathetic people must come forward to help them to overcome their problems. These sympathetic people should involve themselves in their problems and motivate them to lead a happy life. The most valuable gift is to spend time in the company of someone's love and sympathy. For this you have to motivate others to cooperate in this good deed. There is a wonderful law of this universe that if you maintain good wishes and sympathy towards others, then at a time of need you will not only receive sympathy from these people but also from others also.

It is through sympathy that a person becomes aware of his service towards others. Anyone can adapt himself to flexible and mature people but it is a challenge to adapt to those who are very rigid. Because to adjust to changing situations and rigid people is an art.

Those who are good natured, capable, great and humble always receive love, respect and sympathy of others naturally. However, you cannot maintain sympathy towards those people who have an insulting, violent and hostile attitude. If you maintain love towards criminals, sinners and poor people and love, mercy, a forgiving attitude and sympathy in a place of revenge then how much this world would be benefited. Remember one thing that when you are sympathetic towards others you are in fact giving something. You are not doing it as a duty but because such people need your sympathy.

The world assumes that a particular person is evil due to their ignorance, however, how can you become merciful towards such people? The future generation will remember those people who had showed love and sympathy to needy people by bringing happiness into their lives. None other than great Mother Teresa and Mahatma Gandhiji, who were lively idols of love and sympathy, are sources of inspiration for our forthcoming generations. Can we learn from them?

It is natural that whenever you give validation to someone's emotions, or if you patiently listen to their viewpoints and give them credence, then you find that their love and respect flow towards you. Whenever there is a flow of love for one another at that moment people enter into each one's heart. It is through this door of the heart by which a sympathetic person enters and brings about unity.

Swami Ramtirth said, "When a person experiences unity with another it is as if he becomes engrossed in the other person and then experiences Unity in everyone. There can only be such stable unity where there is oneness of mind."

It is impossible to judge a person impartially without understanding his inner state of mind. This introvert nature opens the door of sympathy towards others. It is from here that unselfishness, divine love and bliss start and the fragrance of mercy, love and respect spreads while the polluted air of hatred, anger and insult vanishes.

The greater the intellect and heart, the greater the sympathy, and the light of happiness will spread to that extent. At the same time, the area of success in his life will also be to that extent. Spirituality and science is also concluding the fact that there is a wonderful balance, unity and harmony between this vast universe and nature. Where there is brotherhood there is a loving interaction between nature and human beings. In this unselfish true sympathy man experiences the divine sight of supreme mystery, justice and truth.

That is why one dimension of sympathy is to be merciful, kind and non-violent towards everyone and the other dimension of sympathy is not to torture the weaker person but rather to overcome rude behaviour, revenge and anger towards them. It is one dimension to be happy in the others' progress and prosperity and not to be jealous and show hatred.

Sympathy is a Must, Regardless of Whether the Person is Capable or Incapable

The pride of humanity and the foundation of good wishes are to maintain sympathy towards everyone. Man commits bad acts due to various reasons such as ignorance of the outcome of his actions or due to rigid habits or lack of sufficient knowledge. It may be possible that a soul may have been very elevated in the past, therefore, why should he not be elevated in the future? The only quality required is the personal touch of compassion.

Let anyone come in direct contact with you irrespective of whether he is degraded or divine. But always maintain good wishes towards them. If someone behaves rudely with you, still have mercy on that person by consoling yourself with thoughts such as, it is not his fault, but he is bound by his own weaknesses. Thus, we must motivate him to overcome his weakness or help him in transforming his habits. Suppose you find fire spreading everywhere, you would endeavour to extinguish it. In the same way, it is the duty of all souls who have mercy and sympathy to see that they maintain sympathy towards all irrespective of whether they have weaknesses, negative habits, cowardice or an insulting nature.

A great soul is one who shows sympathy towards all by understanding their pain and difficulties. He continually becomes involved in removing their pain and never hates their sinful actions but always keeps a positive attitude whilst thinking of how he can help them to overcome all weaknesses. Just like myself, if not today, then tomorrow he will attain love, bliss and peace of mind. Just as nature gives all its wealth freely to everyone without differentiating, in the same way great people will not differentiate between people whether they are capable or incapable, friend or enemy, good or bad, etc. while giving love and sympathy. Such great people can listen to the sounds of destiny everywhere in this world drama, which is not only predestined but also beneficial. Because the formula of this universe lies in its destiny. Then why not make others full with by giving freely and donating sweet blessings. Such people must always keep such words in their minds.

Always remember God and your last moments. Do good deeds to others and forgive.

- May your life be free of all problems. May God offer love, sympathy and Godly service as the supreme aim of your life.
- May God make your worship, meditation, devotion and dedication be focussed towards this supreme goal.
- May God make your life blissful. Let truth come on your path soon so that there is no place for negative thoughts in your tender heart.
- May God shower fame, wealth and prosperity in your life so that your life becomes a source of inspiration and blessings for others. The only effort that is needed at this point in time is practice.

To Find Fault with Others is an Obstacle to Sympathy

Gautam Buddha said, "It is easy to find fault in others but difficult to see our own faults. The general tendency of people is to spread the weaknesses of others but they make effort to hide their own weaknesses just like a clever gambler who hides the dice of defeat."

Dale Carnegie said, "In 99% of cases it has been observed that no-one blames himself for his faults though he has done the greatest."

David Greyson said, "Whenever I feel like finding fault in others, then its from myself I start and I find that I cannot go further."

Unfortunately today we take great interest in discussing others' weaknesses and we inculcate bad habits unknowingly in our life. People are experts in discovering those weaknesses which are merged within. I wish if they had used this skill in discovering their weaknesses, then this world would have been a heaven-like place. Now the question arises that if they know very well that fault finding is a harmful habit, then why are they compelled to do so day and night? Let us discuss this topic in detail.

Generally there are two different ways of exhibiting human actions.
- The action that comes from knowledge in which the word, 'self' vanishes.
- The action that comes from ignorance, in which 'self' and 'ego' are united.

There are two types of action that come from ignorance.
- Such actions which you fail to understand that you should not be doing while performing them. In other words, a lack of realization of the outcome of these actions would be painful.
- Those actions which you should not have performed.

The illusion of this is knowledge. In other words, illusion of understanding that we are aware of the results of both these actions. But the reality is entirely different. It is our ignorance towards those actions. If seen from the viewpoint of experience then we are ignorant about subtle results. We just believe in others' certifying that this is good or bad and on this basis we perform actions for inner satisfaction or materialistic profit and find depression in our later life.

People are Ignorant about the Right Work Philosophy

People are ignorant about their duties as to what they are expected to do and vice versa. No individual would put his hand in extreme heat. This is because he knows that if he does this he will have to bear severe pain and lose his hand. He will never put his hand in the fire knowingly. This is called the true knowledge towards fire or equality in knowledge and behaviour. Let us now observe the second dimension of unequality in knowledge and behaviour. Most of us are aware that anger is like a strong volcano which can destroy our happiness and peace of mind. In spite of having knowledge man carries out bad deeds due to anger. He may be forced to perform negative actions either due to his habits or other external excuses. In this way bad addictions like alcohol, tobacco, LSD, cigarettes, heroin, marijuana, brown sugar or bad habits like anger, sex lust, greed, selfishness, ego, etc can destroy a person's life completely. But one thing is definite that both family and social lives of people are being destroyed due to the above-mentioned reasons. Man becomes addicted to these drugs or bad habits and whatever wrong action he does he is absolutely ignorant about the long term serious results. He may justify himself in understanding the knowledge but the truth is that he is completely ignorant about the right knowledge of action.

All knowledge which one takes up to a height of perfection and divine knowledge can easily bring transformation in a human being. Is it so difficult to implement in life? Why not? Indeed, man can become happy by inculcating these values in life. He fails to do so because he remains ignorant about the possible loss or he understands the knowledge incompletely. Sometimes a voice arises from his inner mind or others' viewpoint that 'this is wrong,' but that faded understanding gradually disappears instead of becoming clearer.

Reasons Behind Undesirable Actions

Some people perform actions to experience immediate benefit but fail to see the long term results.

He fails to realize the philosophy of action and that his present sorrow is due to wrong actions in the past and that today's instant reward may be the cause of him experiencing sorrow in the future.

Those actions which bring instant gratification are performed consciously. However, other actions that appear to be beneficial but have a detrimental effect and people are not aware of this. Some actions are unrighteous but people are still attracted towards the instant gratification and finally they become helpless and continue to eat the poisonous fruit.

For example, consuming alcohol is undoubtedly a bad habit but offers temporary satisfaction to an alcoholic. He feels that alcohol can liberate him from stress and attain bliss and peace of mind. The instant gratification masks the true knowledge that consuming alcohol is a bad habit. He feels as if today's pleasure is much more valuable than ideal values in life. That is why such teachings or knowledge can never become a lesson in his life. But sooner or later when the doctor warns him that if he does not overcome his habit, then he may die due to liver failure, at that moment he realizes that alcohol truly is a bad habit and that his life is more precious than his pleasure of consuming alcohol. At this point he makes the right judgment.

As and when man starts to understand the immorality of his actions, slowly he starts to become liberated from them. The elements that were offering him happiness until yesterday, he now starts to break his relationship with them. Now his image of perfection starts to become deeper as he develops disinterest in the world. He understands that the reward for bad actions is always sorrow.

It can be concluded from the above discussion that all bad habits which degrade one's life such as selfishness, hate, ego, jealousy, and ignorance should be overcome. In other words, man does not know what he is doing or why he is doing it. This would be the subject of mercy and sympathy in the eyes of great people. Those who are suffering do not need hate and insult, but rather mercy, sympathy and forgiveness.

Man's Viewpoint is to Find Fault in Others

Freedom is man's birthright and every individual wishes to think independently and live without being dominated by others. But surprisingly, one who wishes to be free from all bondages wants others to think and act according to his own

Thought– A Sight to New Life

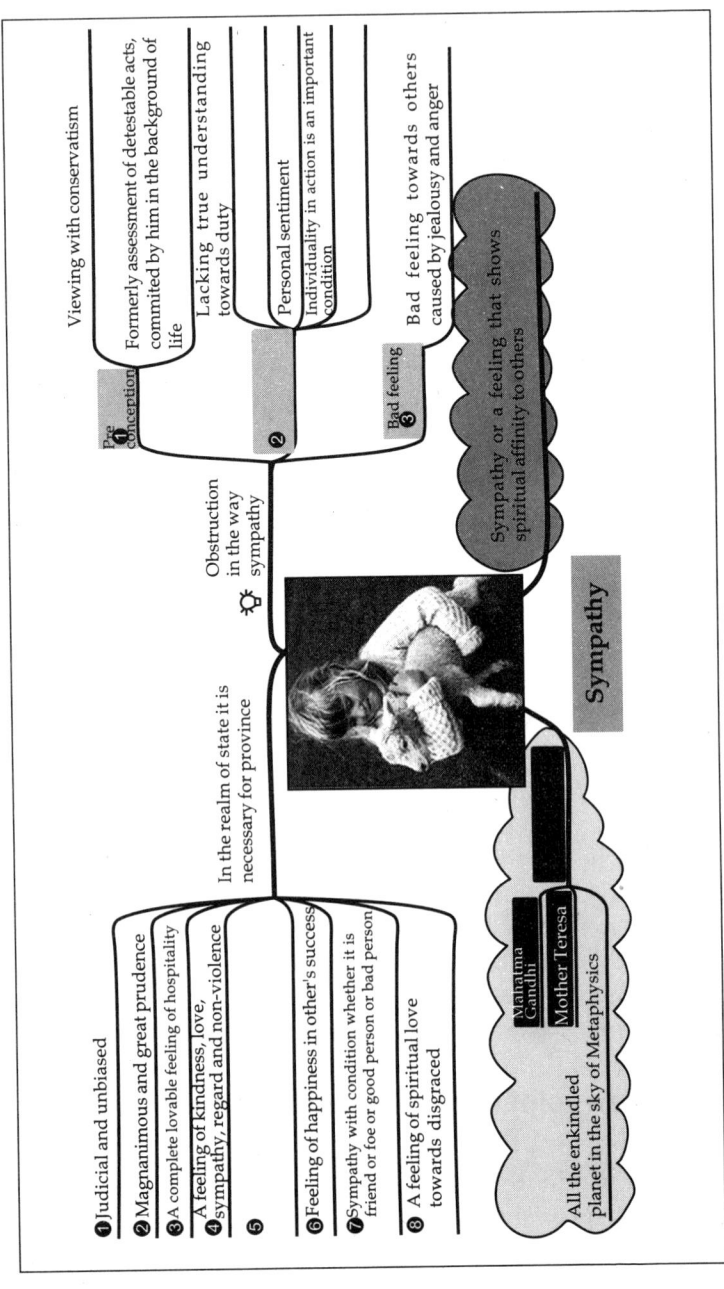

Sympathy

- ❶ Judicial and unbiased
- ❷ Magnanimous and great prudence
- ❸ A complete lovable feeling of hospitality
- ❹ A feeling of kindness, love, sympathy, regard and non-violence
- ❺
- ❻ Feeling of happiness in other's success
- ❼ Sympathy with condition whether it is friend or foe or good person or bad person
- ❽ A feeling of spiritual love towards disgraced

In the realm of state it is necessary for province

Obstruction in the way sympathy

❶ Pre conception
- Viewing with conservatism
- Formerly assessment of detestable acts, commited by him in the background of life
- Lacking true understanding towards duty

❷
- Personal sentiment
- Individuality in action is an important condition

❸ Bad feeling
- Bad feeling towards others caused by jealousy and anger

Sympathy or a feeling that shows spiritual affinity to others

Mahatma Gandhi
Mother Teresa

All the enkindled planet in the sky of Metaphysics

will. He wants others to be tied in the chain of thoughts so that he remains within the prison. And when the other person fails to accept him, then this person would not like him. In other words, that person is bad. Fault finding in others and insulting others starts at this point. Statements such as "We are good, our thoughts, our attitude, our principles, our religion are superior to all the others." All these arguments, whether religious, beliefs, national or international disputes are due to the attitude that "I am right and the rest are all wrong." Today all religious disputes are the result of attempting to prove the authenticity of perfection. If anyone wishes to be liberated from this evil attitude, then he has to get rid of his biased thoughts and become neutral.

To Act Differently is a Challenge in Life

This vast universe is a huge stage where everyone plays their part. It is natural that each one's actions and attachments will be unique. And that is why it is also natural that their thoughts will also be unique. The moment an intelligent person becomes aware of this universal law that all souls are actors on this stage, playing a unique role, all his past assumptions and fault finding finishes. The moment he realizes this truth, all the dirt of his mind vanishes. In this state he allows others the freedom to be themselves. Therefore, where is the question of blaming others?

Man Becomes a Deity only After Being Hurt

Freedom is man's nature as well as his good fortune and birthright. It is God too, who neither interferes in desires or actions of human beings. Anyone can freely have a right to choose his actions as per his desires. He is solely responsible for his choice of action, emotion and thought. He is responsible for the outcome. According to the philosophy of action, the moment he does something negative due to the vices he becomes trapped in mental and physical traumas. And after realizing the pain he evaluates his actions and comes to walk on the right path. It is only after being hurt that a person learns how to become a deity. It is through knowledge that man can overcome his depression. There is no reason to blame others because all experience, whether good or bad, helps a person to grow and develop.

People should not look at others with an attitude of finding fault. Such a person always expects others to live up to their own ideals and if this expectation is not fulfilled, he starts to find weakness in the other person.

If you wish to be free from this fault-finding habit then with love and good wishes be indifferent to other's weaknesses. Before pointing out other's weaknesses we should ask ourselves the following:
1. Did I become free from sin?
2. Is there any weakness still present in me?
3. Has God appointed me as a Judge to find fault in everyone? We have to be a judge for ourself, not for others. Be a judge for yourself and a lawyer for others.
4. Did God make you a Police Inspector or did you wear the uniform of an Inspector simply to praise yourself?

Remember that important version of Jesus Christ who said, "Who amongst you will throw the first stone who has not committed any sin until now." Such ones who think in this way, without hatred and with love, sympathy and respect can stop the habit of finding weaknesses in others and can liberate themselves from depression and problems.

A greedy person never thinks that greed is bad. Similarly, an angry person never thinks that anger is bad and the same for sex lust. They believe their actions to be justified and that others' actions are unrighteous. They say, "I always tell the truth in front of all people or I am straight forward." Such people try to gain wealth through undesirable means and keep human values at a distance. Some believe they are performing good deeds at the cost of offering sacrifices of man to make deities happy.

In reality there are differences in perception in human beings towards good and bad. The level of understanding and experience differs from one person to another. Certainly, he must be carrying out all his actions within his own level of understanding. Suppose you become angry and it starts to spread. Now how far will this anger travel? This will depend entirely to what extent you have developed your inner powers and divine virtues, such as tolerance, patience, spiritual knowledge, mercy, love, etc.

Let us take for example whether a war may take place between America and the Taliban or between Israel and Philistine. In this situation there are thousands of incidents taking place on an international level. Now you only decide whose fault it is and who is innocent. How will you make that judgment? This is why an intellectual person understands this concept and lives a peaceful life by keeping a distance and not finding fault.

That is also why a holy person always keeps a feeling of brotherhood and considers the whole world as a loving family and does not register anyone's weaknesses on his mind. Such holy people assume everyone as a child of the Supreme Soul, God and all souls are brothers. Such pure people interact with everyone with a sweet relationship and thus leads a blissful life. They do not degrade others by insulting or forcing them to act as per their likes and dislikes.

Forgiveness is the Greatest Jewelry

Saint Francis said, "Forgiving others means to qualify oneself for forgiveness."

Swami Vivekananda said, "Forgiving means not to become angry on hearing some one's bad speech."

Premchand said, "Forgiving is the supreme human emotion, but not mercy. Mercy is that charity which grows on yellow land. Whereas, forgiving is just the opposite to mercy which grows on thorns. Mercy is that edge which flows on a flat plain, forgiveness is that edge which flows on rocks and stones. The path of mercy is straight and easy whereas the path of forgiveness is complicated and difficult."

One of the unique inner virtues of human beings is forgiveness. If someone commits a mistake either due to ignorance, then at that time it is your duty to interact with love, respect, by not taking his mistakes to heart and not letting him feel inferior or guilty. Generally people understand forgiveness in their own way. Suppose a person steals your hard earned money, say Rs 10,000, would you not file a complaint at the police station? Or would you forgive him and just wait and see if he steals your money again? No. You would definitely try to get your money back. If the thief is punished in court then there is some benefit in that. Firstly the karma of his wrong deed is settled and secondly he may give up his habit of stealing. In a sense you are helping him.

There is a Japanese saying, "Forgive the one who does not feel guilty because it is a waste exactly like that of drawing lines on water."

A famous statement of Jesus says, "If someone hits you on one cheek, then offer the other cheek to that person". In other words, he will feel ashamed of his bad action and in future may save himself from this evil act. However, this would have no impact on foolish people. Indeed if such people find some monetary gain in cheating you, they will disfigure your face by slapping your cheek. Such people will spoil your whole life. Let us look at an incident of this and reflect on how to inculcate forgiveness.

Once upon a time a priest was preaching on forgiveness in a church. However there was an evil person sitting in the church who decided to test the priest as if God has appointed him to test everyone. There are many people who are evil minded think that they themselves are God. As the sermon ended the evil man slapped the priest on his cheek. The priest was shocked and continued to look at him, and immediately he remembered Jesus' statement to offer the other cheek. Now he offered the other cheek to the evil man who slapped him hard. Physically the priest was a very strong man and caught hold of the evil man and beat him severely. He shouted, "But brother, why are you beating me, what has happened to your golden sermon of Jesus?" The priest replied, "O fool, I am only preaching his teachings, but I am teaching you a lesson." "Just think, I do not have a third cheek to offer you. Go, you are forgiven. I am doing this for your own benefit and have no feelings of animosity towards you."

Forgiving others is an inner fragrance and well worth developing. Maintain a forgiving attitude towards others but at the same time act with caution.

To Forgive and Forget is the True Solution

Tiruvalluvar said, "Those who take revenge on evil people are not respected but those who forgive their enemies are given validation."

Agyat said, "Forgive the many weaknesses of others but never forgive yourself for even your small weaknesses."

Sharun said, "To forgive someone means to dissolve anger towards that person."

One who does not allow others' reactions, thoughts or actions to dominate him will never be manipulated. Such a person does not like to be dominated but prefers to be as a king. The moment another insults him, he becomes neutral and his merciful nature comes forth. He does not become angry or use bad language and shows no revenge. As a result of this his mind remains peaceful and loving and he saves himself from the fire of revenge.

It has been observed that people are more merciful towards children. It may be that a child is insulting you or throwing a tantrum but still you remain calm, why? Because you understand that the child is unaware of what he or she is doing. The child may be angry but may not be aware of its effect on others and it is natural that people will have mercy and forgiveness for it. If you feel any hurt by a child's mistake then one would assume you to be abnormal and foolish. Just as

Forgiveness

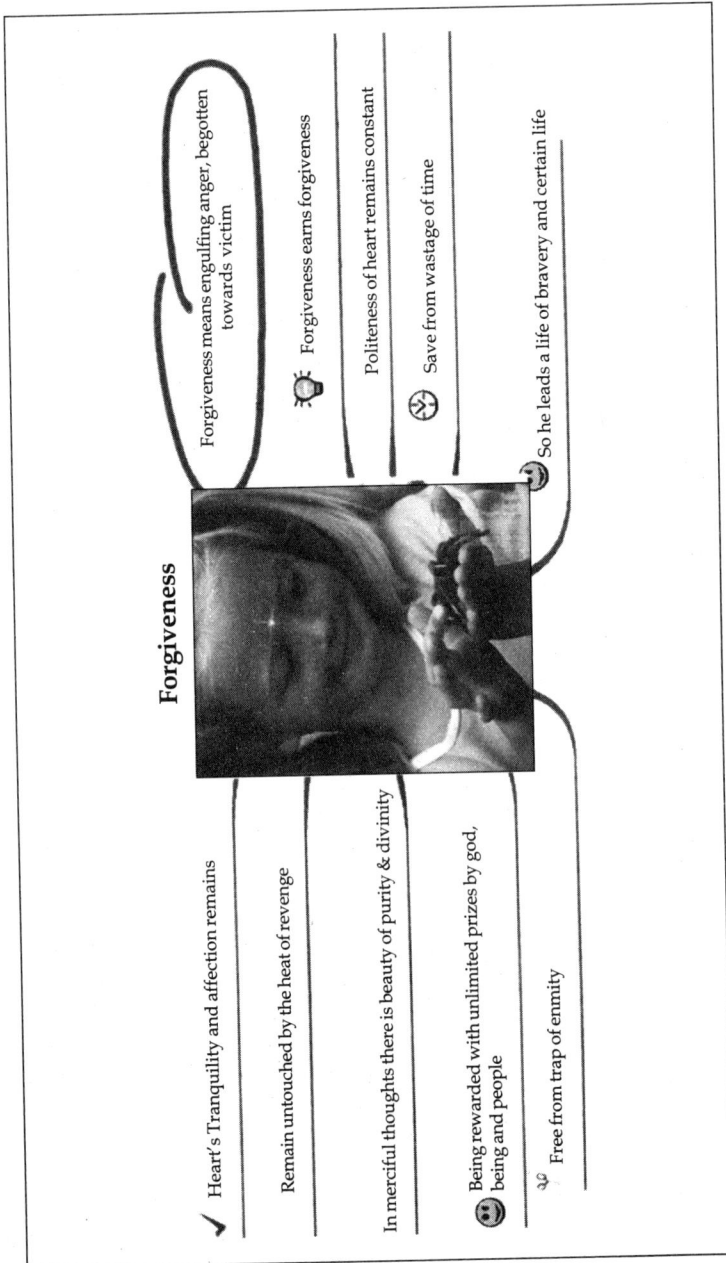

- Forgiveness means engulfing anger, begotten towards victim
- Forgiveness earns forgiveness
- Politeness of heart remains constant
- Save from wastage of time
- So he leads a life of bravery and certain life
- Heart's Tranquility and affection remains
- Remain untouched by the heat of revenge
- In merciful thoughts there is beauty of purity & divinity
- Being rewarded with unlimited prizes by god, being and people
- Free from trap of enmity

you do not take to heart a child's mistake, in the same way great personalities do not take our mistakes to heart, but rather forgive us because they also consider us to be their children. They also become our well-wishers as they understand that our actions are done in ignorance. Jesus also said the same, 'O God, forgive them for they know not what they do.' A man who forgives others receives unlimited blessings from people, nature and God. The foundation of divine virtues and inner beauty is a forgiving nature. An intelligent person is aware that as you sow so shall you reap, and that you are ignorant of these universal laws. Revenge or having enemies can only end by forgiving others and having an attitude of love. The moment you react to an angry person it increases like a fire and you become powerless. It is only afterwards that a person feels the guilt or insult. Often, when a person does something wrong he later repents saying, "I do not know how I could have done such a bad action. I feel so guilty."

Benefits of Forgiveness

If you wish to understand the meaning of bliss, then forgive others mistakes whole heartedly and forget, because one who has a forgiving nature is always light and happy. By dissolving others mistakes, insult and bad behaviour one receives God's blessings and when a forgiving person makes mistakes he, too, receives forgiveness from others. This is the universal philosophy of action in the world.

Important Points to Note

- Such people with a forgiving nature are saved from many mental traumas because they experience bliss, peace and happiness.
- A heart filled with revenge becomes full of bliss when one's mistakes are forgiven, otherwise the heart gives way to disputes and spoils the reputation of a person which leads to depression.
- A person with a forgiving nature leads a life of divinity, purity and beauty.
- A person with a forgiving nature has no enemies and thus

leads a brave, stress-free and blissful life and receives full support from their friends and spend their live in a positive atmosphere.

It has been observed that people feel bad over trivial things and thereby lose their kind heartedness, generosity and love. Ultimately they become rigid and destroy their happy life and day and night punish themselves. It is everyone's duty to save themselves from this painful and depressive state of mind by inculcating forgiveness which brings bliss, mercy, simplicity and good manners. It is certain that forgiveness will bring forth a sweet life filled with a blissful vibration.

With practice one tastes the sweetness of forgiveness and from that moment bitterness and anger towards others dissolves. The hate which emerges from insult and ego, anger and revenge, becomes passive. Such people win the hearts of their enemies and come out of their sinful and corrupt lifestyle. To have a forgiving nature is a source of divine and eternal love which becomes expansive and ultimately all negativities lose their identity.

To follow the wrong path destroys a person's inner powers and valuable time, as a consequence of which his life becomes meaningless.

8

The Greatest Beauty in Life is Love

Just as the soul, the Supreme Soul and nature are eternal, in the same way love is also eternal. If any element of this universe is omnipresent, then it is love. It is love which is beyond the boundaries of any country, or life and death. One who tastes this nectar of love becomes liberated from fear. He neither fears being in this corporeal world nor does he fear the incorporeal world. Swami Vivekananda spoke about the greatness of love by stating, "What is that force which brings elements to unite with each other, that unites atoms and attracts planets towards each other. Love not only attracts human beings towards each other but also animals. It pulls the whole universe towards its centre.

Shri Aurobindo said "Love cannot be offered individually as charity, but still it is melodious in its nature".

An English poet Shelley said "Love is always melodious whether it is given or received. Love is as visible as light".

William Blake said, "Love doesn't make its happiness as any goal nor does it worry but it gives happiness to others and converts hell into heaven".

- Love occupies the highest place in all the laws of life.
- Love survives for its own sake and its prize is love itself.
- Its pleasure and bliss are necessary.
- Amongst all spiritual achievements, love and sympathy

- Where love is an indication of expansiveness, then selfishness is an indication of narrowness.
- Life is meaningless without love.
- Love is the powerful medicine of life.
- Love is a light of goodwill. Love is that emotion which is egoless and enjoys a state of surrender where it offers peace and bliss to everyone with an unselfish attitude.

The first formula for the transformation of the soul is unselfish spiritual love. Love is one of the greatest forces in the universe. Love is a flow of that nectar of which one drop can destroy poisonous vices of previous births. Poisonous vices of human beings such as hatred, anger, sex lust, jealousy, etc can only be extinguished by pure love. Love blossoms like a flower in the hearts of human beings and its blossoms create good wishes, the fragrance of true love. There is no doubt as to the importance of the role of love in life. Just as there is a bridge between the breath and the body, in the same way, love is a bridge between the soul and the Supreme Soul. Love is food for the soul. It is that hidden energy through which we celebrate an auspicious union with God. Meditation + Love = Experience of Bliss. All types of love in this universe become unsuccessful except love of the soul and the Supreme Soul which always succeeds.

No-one in this universe is deprived of this love. Love is the nature of life and its form is endemic. Love has a variety of colours and forms. The one aspect to bear in mind is its direction and whether it is right or wrong, so let us understand in detail the different dimensions of love. These can be broadly classified into three forms:

1. Materialistic love which consists of love for wealth, money, property, cars, diamonds, jewelry, etc.
2. Love for human beings.
3. Spiritual love, where there is love for God.

Materialistic Love

Today, the age through which we are passing is known as

the materialistic world where the shops are filled with attractive goods. In these times the consumer is regarded as a king in the marketplace. This consumer-oriented culture has put 95% of mankind in this materialistic craze and today's disillusioned man is spending his life believing that this is love. Is not love flowing in the wrong direction when life gives priority to materialism? Why, then are we trapped in this materialistic love in spite of knowing that spiritual love is the foundation of bliss in life?

The basic requirement to experience love is to surrender. Suppose you have a one thousand rupee note; there is no distance between yourself and the note. The money has completely surrendered to you. It becomes your obedient servant and follows your advice and raises no objections. There is no longer any distance between you and the currency note. Both become as one, surrendered in each other's love. You may feel love from being surrendered in this way, but in fact this is a state of illusion.

Money does not have any consciousness of its own. Neither does it have any state of mind as it is lifeless. It has no economic value of itself, but rather its value is dictated by society. It surrenders itself to a thief in the same way that it surrenders to a saint. It can be used in any circumstance; it is ready to sacrifice. You may go to the market and buy goods or keep it safe in a locker. It is the most obedient object which does not create disputes because it has no soul; it is lifeless.

Why Do People Love Wealth?

People love wealth because it brings various types of security. It feels like nectar and creates the illusion that it will remain with us forever, unlike a human being who may be your best friend today and your enemy tomorrow. It is also possible that a friend can die. We can trust love, but who will trust death? Because death is unpredictable, there is always a danger of insecurity in relationships.

Wealth can be exchanged between individuals and can be

bought and sold. For example, a television set can be exchanged and a new one can be bought. One home can be sold and another one bought. If you become bored with one car, then you can sell it and buy another one. Now a car can never cause you such a problem that it refuses to be sold, so it is easy to fall into its love.

However, it is impossible to do this with another person. Each individual in the universe is unique. No one individual can be compared with another. As far as work is concerned, one person's place can be substituted by another, but it is impossible as far as relationships are concerned. However, this concept is different if someone regards her husband as a servant or a wife as an object of wealth as was the case in earlier times. In this context, it does not remain as a relationship but rather as a possession. Like an object, it can be exchanged, but a human being cannot be replaced. There are innumerable objects of a similar kind, so their absence can be replaced. But there cannot be innumerable human beings of the same type, thus their absence can never be filled.

Who is the poorest man?

There was once a saint who attained a lot of wealth. He announced in the neighbourhood that whoever was the poorest person should come to meet him and he would be entitled to claim all his wealth. Many people went along to meet the saint but left in vain. According to the saint, not one of them had come who could be called the poorest in the village as per the condition. One fine day a rich man from that locality was driving through the village. On seeing him the saint immediately threw his bag of wealth into his vehicle. The rich man became very angry because he knew the condition that had been announced by the saint. He ordered his driver to stop and angrily said to the saint, "How can you insult me in this way? Am I the poorest man of this locality?" The saint smiled and said, "If you are not the poorest man then why are you such a miser? Don't you wish and strive hard to increase your wealth at every moment? Didn't you pray to God in the temple to become a famous and rich man?

Unselfish love relationships deliver
from all burdens

The beggars that you find in the street may fulfill their needs with just a little wealth, but not you. You need far more wealth than those beggars so tell me, have you fulfilled my condition or not?"

It is greed that is the gateway for all other evils. A greedy person always remains poor though he may accumulate massive wealth because, together with wealth, his demands go on increasing. He lives his life in deficiency. How, then, can he become happy? There is no greater insult than being called a miser and to be a miser in love with money is unattractive. It is of the utmost importance for a human being to remain soul conscious and alive because objects are lifeless, passive and have no soul. They are rated less than human beings. If we love material objects then we also fall and are rated at the same low level. Whenever a person is defamed it means that he has fallen in love with a commodity which is rated lower than humanity. In the same way love is unique and we can create a loving relationship and accordingly bring about changes in our form because in one context we have offered ourselves into its hand. It is not only an internal shift but also an external form as we start to bring about equality. The love of objects not only creates a greedy personality, but also brings about a different facial expression. People of different countries have varying facial features and expressions. This is due to environmental factors and the different cultures of each particular country. Psychiatrists have also discovered similarities in the faces of lovers. Equality in the features of parents and children in their inter-relationship has also been discovered. The moment a human being starts loving objects, he starts becoming like the object. This is why a no-one does such degraded actions as a miser does. There is a saying "Where is Raja Bhoj, and where is Gangu Teli", both of these are incomparable. In the same way the soul, a point of light, is blissful and loving, whereas objects for which man craves are so small and degraded compared to the greatness of the soul. Materialism does not even come close to the concept of humanity for man's heart always remains attached to wealth. His property is tinged with violence, dishonesty and falsehood. The life of a greedy man does not remain blissful and creative, but instead is filled with noise and peacelessness. Wherever there is a craving for buying and collecting objects, in the end everything turns to ashes. This is why it is written, "A man drinks a glass of greed and becomes a crazy fool".

One who loves materialism goes through life accumulating wealth. He thinks that all these luxuries and wealth will bring him comfort and pleasure in life. He postpones his present moment and always thinks that in the future when he achieves a healthy bank balance, owns a car, or a house etc, then he will starting living happily. But such people who are so obsessed with their wealth have not learned a lesson from great personalities in the past such as Alexander, Napoleon, Genghis Khan, Taimur, etc who taught that such golden chances never come into anyone's life. As peace and happiness never came into the lives of these great personalities in history, then why do you believe in the wrong notion that you will become the happiest person in the world by accumulating wealth?

In this world one who is crazy for wealth is a very restless person. He is restless because he aspires to accumulate more and more. If he were to step back and relax he would miss out on accumulating money. Such a life is always filled with misery. His face never remains fresh like a rose emitting fragrance. His life neither becomes a song nor music. Such a crazy man hates all human beings. He is unable to speak to his wife and children with a smiling face. This is because he fears that his wife may ask for a new sari or his children may cry for chocolate. Such a man does not love his nearest and dearest because he always has a fear that they may want a part of his wealth. He dare not love others for fear that they may feel entitled to share his wealth.

Surprisingly, such people may look very religious and strong believers in God as they visit temples, mosques and the church. Their love of God is a pretence. Amidst the crowds they are greedy, miserly and great atheists. Only a minority become happy, whilst the rest visit temples with an expectation of getting something due to their greedy nature. Some visit temples for wealth and some go to free themselves of their diseases. Such people have no love for God. In fact, they have nothing to do with God or Godly love. The indifference towards God indicates that they are atheists. In reality, one who always begs from God never attains God. A saying goes "when you don't beg, you get pears and when you beg, you don't get anything". They imagine, how could the Supreme Soul, the wealthiest, have a relationship with a beggar? Still, if you really want to beg, then it is far better to beg from God rather than from other beggars. It is believed that knowledge is superior to devotion. A devotee becomes knowledgeful when he becomes mature. Devotion means a prayer with a hidden wish. Knowledge means understanding without begging for anything and then you attain everything. Then why not put an end to the attitude of begging? This is the reason why it can be concluded that we must never love any material object which is considered as degraded. This would be taking a step in the wrong direction, away from love. As far as possible there must be a turning point in the

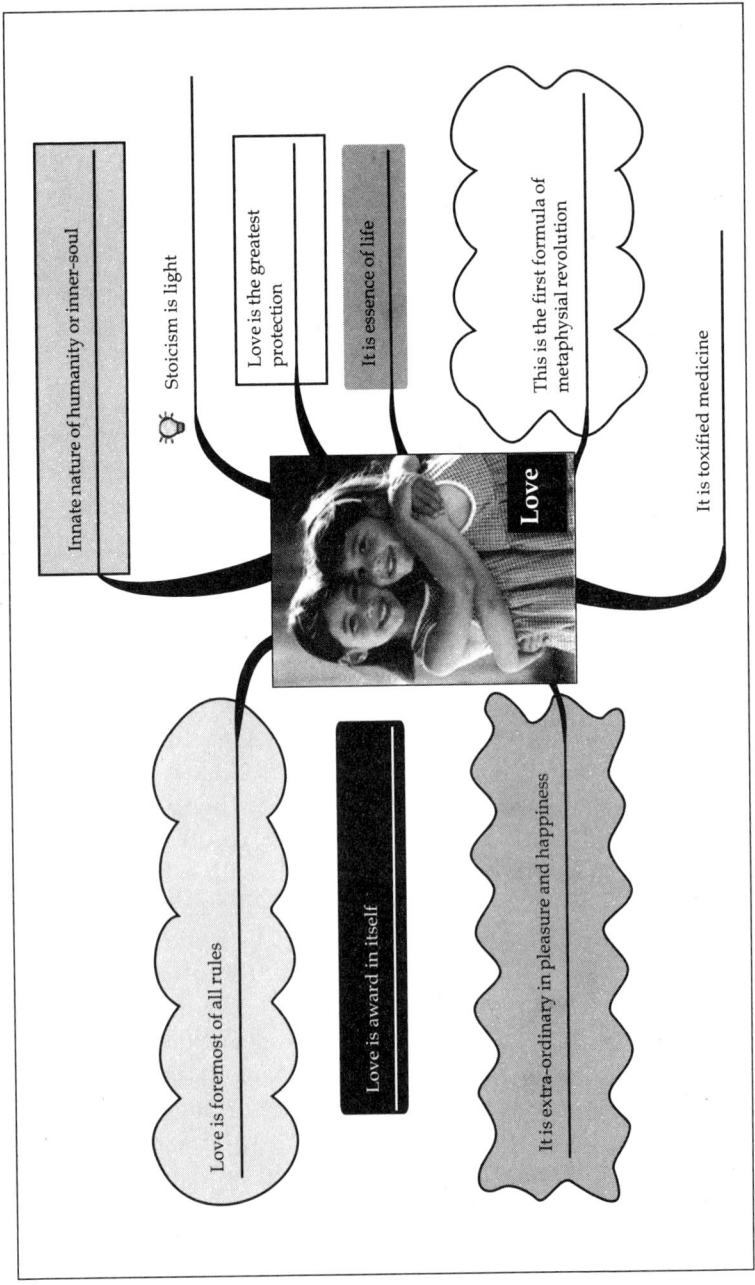

direction of immortal love.

Love for human beings

Human love is a melodious love symbolizing brotherhood. However, this love has less consciousness than divine love. It is said that artificial flowers never fade. They can be washed whenever you like and once again their original freshness returns. But still, these artificial flowers cannot replace real roses. You will never find honey bees and butterflies flying around these artificial flowers. Even though flowers which blossom in the morning may lose their freshness by the evening, still real roses are, after all, real. And that is why the moment we start loving another person, we start giving them flowers to prove the love between each other. At this time one starts to lose attachment to objects. He starts to feel indifferent towards wealth and his love goes deeper. In short, the artificial loses its importance in comparison to something real and alive. Human love degrades materialism and its existence weakens.

Human love is not superior love as people come into conflict with each other due to body consciousness, the darkness of egoism. In love it is essential to surrender oneself, that is, to destroy body consciousness. Human love would be elevated in the absence of body consciousness. However, there are many obstacles in destroying the ego. This problem exists in every relationship whether it is between husband and wife, father and son or between friends. Conflicts are prevalent in all relationships primarily as to who will bow down to whom. One may say, "First you bow, you listen to me, you have made a mistake or it is your mistake and that is why you first have to apologise etc." Ego manifests itself in many different forms. A small child exhibits his ego by crying loudly, and in the same way, his father exhibits it by beating his child or scolding it. This is why a greedy man's life may be peaceful in a way as he has no relationship with outsiders and therefore no question of conflict arising. If there were conflicts, then his wealth may be lost and a greedy person could not tolerate such a loss of wealth. But in the case of human love conflicts are constantly arising. A wife may consider her husband to be God, or a deity etc and consider herself to be a servant, but this is all pretence. In reality, she does not believe this internally.

If a wife bows down to her husband or surrenders to him due to ego, then the expectation of love would be much less. In this situation the husband regards his wife as an object and less as a human being. In the past people used to consider their wife as wealth and treated them as objects. That is why today women challenge their husbands in the name of love because they have begun to understand that a wife is not an object, but a soul. On the other hand, if a husband surrenders himself to his wife, then he would be regarded as hen-pecked. Would any man enjoy being dominated? This is the main reason why so much unrest arises in relationships. There is constant effort to dominate the other person. If one does not surrender, then conflicts arise and if one partner does surrender, then the attraction reduces. If any person has experienced human love he will know that he is capable of attaining happiness through Godly love. In this circumstance, on the basis of this experience, he will rise beyond human love and put in effort to go deep into Godly love. Due to a little happiness received from human beings, he starts his journey towards Godly love.

It has been observed that whatever depression is experienced in human love, it is due to lack of surrender and to ego. Surrender will be easy if we overcome our selfishness. It would be meaningless if we cut our relationship because they are just like you. There you need to possess a forgiving nature and sympathy. There is no need to run away or hate them. The greatest obstacle on the path of love is ego. Ego means lack of right knowledge and lack of experience are the needs of human beings to discover alternatives to overcome these two weaknesses. In short, these two hurdles can be overcome through Godly knowledge and Rajyoga Meditation.

Spiritual Love

Godly love is not only wonderful, unique but also universal. Godly love gives more happiness in which there is no strife or depression. One who loves God always experiences contentment and imparts spiritual love to everyone. The only path through which this Godly love can be attained is to remain detached from body consciousness.

The ladder to reach to that supreme love is where you surrender yourself. God is an incorporeal point of light. God does not have arms and legs, but our emotion of surrendering to Him opens all doors to all achievements. Human love has two directions; firstly, whereby a person wishes to enter into a world of objects and experience like the king who used to lie on a bed of gold and yet burn in the fire of hell (You must have heard about the story of King Midas, who was blessed by God that whatsoever he touched, would turn into gold.) The second option is that you can enter into heaven if you love God. That is why the depression which comes from our relatives teaches us a lesson to love God more intensely. The sorrow given by people motivates us to lean towards Godly love.

If once this fire of love emerges for God, then that person may not feel satisfied without remembrance of God. Then his situation becomes like a fish that cannot remain outside the water for a long time. The state of mind on the path of Godly experience is most blissful. One who surrenders his life to God with self-confidence and love becomes so strong mentally that he easily comes out of critical situations just like pulling a hair from a piece of butter. He not only receives fatherly love from God, but also becomes merciful towards others. The love and merciful blessing of God acts like magic which transforms depressed hell into blissful heaven. This true love converts human beings into deities in a real sense. In this state true success, true happiness and a prosperous life become a part and parcel of life and it is Godly love which destroys all vices and weaknesses for ever. It also liberates us from all types of stress and fear. We only need divine, Godly love.

The law of all laws is 'love'

Once upon a time, a question was asked by a man to a priest, "Tell me, which is the principle for purifying life and attaining bliss. I cannot implement all the principles in life because I am uneducated and ignorant about religion. Tell me any simple principle by which I can become pure." The priest remained silent for a few seconds and then replied, "Begin to love others and all your principles will be completed. There are thousands of principles but out of these, which principle will you implement? Besides this, see your life is so short." Here we recall those versions of God, "O my dear children, don't waste your time in small things. Sometimes your eyes may betray you or your ears, that is, sometimes a dog may enter or a cat or sometimes a tiger in the form of weaknesses may attack you. That is why you should start loving the Point of Light, God so that all your weaknesses will be burnt in that fire of love. The foundation of this union with God is nothing but love. You will become effortless in implementing all principles if you establish a relationship with this ocean of love, namely God because one who loves God will start loving all directions given by Him. This makes the person follow the principles easily in life. There can be no principle achieved without love. All laws are unlawful without love. All good manners become bad manners without love. One who becomes engrossed in Godly love, his life automatically becomes disciplined. It is unselfish love through which you continuously get the nectar of divinity. One who becomes loving can never steal anything so how can he be violent? How can he insult anyone? One whose love is towards the soul, he is one in whose life all thorns fall away because love brings forth only flowers. How can anyone show anger, hatred, animosity or competition if he loves? For example, one who loves can never become a greedy person. If you want to be a greedy person, then do not talk about love. A miser can never love anyone because love is dangerous for him. Love means to share. Love has only one language, "share with everyone without expecting anything in return." In a normal course of time, when a person loves another person, the former always is filled with an emotion of giving. A lover gives his love to another instead of an object. In other words, objects become meaningless in terms of love. Generally, we give everything we possess to other person who we love. Kings have lost everything, even their kingdom in the name of love. Even their kingdom looked inferior by kings for this short-lived temporary physical love. But a miser can never share or give anything. How will he love? One who loves wealth can never love his life. Such a person will not have any connection with his life. So remember God in a loving way and then spread vibrations of love to the whole universe. The unselfish love which is received from God should be imparted in the same pure way.

Lau Tse said, "A saint produces thoughts and his own principles by remaining in silence. Just his presence gives way to superior actions".

Kabir said, "Your easy devotion can give you immortality."

If you observe the movements of nature you will find that it is moving effortlessly, easily and with freedom. This principle of neutrality is actually completely based on love and the principle of harmony. The huge motion of nature is flowing smoothly such as flowers blossoming, fruits emerging, birds chirping in the open skies, rivers flowing, fish swimming, seasons coming and going, rains pouring; nature is colourful and filled with sweet sounds and its energy is flowing naturally.

When this vast nature can flow so easily, then our effort can bring success in life by establishing loving soul conscious relationships and harmony. Due to continuous hard efforts, the formula of maximum success in life will be meaningful only when the foundation of all actions is unselfish love. On the other hand, if we aspire for any kind of power such as wealth or status or relationship, etc, and try to dominate others, then due to these our inner energy is destroyed. In this way, the effort to acquire more wealth and safeguard one's self respect would be to run after happiness. But your every action inspired by unselfish love fills you with so much energy that you can easily succeed in achieving everything.

Whatever You Wish for Yourself Wish for Others

There are two important aspects about love. Firstly, love everyone because the whole world is thirsty for love. Secondly, to receive love from God. I am strongly in favour of this second love. Suppose we offer someone impure love then this comprises sex lust, anger, greed, attachment, etc. and are the vices of many past births. In other words, our love goes through different expressions, desires and aspirations. Our heart which is away from the purity of love is a closed room from which only the bad smell comes out. There is only suffocation in this degraded atmosphere. Hatred is that lower level like a closed room from which the bad smell of selfishness comes out. If you wish to stop this bad smell, then you will have to come out of this dark room. Otherwise, this love will lose its purity and sex lust and attachment will form its ingredients. The pure light from love exhibits from those souls who lack sex lust or desires. Love is a form of charity. Desires are something in the form of begging. There is a vast difference between love and desire and that is why there is always sorrow in desire. Thus, all types of love fail except love with God which succeeds.

Let us imagine that if we love someone and expect something in return, then it becomes conditional love. This expectation is nothing but a desire to receive pleasure from that person. This will create a sense of being dominated. Love is a universal phenomenon which makes the person feel like an emperor. That is why a viceless person can only give love.

Love Without Effort

I had read somewhere .... Once upon a time, a saint had gone on a pilgrimage to the Himalayas. The peak was high. He was sweating profusely and became breathless. He saw a girl of about 10 years who was holding her younger brother on her shoulders and was climbing up the hill. She looked tired and hot. The saint approached her and with sympathy and love said, "O daughter, I am also tired, you too look very tired. You are climbing with such a huge weight." The girl with an angry face said, "O saint, you are walking with a heavy weight too, what I am carrying is my younger brother, not a weight for me." Don't you know the magic of a loving relationship. Love goes beyond the law of gravity. Though the weight of her brother was comparatively more than the bag which the saint carried but still love for her brother made her feel weightless and effortless. If we are on the constant path of attaining immortal bliss, truth and Godly union, then you have to definitely pay for it. But there is no effort in Godly love. It is possible to be in remembrance of God continuously but, of course, a little difficult. But if you connect your intellect with God by establishing a relationship, then there would be no hard effort.

Obstacles on the path of love

Generally, there are three obstacles on the path of love. They are body, relationship and objects. But Godly love can easily cross all these three obstacles. Godly love is such an element which can take us away from this world. It is such a source that whilst it is within this world it can also take you beyond this world. Godly love is that subtle ray which brings the Godly world and subtle world to the earth. Due to the help of these rays, we can go beyond the darkness of ignorance and reach to the Sun of Knowledge. You must have observed or experienced in your life that whenever you came in contact with unselfish love, you felt as if there was no barrier between you and the other person, like two lovers meeting after a long time. All limits are broken and all barriers are surpassed. Each one unites with the other in love. In this union, there is no realization of either time, place or any object, person or even the world. When two lovers spend hours and hours together say, "O, we did not come to know how time just passed away." There is no effort in love and that is why love

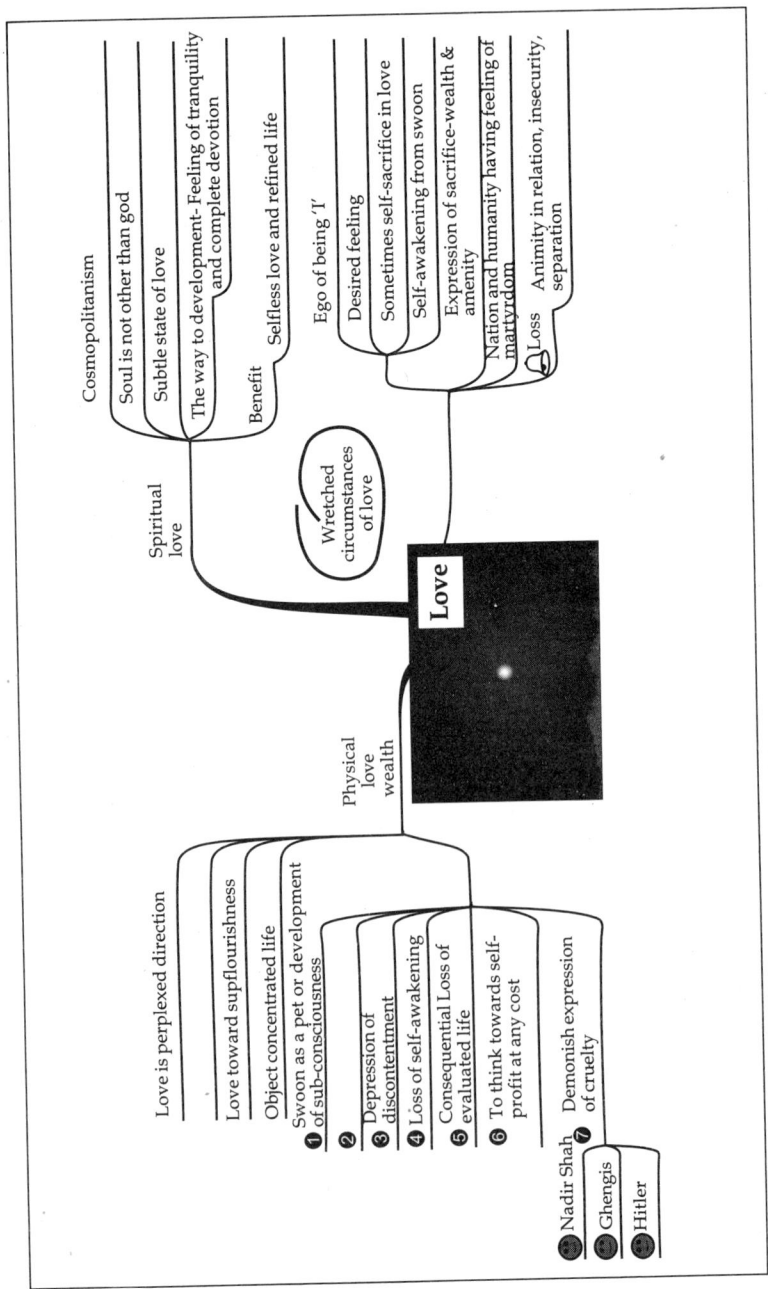

is indifferent. When two lovers get so much happiness in physical contact, just imagine how much bliss the soul will experience in Godly love. All boundaries are passed in this moment of great bliss. Two become one, that is why love means.

Biological impact

There is a centre in the brain called the hypothalamus from where love and other desires emanate. It is love which makes a person come alive. Blood contains endocrine glands which become mixed with dopamine, narefinofrin and filial ethylamine chemicals. If filial ethylamine process goes on for a long time, then along with adequate hormones, amphetamine starts to be produced in a natural way and a person starts living with happiness in his life.

Love is an Art, Learn It

Love is an art. Who does not wish to have respect and love in their life? Love is the foundation of cheerfulness and liveliness. If you wish to attain love and respect, then you have to become capable of expressing love yourself. It is essential to become capable of attaining love.

Your interaction with others should be royal and respectful. Your speech should be sweet and you should have a cheerful face. You can become capable of receiving love when your attitude is honest towards your work.

In this world, if you wish to do anything then it is only love that will help you achieve it. Love is not publicity but a silent prospectus. That is why love expects sacrifice. It is meaningless if you try to buy love by giving wealth. A lover has to surrender himself for his love and he who has given everything becomes a king. Love is attained only by paying something. That is why people sacrifice their life for perishable love. They tell each other that if not in this birth we will meet in the next birth. In short, love is a greater event than life.

One who gives something receives something in return. If you wish to make your life loveful, then you should learn to give love. Love is not something which can be drunk in a glass. Love is something which you only receive when you give. Love is not a commodity, but an emotion or feeling. Love is not like money which you can give to anyone. It comes within only when you start donating it. Love is an innate emotion. On the other side, it would be wrong to say that we lack the stock of love. The very nature of the soul is love. But that nature has to emerge. By loving it can be manifested.

Let us take an illustration. Suppose I am sitting and someone tells me "You don't have the stamina to walk". Will I say, "Yes, I don't have it." I would rather say, "The possibility is there." If I start walking, I will walk and automatically stamina comes. Suppose I say, "Where is the energy to walk, first give me the energy and then I will walk." This becomes a meaningless statement. In the same way, love is produced within you only when you start expressing it. So love is an art. Love is a charity, not a begging instrument which can be demanded at will or from another person. Love is just like swimming. If you step into a river and start swimming, it is then that you learn to swim. But if you say that first let me learn to swim and then I will get into the river, then you can never become a swimmer. You receive love only when you start giving it. Love must become an art of living. Look at everyone with love. Look at everyone in a soul conscious way with the feeling that this world may also become elevated. Look with love at nature also. The poet Milton said, "You should remove your shoes with love and thank them because these shoes have saved you from thorns". In a nutshell, our actions should be loving and the ocean of love will always be with us. It is not that if you fall in love, only then will you start loving. But in fact, if you start loving, then your love increases.

The Last Leap to Achieve Complete Love - Perfection

Once upon a time a king came to meet a saint. The king had great devotion and love for the saint. So the king took a wonderful diamond necklace in one hand and a beautiful rose in the other hand to offer to the saint. The moment the king went closer to offer that precious necklace, the saint Buddha said, "O king, throw it away." The king was shocked because he never expected such a response from the saint. But the saint had to throw the necklace away because he was ordered to do so. The king thought, let me give this rose as a gift because the rose was rather unique compared to the necklace. But the moment the king took the rose in his hand to offer to the saint, he said, "Throw this away too". The king became more tense because he had nothing to offer the saint other than the rose. But the king threw the rose away . The king immediately remembered his 'self' and thought of surrendering himself. The king closed his palms and bowed in front of the saint. The saint replied, "Throw this away also". All those disciples of the saint, who were present started to laugh. At that moment the king realized that "if I surrender myself, it is also a part of my ego. This ego of 'myself' has to be thrown away too, only then can I surrender myself, because this is also a portion of ego". The king surrendered himself completely by falling at the feet of the saint. The saint, with a smiling face said, "O king, your understanding is great."

The Supreme Soul, 'God Shiva' says to surrender means one who has destroyed his 'ego'. Such lovers have four qualities in them namely, love, closeness, courage and all relations with God. To surrender means remembrance of God in every breath. Complete surrender means to surrender oneself in all relationships, surrender body, wealth and time. Let us keep this mystery formula of surrender and churn over it because it is impossible to get the fruits of love without surrendering oneself.

'Surrender' is the beginning of a happy life and a milestone for a progressive life. Man has to face many obstacles on his way while reaching the goal from surrendering to completion. But one who starts to understand this mystery starts experiencing bliss in his life. When our faith and confidence develops for Almighty God, that He is our great defender, then our surrender to Him becomes easier which liberates one from all tension. So surrender means not to keep any relationship of any past life or bad habit and to begin to experience this through attitudes and emotions. If I surrender 'myself' to God, then I am surrendering whom? In other words, surrendering the egoism of 'I'. Who will think about the result of ego and its purpose? And a surrendered person who thinks and does actions according to God's orders, his purpose and reward become auspicious because we surrender all decisions into God's hands.

Remember that all egos can be destroyed by Godly love. Therefore, on the one hand we strive hard to destroy ego by knowledge due to which it becomes easy for us to surrender. On the other hand, if we surrender our egoistic actions and their reward to God then our life becomes full of fragrance. Now contentment and completeness start in one's life. If you surrender that ego of 'I' to the Merciful God, then you will open the doors of blessings and wasteful thoughts which you have surrendered will be converted into divinity. All waste will be converted into diamonds and pearls. In short, surrendering oneself is a creative power.

The beginning of surrender, godly love

Surrender is the beginning of spiritual progress and a ladder to reach to a divine higher consciousness. But the origin of surrender is from Godly love. The pure remembrance of God brings immense bliss, so imagine how much love you will gain if you establish all relationships with Him. That is why a loveful heart can easily attain the qualities of surrendering. Love gives rise to surrender. Therefore, the devotion of complete surrendering in Godly love is not only spiritual progress but also a ladder to reach to a higher consciousness. You fly so high that you cross all barriers. Godly love makes your life progress. It is through Godly knowledge that we overcome all sorrow and vices in life. We make a resolution that we have to surrender our mind and intellect to God. This phase is the period of transformation in life. It is easy to surrender body, wealth, relationships, but it is difficult to surrender the mind and intellect which consist of invisible habits. It is at this stage we become an instrument of God. Our surrendered life becomes an empty flute. Now no sound of any desires of action or thoughts comes out of that flute. It is up to the will of God to put a voice to his lips to create a sound. Otherwise, that sound will be soundless and empty and just the instrument will remain. It is God's wish to decide in whatever manner He likes to play the flute. There is no signature which remains at the end.

One important aspect of surrender is that you do not become lazy and passive, but much effort is needed for real transformation. It is essential to become egoless by overcoming the ego of 'I' throughout life. In other words, God says, "Make a big effort with will power, only then will your surrendering be worthwhile. " On the other hand, our experience says that all those invisible actions, habits or any other obstacle make us depressed, sad, nervous or stressed during our effort. Then at such time, if you fail to be stable mentally, then become easy natured like a child by establishing a loveful relationship with God and offer all your problems to Him. Give all your tensions, wasteful thoughts to God and become light. Then you will definitely experience that all your obstacles which seemed to be like mountains become as soft and small as cotton wool. All your problems will automatically fly away like cotton wool in your daily life.

To Surrender to God is to Experience Newness

This means to realize death along with the experience of newness of life. Both experiences go hand in hand – Second death and second birth. The first experience of death is the experience of soul consciousness, in which we understand that, "I am a point of light, a soul who is immortal". The meaning of new birth is the experience of immortality, newness in the way of life, new development and death of old ways because now our memory has changed. All our old beliefs have broken. Complete surrender means to die mentally. Our body remains alive but our mind, intellect and old habits change. In other words, it becomes possible to destroy ego. At the same time, a new, healthy, auspicious and beautiful birth emerges. The eyes are filled with a new healthy energy, the legs with strength, a joyful heart appears as if a few seconds before life was like a desert and has now become a sweet honey garden. The sound of birds, a dancing peacock and fresh air rustling in the wind are felt.

If your life is surrendered to Godly love, then you can experience bliss, love, peace which make your life joyful and new. Therefore, Godly surrender is a wonderful incident in life filled with bliss which cannot be expressed in words. It can only be lived and experienced. One who has surrendered his life to God, to him even God surrenders. In other words, Godly property such as knowledge, divine virtues, powers, etc become his property. That is why, if Godly love starts from the height of surrender, then it becomes beneficial and attractive for mankind and only then is complete love manifest in human life. This makes your life successful and prosperous.

Fragrance of Dutiful-Life Far From Selfishness

9

Unselfish Action is the Fragrance of Life

In the past societies grew in prosperity in an atmosphere of happiness, bliss and peace. People from all corners of the world are searching for the secret of how people remained happy without the luxuries and comforts of life. However, today we possess everything but still feel ashamed to call ourselves human beings.

In the 21st century impatience is the dominant force in life. Man needs to pass through a spiritual revolution and self introspection, otherwise it will become impossible for man to survive on this earth for much longer. The need has now arisen to connect human beings to their original nature. For this it has become so necessary for modern man to give credence to spirituality. It is essential for human beings to inculcate spiritual values for a successful and prosperous life. What is right action and its reward? What is the universal law? What is consciousness? Who am I? What is the connection between the senses and action? Why is man so depressed in spite of having all luxuries and comforts? It is necessary for everyone to re-think once again. Let us look at the relationship of actor, action and its result in our lives and how much it affects our way of living.

Swami Vivekananda said, "Action is an unending manifestation of human freedom. Our thoughts, speech and actions are threads of a net which we keep weaving around us."

Every individual is confused as to which actions are to be carried out. Whatever way he wishes, he has freedom of choice, but often the wrong choice is made due to his unconscious habits. But one thing is certain, and that is whatever choice is made in whatever circumstances, his actions will definitely bear fruit, whether good or bad. Suppose the majority of people knew that they are free to choose any action, then they would never carry out any actions under the influence of another person or through their own mechanicalness. However, they forget that if they would pay attention to their actions they could overcome all bad habits and remain as an actor on the world stage. Whenever you carry anything out always reflect on the outcome in the future. And also think about the happiness or sorrow that may be caused to both yourself and others.

Every action has an equal and opposite reaction. This is the universal law of action – reward

The universe is a huge echo whereby your sound comes back to you. In life every action, emotion and thought are like a boomerang. Life is also an echo, whereby all sounds are firstly encoded and then finally decoded. Here every action has an equal and opposite reaction. A depressed seed will always bear depressed fruit. Thus try to understand the universal laws. No person wishes to bring sorrow upon himself but unknowingly a depressed person will pull himself down.

You cannot expect mangoes from a neem seed

Sometimes we forget about the actions which we have performed and it takes time for them to come to fruition. When the fruit of past actions come to us we wonder why we are in such an unfortunate situation. Just as we never expect mangoes from a neem tree, how can one expect sweet fruit from a depressed seed. You may repent but remember that one seed contains several times more fruit when it becomes a tree. You cannot set a goal when you are already on the road. You will attain only those things for which you have made effort. If you wish to visit Calcutta in India and you reach Mumbai, then one thing is sure, that you did not sit in Kalka Mail of Calcutta. We desire one thing and do something different. We desire to love and be loved and instead give and receive sorrow.

The Philosophy of Action

Depression is a result of past actions. The account of actions is accurate. Depression is a kind of debt which a person has to pay off even though he does not wish to do so. Then why not embrace this moment. At the same time one can learn from this state and bring some correction into one's life. A little hardship in life brings experience and maturity in the art of living. There are many occasions in life when we receive an intuition from God that we must not carry out certain wrong actions. The most powerful instrument to end the impact of bad actions is through Rajyoga meditation. It is through this method that one can purify the dirt in the mind. This is one of the simplest techniques available and anyone can change a depressed state of mind into a happy mind and thereby achieve success and prosperity.

If you wish to lead a happy life then it is necessary to be perfect in the art of living. One philosophy of action is "Whatever work we do, we definitely reap the reward." Every action has an equal and opposite reaction. There is no-one in the world who can remain without action. For an ordinary person it is sometimes difficult to judge good and bad actions. This often happens with people who have set themselves on the path of a preset goal. Those who have faith in God and the laws of the subtle world or those who are either intelligent or have a thirst for discovering bliss and wish to live a divine life, let us discuss for their sake the differing aspects of actions.

Man Lives in the Expectation of the Impossible

Jesus Christ said, "Do unto others whatever you would have done unto yourself."

But we behave in just the opposite way. If you observe yourself throughout the day from morning till night you will find that around 80% to 90% of thoughts and actions are negative. Then how is it possible to expect positive responses in return for this?

We hate others and always expect love in return. We speak in a rude and harsh manner and expect sweetness in return. We insult others and expect praise. We curse others and expect blessings. This is to be one's own enemy, so how can one befriend others.

How is it possible that I double-cross others and expect them to trust me in return. Human beings expect goodness from others but are trapped in their own vices. Today the majority of people are experiencing that their trauma, pain, depression, stress, etc are increasing. People are going crazy on their quest to find happiness and are chasing after temporary happiness. But the reality is that real happiness is slipping away.

Just as ripples flow out from a stone thrown into a lake, in the same way wrong speech and actions produce a wave which spreads from one corner of the world to the other. These waves have harmed many people and you are solely responsible for this. It is possible that this vibration may not affect strong people but those who are mentally sick may experience an adverse effect. You may not be aware of how harmful a negative vibration can affect another and how this comes back to you. There are no actions that go to waste. If you wish to experience the scientific impact of good and bad vibrations, then sit in silence and pass through a group of holy people and then pass through a room of gamblers, alcoholics or a prison. You will quickly understand the difference in the vibration of these places.

What is the Next Step to Be Free of All Problems?

Always be filled with good wishes and good feelings towards everyone and nature. This has two benefits. Firstly, you will not have time for bad wishes and your power will be channeled in a positive direction. Secondly, your good while can produce good feelings in others and instead of a loss your book of auspicious and good deeds will start to increase.

What is the Secret of Detached Action?

Today, whatever obstacles human beings encounter in their lives are due to one reason only, and that is attachment to the action. In this world the attraction toward action is due to its fruit and the desire for reward. If one were to receive the reward prior to the action he would never carry it out. Thus the attachment to the reward creates attachment to the action. This reward may be in the form of wealth, position, fame, to name but a few. Thus, effort which is put in to acquire wealth may be an attraction to satisfy one's desires. Money is capable of buying all those things due to which your sense organs may be satisfied. Money has no importance in itself, but what it can buy brings satisfaction. It is the attraction of the senses that propels one to make effort to achieve something. The real value of wealth lies in its ability to satisfy the senses.

The secret behind great personalities was that they had no attachment towards wealth because they had lost interest in satisfying the senses. Today, people are striving day and night in earning wealth in unethical ways just to satisfy the senses. One can buy everything with money but not peace, bliss and happiness. Money ultimately brings depression. Now the question arises in the mind as to how human beings may be free from the attraction of the senses.

Today man lives in ignorance of who he truly is. The realization of the true power of the soul is the foundation of peace. The soul is so close to the body and its senses that it assumes itself to be the body. You can experience yourself as a soul detached from the body by closing your eyes for some time. Now this is even possible in science. Suppose all your senses were switched off, still you would exist. Imagine that you cannot breathe, see or hear and the sensation of touch is lost, then what would be your experience? You would experience yourself to be pure existence. You have to overcome the attachment of the senses. Any person can be free from the attraction of the senses, but one who experiences that he is a soul, detached from the body, can easily overcome the senses.

For this, whenever you feel thirsty or hungry or feel pain, at that time ask yourself where is the feeling of pain or hunger located within yourself. Then you will realize whether your stomach felt the hunger or yourself, whether your body was experiencing pain and thirst or yourself. Your inner realization will make you experience that you are a unique authority detached from the body. The bondage of oneness of yourself with the body will begin to break and you will start to realize that you are a soul, a true authority. Once you realize this, then the attachment towards action and the senses will become weaker. This does not mean that you will not feel hungry or thirsty, indeed you will experience bliss. The root cause of all disorders in the body is due to attachment of the senses. Necessities have their limits but desires do not. One can manage on a little food but there is no end to taste and the day a person is free from this vicious circle of the senses, that day he will be free from the impact of nature.

Detachment and Practice is Essential

Detachment is the beauty of family life. There are many secrets behind this Godly formula regarding detachment. In the world all are selfish and vicious and everyone is untruthful. Families are broken up and relationships break down. However this is not detachment. True detachment is loving and one does not run away from responsibilities. Become a source of purity by getting rid of the impact of success and defeat and overcome all obstacles on the journey to your goal. Detachment is a realization of internal purity and becoming a well-wisher for the whole world. We are not detached because the world is meaningless, selfish or untrue, but because we can overcome the layers of subtle weaknesses in the soul and manifest the bliss and a true light of love. We have to inculcate detachment because our powers are misused in wasteful things. These energies need to be channeled to destroy negativities. It is possible to cross the boundaries of so-called man-made social customs and discover the inner power to attain immortal bliss. Detachment can dissolve the hatred in the world and open the door of truth.

The meaning of detachment

Detachment means where there is no thought of anyone, no pull of the senses or expectation of peace and happiness. This experience of detachment comes only by living an intellectual life. You may have experimented running after a rainbow of happiness only to find that there is nothing there at the end of the rainbow. When you walk along the path of desire only one lesson is learnt and that is, instead of happiness you receive sorrow and at this point detachment takes birth. This experience of defeat in fulfilling desires brings detachment.

A second meeting of detachment

Detachment is the original nature of the soul and the Supreme Soul. If firm detachment is created towards these immortal truths, then it can easily be shown towards the poisonous vices. When a soul is united with the Supreme Soul in love, then detachment towards the vices arises. We must never make detachment our strong goal in life because we have observed that such detached and depressed people who have misused this detachment in the wrong direction have made their lives, society and country go against them. In the correct sense detachment gives rise to self confidence and Godly blessings and no-one needs to beg for anything to attain a reward. The nature of the soul and Supreme Soul is so divine that all material and spiritual achievements are easily attained.

Many people show detachment in their lives but not in such a way that it cuts through desire. The taste of the experience of detachment is lost in the desert of habit. Detachment is an attitude or emotion. Practice is an effort. For example, there was a poor man who used to have happy dreams and think, "I wish I could get 10,000 rupees, then I would spend my whole life in happiness." An ordinary man also has the same attitude towards earning wealth. That person may get 10,000 rupees, but still his mind may be filled with vicious thoughts as the dream is shattered. Wealth has come into people's life but has brought new problems with it. New desires develop and for a short time the dream can come true, but then one needs one lakh and then two lakhs etc. One's life goes to waste if there is no detachment. You do not attain wealth free of cost but it has to be achieved by values in life.

What does practice mean?

Whenever old habits or desires betray us, at that time we must control the senses by continually remembering detachment, otherwise the line of attachment will be set in stone. It is very interesting to note that everyone in the world experiences attachment. Each time a person commits sin, he promises not to do it again, but it continues and has done so for many births. But now we have to practise detachment in such a way that whenever bad habits arise in our mind, at that time we remember detachment. What is to be remembered in this situation? You have to think about the consequences and the promise that was made to finish it. When remembrance is strong and the attachment is overcome a new power is generated and negative thoughts and habits cease. Gradually an inner balance is created and whenever desires do arise, at that moment, the remembrance of detachment is strong.

The meaning of practice is simply to be detached to whatever comes your way in life and to create new powers. Buddha sent all his disciples to a mortuary to see the corpses and they realized that the body is perishable, therefore, there is no point in having love for it. After three months of being there their attitude towards detachment developed. Their inner sight understood "O children, this world is a graveyard; there is no use in loving the body." The world is to be destroyed, so what is the use of being attached to objects and nature. All that is needed is to stay in remembrance and have strong willpower and detachment will come easily.

Which Actions are Desirable?

Two ways of expressing action

Firstly, actions arising from ignorance and secondly, actions arising from knowledge. Actions arising from ignorance consist of ignorance and ego, whereas actions arising from knowledge are without ego. In this state we are an instrument or a channel. Therefore action combined with knowledge is always egoless. We think that all actions associated with sorrow and peacelessness are out of ignorance and those which do not tie us generate bliss and peace.

What are the Different Forms and Colours of Action?

We should understand clearly the difference between action and reaction before entering into the world of action. There are two types of actions.

Some actions are natural over which we have no conscious control, e.g. sleeping, breathing, hunger and thirst. However, if anyone does pranayama, then the action becomes a reaction. There are some over-reactions such as desire, expectation, belief, custom, and tradition which are affected by genic bondages. We become servants of the reactions. There are some actions, known as reaction under which we are trapped, reason being slave are due to our desires, traditions and old sub-conscious habit body consciousness, ego and the vices. The question arises as to "What is an action?" A true action is only when man realizes that he is an immortal soul, a point of light residing in the forehead, an action without any compulsion.

Today man is moving through a transition and progressing through science, yet on the other side he is surrounded by both physical and mental diseases thereby losing his original nature of bliss, love, peace and happiness. He is becoming increasingly depressed, stressed and peaceless. All human beings desire to have subtle divine bliss, an imperishable bliss

The way there is fixed time for all seasons, one fixed life cycle for humans & plants, in the same way, there is a fixed cycle for the world drama which goes on repeating automatically.

and peace. For this, one needs to bring about spiritual transformation in his old way of living. Auspiciousness and newness in life is only possible with constant practice. Today, the state of mind of the human species is very pitiful. They have progressed in ways which never existed before, yet in spite of this progress in science, life is like living in hell. Today, humanity is standing amidst great confusion. On the one side, science has invented new technology to give human beings luxury, comfort etc and on the other hand society has become more unhappy, peaceless and dysfunctional.

Godly knowledge helps in differentiating between right and wrong actions. If an action is carried out with this understanding and good wishes, then such an action will not create any bondage. Thus, it is most necessary for us to understand the difference between action and reaction; otherwise from morning until night we react due to the vices or consider every act as an action. We have to save ourselves from this dangerous mistake in order to become liberated from these mechanical reactions. We have to save ourselves from reacting from the outset and stand ready to act. This is necessary to free ourselves from the trap of reactions in order to experience bliss. The question arises, "Why should we carry out actions?" There is a saying "An idle brain is the devil's workshop". In other words, if you don't perform any actions, you will become trapped in reactions and thereby become even more mechanical. Not only will you miss the nectar of bliss of the soul, but also the experience of being a master. Thus it is necessary to perform action. Let us understand every action in depth.

The philosophy of action is very subtle and also a mystery. Whether a person is a saint or ordinary man, he must be aware of the subtlety of action. There are many actions which we believe are actions, but in fact are reactions, or responses to actions. Suppose someone insults us, the anger which this generates is a reaction and in response, if we speak angrily in return or fill ourselves with this negative emotion, then this would be called a reaction or a responsive action. In the same way, if someone praises us, we become happy and as light as a balloon. This is also a reaction. These types of reactions happen throughout our daily lives. There are such actions as insults, praise, respect, disrespect, love, hate, etc which are external influences known as productive actions. It is as if someone switches on the electric light and the bulb lights up and when switched off, the bulb goes off. These are productive actions. Suppose someone insults you and you burn yourself, this is also called productive action. On the other hand, if someone insults you and you respond with a smile, then it is not called a productive action, but rather easy action. Thus, the meaning of action is ease. Reactions are nothing but motivated action. Motivated actions are like slaves. When someone expects an action from us, then we can never be called a king. In short, easy action can be performed only by one who is a free bird and a king. In other words, a human being can perform superior actions through Rajyoga meditation. That is why, if one keenly observes, you will find that most of our actions are reactions and there are no actions which are not combined with desires and expectation.

Action Without the Desire for Reward is Possible

Firstly, all of us believe that the reward of superior action is always joyful and blissful. But if we go deeper, we will find that superior action and bliss are not separate, but rather they are united. Bliss is the outcome and not a reward. It is, in fact, the nature of the soul. A person can attain soul consciousness without carrying out any actions if he so wishes. Generally, all actions in life are motivated by an internal or external motivational force. All human beings possess the power of action. A person may either be drawn to perform an action or try to run away from performing an action or becomes distracted. Within us we find hatred or love, attachment or detachment, respect or insult. These opposites are not two separate powers. Indeed they are two edges of the same power. Generally the world of action is divided into these two opposites such as attachment – detachment, friendship – rivalry, hatred– love, etc. If love consoles the mind by creating happiness, then hatred brings about the poisonous fruit of depression. Attachment creates a false feeling of happiness whilst hatred becomes a channel for giving sorrow. One who goes beyond these dualities attains a selfless yogi life, however, this does not appear to be easy. There are basically two reasons for performing actions; either for receiving or rejecting. The motives for actions change, otherwise how could one perform any actions at all. Let us observe these points in more depth.

Western psychiatrists believe that unmotivated action is impossible. They challenge that no action can be performed without a motive. However, this is not correct, why? Because their investigations are mostly with psychic people. There are heights as well as depths in status amongst human beings. They can either reach their peak and become deities or super human beings or fall down to the level of a devil. Great personalities of India have proven that unselfish actions are possible. Great personalities such as Shri Krishna, Shri Rama, Mahavir, Gautam Buddha, Shankar, Naarjuna, Ramanuj, Thiruvallur, Prajapita Brahma, all reached the peak of humanity.

Cultivate a Playful Attitude

A few tips to keep in mind for unselfish actions

When we play, we play happily without creating a margin for either hatred or love. Nowadays competition has destroyed the originality of play and games. Because of this competition, people consider play to be an action. An intellectual person can turn their actions into play. Chess is such a game which, after some time, wooden elephants and horses appear to look like real ones and often the game becomes so serious that it is as if a real war is taking place. Supposing you lose in this false war, then the feeling of sorrow emerges within oneself. Children, however, do play, and because their actions are unmotivated it is joyful play. They don't have any attraction to the fruit. Their simple, playful attitude brings them immense bliss.

Let us take another example of play. Great personalities of India such as Mahatma Gandhi, Nehru, Khudiram, Chandra-Shekhar, Bhagat Singh, etc never thought that India would attain its freedom or that they themselves would be assigned a superior position in the hierarchy. But they did actions and devoted their lives to their work. The actions they performed for attaining freedom were not only blissful, but also desireless. Suppose a person is walking along the road early in the morning and you ask him, where are you going? He would reply that he is going for a walk and not going anywhere in particular. However, when this same person then happens to go to the office in the afternoon or goes shopping and you analyze him, you would find that the freshness of the morning had deteriorated. The spring in his walk and the experience of lightness from the morning is now missing. Now he is walking with a burden in his mind, why? Because the action performed in the morning was an unmotivated or reaction-less action. But some people assume roaming as an action and spoil its divinity. Some are roaming due to various reasons such as medical cures to fight diseases, etc. Then his roaming becomes a condition. He has to either walk for two miles or five miles distance. If he becomes tired, still then he has to roam. Then his roaming becomes a duty for him. But a happy person can come back to his origin from anywhere because he need not fulfill any condition. Then this action of roaming becomes an unmotivated action. Many times you must have experienced that your body is strong enough to run in the early morning when the breeze is cool and fresh. This strength that comes within you to run is due to unmotivational power. Sometimes you become so excited that you start singing in the bathroom. These are all desireless actions. You know that by singing you will get nothing but you become so excited that you start singing. In the past villagers used to sing and dance happily when it was time to harvest the crops, There was no motivation behind singing and dancing and their crops would not grow because of this. It simply became a celebration and play for them. Such a blissful action can be performed without any desire for reward. The festival of Punjab, 'Baisaki' is a symbol of this celebration. Here in Mt Abu also we find that Bhil, Garciye tribes work the whole day and sing and dance for hours in the evening and later go to sleep.

So action in the form of dancing is going on, but the energy of action is flowing out in those actions without any love or hatred. And the dancer is experiencing complete bliss. It is not that after dancing the happiness will come to him. All actions can become unselfish but by introspection we can perform those actions which are free from desires and expectations, free from love or hate. We can perform actions in a blissful manner. If our attitude changes towards action by considering it as play rather than duty, then there is no need to go through seven days session. But our actions will go on keeping us fresh by giving us immense happiness.

Life is Energy

Power cannot be destroyed or go to waste. It always exists. Let us take an example of a child who goes on walking or jumping from one place to another. It is difficult to make the child quiet by asking him to sit silently. It is rather difficult for older people to understand why the child is always running or jumping for no reason. They believe he is being naughty. But a child is always full with fresh new energy. Thus, though a spiritual person may reach old age, his mind remains as fresh as a child. It is due to wrong habits that our powers deteriorate in the dualities of life such as love-hate, attachment-detachment, etc. An understanding says that internal power or energy gives rise to action but not hatred or love. We have never come out of the duality of reason to perform any action. Whatever changes we find in nature are without duality. So one thing we need to understand clearly is that the birth of action takes place due to inner power but not due to love or hatred. And when energy is converted into action it becomes a superior knowledgeable action, which is possible without any duality.

Can All Actions Become Acting?

The question arises whether mechanical productive actions can be performed by inner motivation? Yes, it is possible. One who attains bliss from unselfish action in his karma yogi life, from his shop to his factory, can perform action without any desire of reward, just by inner motivation. There is only one reason for this. It is necessary to have newness in nature of human beings. This is the reason why people prefer to perform different varieties of actions. If someone loves to run a factory, then he will never produce wrong things at the cost of a consumers' health and will not exploit workers by increasing the working hours or paying less wages. Now he will consider workers not as servants but as friends. He will establish a good relationship between the boss and employees.

I strongly think that if you wish to bring equality into the world then it can be possible only by a spiritual personality. This can neither be done by congress nor communist or socialist parties. Here neither the law of Karl Marx nor Lenin would succeed. If a person owns a shop he still cannot exploit the consumers but would have good wishes that all are the children of God and we are all brothers. This melodious relationship of brotherhood can motivate him to do blissful actions. He would rather gain less profit and provide a good service. His taste or reward would be in elevated actions rather than profit. Saint Kabir also agreed in this philosophy and that is why he used to tell his customers 'Ram, I have knitted this bed sheet with love in God's remembrance, so wear this with love." But a layman always thinks about profit regardless of whether the consumer's health is affected. When he increases the bank balance by profit then he experiences the bliss. He may not have any attraction in buying and selling but he is more focused on the profit margin. But imagine if a person does not experience happiness while performing an action, then how he will experience happiness from the reward arising out of that action. Because action is the seed and if the seed itself is poisonous then how can the fruit be blissful? Thus, any action can become unmotivated.

Action Can Become Joyful

Who does not like to play? Who is not interested in dancing and music? Who does not wish that his life is spent in playful dance and music? There was a time, human beings used to spend their life in excitement, fun and entertainment which was known as the golden age. But today we lack that charm. Actions are an unbroken part of human life about which we have many misconceptions and bondages through fame, position, love, hatred, desires, expectations etc. Can actions become joyful and harmonious in our lives? Is it necessary for us to perform actions with stress and tension? It is possible to create a state of mind where actions become joyful and life is filled with happiness. Experience says that it is possible if we put some hard effort in the right direction.

Emotions are More Important Than Actions

Generally, it has been observed that people do not feel their actions as important and attractive. Others actions seem to be very important and appealing. People do have great respect towards those actions which can offer them some national or international award or if they reach the highest post in society. But experience says that this attitude is wrong. Great personalities are better known when they succeed in performing small actions. Whatever actions we do are not important, but it is important how we do them and with what emotion we perform them. Make sure to make the foundation of action i.e. attitude, powerful and everything else will automatically become powerful. All ups and downs in human life depend largely on ups and downs in emotions and thoughts. Your emotions are reflected through your thoughts and accordingly you interact and perform actions and finally cultivate habits. This cycle keeps man moving in building either a good or bad life. So always try to remain in the shadow of good actions. If your inner emotions are pure and clean and you are a highly intellectual person then your action naturally will be sinless and joyful. If you perform that action with complete concentration and skillfully then the same action becomes meditation. Thus, whatever action you wish to perform, do it with complete awareness. Action must not be performed only with the intention of money, fame and position but it should become devotion. You must add meditation to your actions.

You can become a great personality if you possess Godly love and think that "I am the luckiest person who has been chosen by God to render services to all human beings." If this emotion is present within you, then there can be no other happier incident in your life which can prove to be helpful in transforming your inner and outer world. Generally, whatever action we perform there is always a desire to receive something in return. For instance, money is necessary for living but we must not assume it as the ultimate truth in life. Let your life welcome it as a by-product. But perform action with an unselfish attitude so that others attain happiness and cooperation from you. Then you will find unexpected happiness and unlimited solutions coming into your life.

Realisation of Action Without Reward is Essential

It is meaningless to expect reward for unselfish action. When you repeatedly experience that desire for reward it is a waste, meaningless, sorrowful, etc only then will your unselfish action bring good results. Every one desires a reward but ultimately they become depressed. The first thing is that sometimes you get the reward which you had expected and sometimes not. At times he may get the desired reward but it may not bring that much happiness. From people to objects in this universe, you may imagine that all your aspirations and expectations are fulfilled. But did you become happy forever? No. Then new desires arise which people expect that at least will bring them happiness. This way of desire for reward can be understood when one sees that the mind searches for that which it lacks and whatever is present brings sorrow. He fails to think that the one thing that he possesses today was not with him in the past and at that time did not he think that if he gets it he would become very happy. One who is postponing for tomorrow or one who is expecting reward is not an intellectual person. There can be no future and whatever is here only exists in the present moment. And one who believes in this present moment should forget the desire of a reward. This moment is an action and action is always done in the present. Performance is in the present moment and this is in your hands. The reward which you get will be in the future. Action can be performed only now. In reality, there are many uncertainties which are associated with reward, because reward is a mixture of the effort of many people. Even though a person is living with an expectation of reward, still he will always hope for something or other. The person who lives with an attitude that, 'I am performing action but if I don't get anything in return it does not matter," such people can be content even with one piece of chapatti. One loving glance with good wishes can make him happy.

Ask the viewers of America why millionaires of New York are feeling meaningless and worthless even though they have almost fulfilled all their desires, their safes and bank balances are full, but still they keep grumbling that life is meaningless. The mystery of action lies in this philosophy that the desire for reward is meaningless and a person who understands this will never run away from his actions but will perform action as a hero by becoming neutral.

Perform Conscious Actions and Be Neutral

By remembering that, "I am neutral," immense power accumulates within you, so that no circumstances can make you unstable. A neutral person considers problems as a gift and thinks that problems make you more experienced. He considers exams as a play and performs actions as an actor. He is not nervous while seeing the scenes of life but enjoys every moment with pleasure. He experiences huge problems to be as small as mustard seeds. O Dear Souls, are our actions performed in a state of complete awareness or as a mechanical life? Just like how you switch on the plug of a bulb, in the same way if someone insults you with bad language or if we angrily insult someone, our thoughts are like electricity which flows within our mind. When we become angry we fail to become neutral towards our thoughts and fail to analyze the cause. Whenever you become angry you have to be careful that you do not suppress it but do not express it either. But a third state of awareness is known as the fragrance of neutrality whereby we become neutral and analyze the anger. Go on observing the inner emotions just like waves of the ocean. Keep looking at them neutrally without any judgment and you will find that by self introspection your anger will vanish. Are we performing actions by remembering that "I am different, my body is a different entity from me and the action is done by my hands?" or "I forget when my hands started to do the actions until the actions were complete" Always go on churning "I am a Soul and I am using my sense organs to perform actions", for only then will you succeed in creating a great life.

Thus, always remember that you are a guest in this universe and your body. Keep a balance between action and meditation and you will find that people will appreciate. Such a soul who becomes a companion of God liberates himself from all bondages and comes out of his depression and attains a blissful life. In reality we perform actions with a desire for reward. So the first thing which we need to understand is that so much of our energy is consumed in desires that ultimately we do not have any left to perform actions. Thus, we become interested in the future reward. The more you desire reward the more inferior become your actions and vice versa. The more desireless the action, the stronger will be your action. You will find that the expectation of reward increases naturally. If you perform actions with strong self confidence, faith in God and with a surrendered mind then definitely you will attain a blissful life and selfless yogi life.

Man performs actions which are either associated with the past or future. If he leaves the past and future to God and simply acts then definitely he will succeed in achieving his goal. Hence, a person can devote all his present time, thought and power in performing elevated actions and he can have good wishes towards God that the action which is performed is for Godly service and whatever fruit he gets in return will be used for mankind. Thanksgiving towards God due to happiness can make him feel "O God, how lucky I am to become your right hand in creating a new world." This elevated action of not having any desire for reward can bring happiness into this life. A person's life will be full of unlimited fruits, and with self confidence and courage he can surrender himself to God without any desire for reward. Thus, action without a desire of reward is possible and is also recommended.

'I' is an Egoistic Notion

The moment the 'ego' of 'I' comes, all your divine qualities fade. It has been generally found that people with an egoistic nature perform actions and finally end up with depression. It is only the ego of 'I' which is an obstacle in your action. The moment you overcome this degraded ego of 'I', you realize your true identity. The ego of 'I' is destroyed and you realize the authority of the true 'I'. This authority of 'I' means, 'I am a soul' and the ego of 'I' is always related to false pride. There is a long list of the ego of 'I' which I will not go into right now. Every action can be performed by overcoming the ego of 'I' whether the actions are materialistic or subtle. If we put the burden of responsibility on God and become light and perform actions, then we will experience lightness and happiness while performing actions because when Almighty God is our companion there is no need for tension.

You must have studied the subject regarding action and reward whereby a person can leave his reward but not the action. In the same way, the remembrance of 'I' as the subject can be left. Now the question arises as to how it is possible to perform an action without the performer. The performer 'I' creates a lot of confusion in life. People have hardly realized themselves as a soul. The memory of the degraded 'I' remains at every moment in our lives and a person who is trapped in this ego gets trapped in a vicious circle of actions and finally experiences stress throughout his life.

Think – Everything is Happening on its Own

Story: A saint was running fast because a hungry lion was chasing him. Who would not love his life? The saint wanted to save his life. He was running until the end where he came across a rock and in order to save himself, he jumped and somehow managed to hold on to a branch of a tree and was hanging on for his dear life. The lion which was chasing him came to a halt. The saint took a long breath and thought, at last health is wealth. At that moment, he saw a tiger beneath

Thought– A Sight to New Life

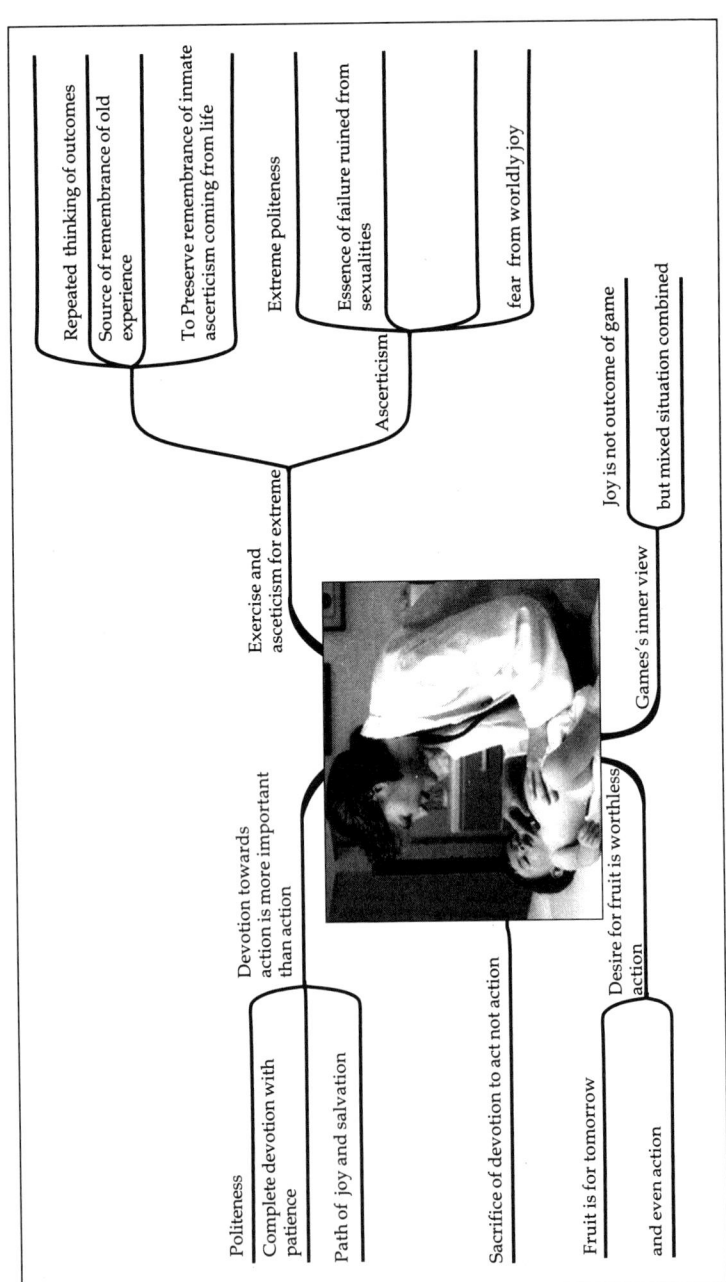

- Exercise and asceticism for extreme
  - Repeated thinking of outcomes
  - Source of remembrance of old experience
  - To Preserve remembrance of innate ascerticism coming from life
  - Ascerticism
    - Extreme politeness
    - Essence of failure ruined from sexualities
    - fear from worldly joy
- Games's inner view
  - Joy is not outcome of game
  - but mixed situation combined
- Devotion towards action is more important than action
- Politeness
- Complete devotion with patience
- Path of joy and salvation
- Sacrifice of devotion to act not action
- Desire for fruit is worthless action
- Fruit is for tomorrow
- and even action

him who was waiting for him to fall. At that moment he looked up and saw that two mice were chewing the same branch. For a moment he was quiet and then a loud noise was heard echoing throughout the jungle. By now he thought of his momentary life and felt that everything was predestined. He was thinking 'If everything is pre-destined then there is no question of tension and suppose I am saved, still these days and nights are like the mice chewing away every second of my life. This is predestined. Now he was smiling as the true knowledge which was free from all tension and fear.

Everything belongs to God but our mind does not accept this truth that nothing belongs to me. But surprisingly throughout our lives we live with the illusion that something belongs to us. If everything is God's then where will 'I' come into the picture? Keep this in mind that in order to keep the ego of 'I' alive if the whole land of 'mine' goes away then just imagine where will the palace of 'I' exist? Thus, surrender everything to God.

It is not mine because of I but because of mine I exist

Generally people think that 'I' comes before 'mine'. There are two uncertainties about 'I' and 'mine'. It is wrong to say that 'mine' exists because of 'I' but the bigger the world of 'mine' the bigger the world of 'I'. A mother's ego is mostly because of her children, her husband and wealth and her near and dear relatives. Let us take an example, any mother who loses her child goes into depression because a part of her personality, that is the identity of the mother, is lost. Suppose we had only one child and her husband also dies at the same time, then her grief will be increased. The reason again remains the same. Now her identity is now that of a widow. In the same way if you separate your sense organs from your body then the identity of 'I' starts to decrease, in the same way mine is related to wealth, relationship, position, fame, etc on which the ego of 'I' is deep rooted. The foundation of falsehood is 'I' and the existence of 'mine'.

The Upanishad says that no-one loves others but it is through others that we love ourselves. None of us likes to be depressed. If any wife loves her husband then it is the wife who loves herself through her husband in an indirect way because the foundation of all comforts and luxuries in her life is her husband. So whosoever tries to feed your ego of 'I' is your friend and whosoever tries to break this becomes your enemy. This state of mind is just the opposite. First you need to prepare the land of 'mine' and then it is possible to build the palace of 'I' on this land. Somewhere there is an equality of 'I' and 'mine'. If you pay some attention you will understand that whatever you possess which you call yours such as my home, my position, my fame, my wealth etc you are an instrument or channel between them. If someone starts taking them away one by one then the whole land of mine will go away. Now you can think if this happens then how will the world of 'I' exist? Thus, start surrendering everything to God. If 'I' is not 'mine' then everything will be fine. Try to understand in this way.

We take birth without a name. However, our name is useful for others and not for ourselves. A name becomes useful when someone calls you amongst thousands of people. Your name which has been put on you is a social necessity to identify you. If you assume to exist only by your name then how can we call you an intellectual person? If your name is Rama, then while conversing you will never say that Rama is talking but in fact you would say I am talking. In general, there is an error between both 'I' and 'mine'.

The way there is a fixed time for all seasons one fixed life cycle for human beings and plants, in the same way, there is a fixed cycle for the world drama which goes on repeating automatically.

Towards Salvation

10

Towards a Stress-Free Life

*E*very individual hopes for happiness, comfort, luxuries and success in life. However, in the majority of cases this is not the case. Even though they were materially successful, sadly they were unable to create a successful life in terms of happiness. There are many such talented and magnetic personalities who may be competent in advising others and may bring solutions, but they themselves are also trapped in their own problems, either physical, mental or social, but there are often obstacles which remain in their life long term for which they have no solution. For this mere understanding and effort are not enough as the root cause is based on unconscious habits. The solution lies in the realization of the soul and a value-based spiritual lifestyle.

There are few amongst us who are such people whose infancy was not traumatic and painful due to which later life is affected by the trauma. The only way to come out of this situation is through the power of thought, willpower, action power, emotional power and imagination power and to continue to practice developing one's inner capacity. We need to develop an attitude of acceptance towards our weaknesses and defeat by remaining positive, constructive and hopeful. Always keep in mind that we ourselves are responsible for our own defeat. The outcome of such positive thinking will be great progress in both our capacity to work and the efficiency with which we carry it out. Those who put the responsibility of weakness on others' shoulders can never transform their own life.

Thus if you wish to make your life elevated then you need to channel both your creative energy and time for character building so that whatever changes are taking place in your life, these will gradually be reflected in your surroundings.

Every individual possesses unlimited expectations within his soul because the soul is knowledgeful. It contains all information necessary to create one's future. Thus, the moment you realize the wonderful capabilities and mightiness of the soul, you can create for yourself a bright and divine future. However, to achieve this one needs self introspection, an analytical approach and patience.

For self-management, one of the most important aspects is to complete one's tasks on a priority basis. In human life there are two types of actions, those which are important and those which are necessary to complete immediately. It has been generally observed that people fail to judge which action needs to be completed first and which ones at a later stage. They become confused. One needs to keep a balance between soul awareness and ambition so that every moment he can make a plan and hence be firm in his decision-making.

If you wish to maintain harmony in your relationships both in family and social life, and if you wish to build an ideal and inspiring self-image, then you need to keep in mind the following:
1. Do you possess sympathy and cooperation towards the needs of others?
2. Are you aware of those small interactions or behavior due to which others are not hurt?
3. Are you consciously aware of the kinds of behavior others expect from you?
4. Is your firm decision very deep?
5. Are you able to apologise from the depths of your heart for your mistakes? For this unselfish love is needed. Is your role of director dependent on your cooperation and

values with others for your inter-relationships and their prosperity?

In reality life is a platform whereby everyone gets a golden opportunity to progress.

The essentials of a good character are:
1. Trustworthiness
2. Emotional and intellectual balance
3. Contentment and an attitude of gratitude.

On the basis of these qualities, great character is built and people accept their directions whole-heartedly. To achieve this one needs the formula of harmony to overcome the mentality of dominating others or convincing them to do as per our own wish. In fact we must try to understand the inner emotions so as to become the king of others' hearts. In this way your good wishes and the wealth of good relations will increase.

The main quality of a successful doctor is that he patiently listens to the problems of the patient. The doctor examines the patient in such a manner that the patient is quickly cured by medicines and advice. Sensitivity and creativity are essential in serving society.

It is of utmost importance to spare some time in one's daily routine on developing the following:
1. **Physical health:** Devote some time each day to physical exercise and a vegetarian diet for a divine and elevated life. In the long term, the impact of this will show in your capacity to work
2. **Mental health:** The study of value-based literature, introspection and daily writings act as a basis for making the mind and intellect strong, thus bringing clarity of thought and development of mental power.
3. **Social health:** Besides emotions there is creative thinking. If any person does not develop his intellect then it is impossible for him to attain success.
4. **Spiritual Health:** Spiritual development refers to knowledge and meditation. If a person wishes to have a stress

free life, then he has to lead a life as described above. Only then will you get an answer to all questions and attain your goal easily.

Today one of the major universal problems is stress. Stress has a negative impact on every age group, whether children, youth, elderly people, male or female. Indeed who is not familiar with this word? Everyone has an innate desire to be free from this painful state of stress. However, some people intentionally neglect the signs of stress. And this is dangerous because it sits in the corner of your mind like a time bomb ticking away. No-one knows when it will explode.

Many researches have been carried out and it has been concluded that stress has a harmful impact on both mind and body, which is referred to as a 'psychosomatic' impact. The negative impact on the body is as follows:
- Joint pain, headache, acidity, high blood pressure, etc.

The negative impact on the mind is as follows:
- Jealousy, anger, fear, hatred, etc.

Twenty people amongst 1,000 are expected to get this disease. It is possible to overcome this negative impact on the body but the negative impact of stress can damage the neurons in the brain. Once the neurons are damaged, they can never regenerate.

Stress causes the constriction of blood vessels, due to which neurons are deprived of oxygen and other nutrients. The negative emotions such as worry, nervousness, anger, fear, hatred, etc can increase the blood pressure in the arterioles of the brain. At times some blood vessels may rupture, leading to brain damage and even death. The other impact of stress is that it causes abnormal lipoid metabolism by disturbing the hormonal system. Lipids play an important role in the function of neurons.

Generally, human life concentrates on five different areas, i.e. at the individual level, family level, social level, work and environment. Human beings have to face opposition in these various five areas. There are basically two aspects. Firstly, the pressure of circumstances and secondly, coping capacity. If pressure is high but your coping ability is strong, then you will not be tense. This can vary in different circumstances. Suppose demand or pressure from your family is more than your coping ability, then there will be stress. But it is possible that you may have a strong coping ability in your office, and here you may be stress free. A survey showed that of five people who were given to face equal external environmental pressures from different people, each one had different levels of stress.

How to Increase Resistance Power to Overcome Stress

If a person accepts conflicts as a challenge, then his capacity to cope increases and stress levels decrease. It has been observed that if a challenge arises then different active inner powers are created in a natural way, which helps human beings to attain success in achieving the goal. The foundation of this challenge is your inner inspiration that an outsider is inspiring you. It is important to inculcate courage, activeness, patience and self confidence. The moment you are free from tension your self confidence increases.

Man generally blames others for problems which arise in opposing circumstances. He always complains that the reason behind the problem is either another person or the circumstances and if you think in this way then definitely your tension will increase. Psychiatrists have discovered that approximately 80% of people blame others. These people blame others for their own sickness. If a managing director blames the union leader or any other person, then the union leader states that the boss is unaware of his discomfort and the outcome is stress. If you observe the day's circumstances in the form of a ball, then you will find that the part which is under your control is very small and the part of complaints is very big. If you keenly analyze the circumstances, then you will realize that which is under your control was to be done by you. You will find within a few days that your complaints will reduce and the capacity to control the circumstances will increase. One of the best examples is the Jewish Dr. Victor Franklin who was arrested by Hitler in the Second World War. His sister was burnt in a gas chamber in front of him. You can estimate that about 99% of war is fought under stress. Dr Franklin found that those who had some goal in life underwent this painful situation.

Man has a wonderful capacity to adjust himself according to the circumstances. Thus, we have to overcome complaining and practise controlling the circumstances. It has been observed that if we start investing our efforts in controlling opposing circumstances, then you will increase your controlling power gradually. You will find that after a few days your controlling power will increase and your complaints will vanish. We have to once again organize our thoughts.

An ordinary man has an average of about 30,000 to 50,000 thoughts per day. The experiences of the sages and scientists have discovered that the lesser the number of thoughts, the more blissful, happy and stress free one is. For this one needs to understand thoughts and the art of organizing them. It is essential to identify good and bad thoughts in order to change the bad thoughts and thereby transform one's attitude. It is rather difficult to change another person or circumstances, but through one's own mental process a person can improve his attitude and be tension free. For this one has to understand the mechanics of stress, accept challenges, increase the boundaries of control, and bring positive change in attitude and practice meditation and relaxation. In this way, everyone can easily attain success and happiness in life.

What is Stress?

When there is a unique reaction or impact on the body and mind due to an incident or circumstances, this is called stress. In this way the impact on the body is visible in that there can be tension throughout the body in the muscles, the lymph node constricts, a higher secretion of cortisal, etc is also observed,.

Professor Hensle has rightly given the word 'Stressed Out' and the stage recommended by him is 'General Adaption Syndrome (GAS) which is very often used in the field of stress.

The moment the level of stress starts increasing in your body, you receive a signal but we neglect this alarm just like a student sets an alarm at 4.00 a.m. before going to sleep. But at 4.00 a.m. the impact of sleep is so strong or due to laziness he oversleeps the alarm or switches it off. He then feels guilty throughout the day for not having used the time.

Let us understand this in a different way. Suppose you contract a disease and your body is full of stress, then your body will exhibit warning signals. If you neglect them then it stops its alarm. Your inner state adapts itself. In other words, resistance power decreases and your disease reaches a critical stage. For some time all symptoms cease for 2 to 4 or even 6 to 8 years. But internally the body is being destroyed. A time then comes when the disease may destroy either part of or all of the body. In this way, the negative emotions such as jealousy, hatred, anger, suspicion, fear, etc destroy the body and brain.

This instance can be taken from the Frog Syndrome. Frogs have a unique specialty in that they can adapt themselves according to the temperature of the environment. Experiments have been done on frogs by boiling them at a low temperature in a vessel. The minute water in the vessel starts to boil, accordingly the frog adjusts himself to the changing temperature. Now the frog must jump out of the jar but he fails to jump out and finally dies. Suppose you take it out of the medium temperature water and immediately place in hot water, then it can immediately jump out of hot water.

It is our wrong lifestyle which makes us ignorant of the excess coping capacity power in the beginning of life. You can also understand it as a balance. Thus, you may come across many such people who are addicted to a bad habit and say, "We have no impact of any drugs such as alcohol, tobacco, etc. We are like Shankar who can digest all types of poisons." For some people, the intake of sugar and salt is harmful but still they never eliminate these from their diet. Just like a diabetic patient must not take sugar and a high blood pressure patient must not consume salt. But there are careless people who are lazy and keep saving themselves by giving excuses. The day when this accumulated power becomes exhausted immediately the body starts showing symptoms. This is the first alarm of stress. We have already discussed in detail the subject of stress in the above paragraphs.

If the problem of stress comes in a person's life he may not necessarily contract a disease because if he puts in effort to overcome the stress and if he succeeds, then his stress is destroyed. But on the other hand if a person fails to come out of that situation of stress, then all symptoms will be reflected through his mind and body. Scientists have done research on different groups of rats which were exposed to unnatural stress and proved this kind of result.

The external environment may be or may not be the same for many but still you will find that two or more people are affected in different ways. This proves that the external environment is not that important but the state of mind of the person is of utmost importance. In other words, his internal capability is stronger than his circumstances.

If you wish to have control over a stressful environment, then you have to be positive towards your life. It is generally observed that our inner state gets divided into two stages. Firstly, thoughts lead to feelings and secondly thoughts are under our control.

True success of life lies in killing the devil of fear with the sword of knowledge and meditation.

The true foundation of any experience depends upon thoughts in the unconscious mind. Doctors have experimented on the mentally sick by hypnotizing them and found that the reason behind these thoughts are that these people had undergone some physical or mental shock in their early childhood. As soon as the technique was given to overcome those thoughts they immediately overcame the sickness.

Killing the devil of fear

Secondly, some people get hurt physically and become sick and still they have better coping power. When asked "How are you feeling?" they reply, "I am fine and feeling better." It was an action debt which is being settled. If there is physical pain, it will be cured, there is nothing to worry about." In other words, though the person is experiencing a painful situation, still his thoughts are under his control. To be stress free your thoughts have an important place in both circumstances Thus, if thoughts are under your control then no stress can affect you. There are many options for controlling thoughts which can be referred to in various books. You can start practising by referring to different aspects such as meditation, positive thinking, positive suggestions, Godly remembrance, etc.

Your stress is coming from the unconscious mind which is giving signals to understand and be liberated from stress. Fear, depression, tension, body muscle pain are gradually knocking at your door. There is no need to become nervous. If you are tired of jealously, then change your thoughts.

Accept jealousy as your friend and as a challenge defeat jealousy with positive effort. That is why you need to meet, greet and beat the tension. Most of the causes of the past and future problems are due to stress. Do not think about past mistakes and feel guilty or become nervous of the future result, simply continue to become introspective.

People say:
- The past is a cancelled cheque
- The future is a promissory note
- The Past is history
- The future is my story.

Freedom from Thought is the Key to Overcome Stress

It has been generally observed that on an average a person thinks around 30,000 to 50,000 times in a day about different topics. This has an impact on about 75 to 80 trillion cells. If thoughts are negative, then its negative impact falls on all cells. For this, one needs to learn the art of thinking for a successful and happy life. Thoughts have been broadly classified into seven parts.
1. Damaging poisonous thoughts
2. Negative thoughts
3. Necessary thoughts
4. Positive thoughts
5. Elevated thoughts
6. Zero thoughts or thoughtlessness

Damaging poisonous thoughts

such thoughts which can have a poisonous impact and can be so dangerous that someone's death is possible. Under this thought category comes jealousy, hatred, revenge, anger, fear, etc thoughts which have an impact not only on you but also on others. Its chemical impact is so poisonous that it can make your blood poisonous and can become a media for disease. We have to strive hard to overcome those thoughts which give rise to such dangerous impact. Fear and anger are most hurting and poisonous vices, that is why it is utmost necessary to get rid of fear.

Negative thoughts

The impact of negative thoughts is not as dangerous as that of poisonous thoughts but their harmful impact can be invisible on our mind and body. For example, one day I was invited to my friend's home. He seemed to look rather depressed. When I asked the reason, his wife replied that there was no loss. The only reason was that where they expected a profit of ten lakhs rupees, they had earned only four lakhs rupees. She said, "We have considered that six lakhs rupees as a loss". They were not happy with this loss of four lakhs rupees. This is called a negative attitude towards loss. A great personality named Marc Rerelias has rightly said, "The way you think in the same way your life becomes." If you compare yourself with others this also comes under negative thinking. We must always stay far away from such a false ego. Every individual has a unique identity and this identification is due to different specialties that he possesses. It may so happen that you may lacking some traits than others. But it again does not mean that you compare yourself with others and feel inferior. Suppose you search for certain traits within yourself, you will find that in some respect you are more deserving and talented. Thus, always think of your self respect and keep it elevated.

Let us observe an example, one of the famous salesman – a trainer, Zig Ziglar had written a book named "Always see yourself from a height." This book contains his biography which describes that when he was a salesman he was a very unsuccessful person. He could not fulfill the expectations of the company. Due to this he used to doubt his capabilities and was always disappointed. One day a company manager met the talented Zig Ziglar and said, "I can see you possess unlimited inner powers. You can do anything as you wish." This statement brought a tremendous change in Zig Ziglar and he was designated as the top Sales Trainer. If such negative thinking can make a person change into positive thinking and make him reach a high position in a hierarchy, then why not you.

The second example is that one day a class teacher told a 14 year old child that his IQ was so low that he could never pass SSC (x std). On hearing this, he became depressed and left his studies. You will be surprised to learn that he lived a very simple life until 17-18 years old and started a job as a waiter in a hotel. When a group of IQ investigators tested his intelligence they found that his IQ was exceptionally high. In other words, he was a gifted child. He started to study after the age of 35 years. He not only became a writer but also the President of the International Association of Mansa Society. You may be aware that the qualification required for becoming a member of this society is an IQ of at least 140.

Thus, always remember one thing, do not let ay negative thoughts enter into your mind from morning until night. Make room for positive thoughts and motivated or inspiring thoughts Understand the magical impact of imagination power and start its improvement. For this one needs to bring divinity of mind and intellect through Raj Yoga Meditation.

Wasteful thoughts

These are those thoughts which have no creativity. These thoughts are neither fit to be learnt nor fit to teach others. These thoughts are just like a weight on our memories and unnecessarily waste our time due to which a habit of wasteful speech and wasteful thoughts are cultivated. These are called meaningless thoughts. Such thoughts do not have any link and as such there is no question of dangerous loss but they do destroy the inner power slowly. So we must save ourselves from these thoughts.

Necessary thoughts

The way life is impossible without action, in the same way life is impossible without necessary thoughts. Necessary thoughts are those which are connected with all types of responsibility whether they are related to family or social or nation or to one's own material prosperity or spiritual pros-

Towards a Stress-Free Life

perity. But one thing has to be observed is that these thoughts are not connected to unnecessary thoughts or harmful thoughts.

One important fact to be noted is that in the case of necessary thoughts, the less you think, the more energy would be economized. Suppose you ate your breakfast and headed off to the office. You are commuting to the office by bus where you are free for one hour whilst on the bus. During this period, there is no need to think about anything, but due to habit you are thinking and your internal energy is depleting. For this little practice of awareness is required. Suppose you are having breakfast consciously, then you can experience the taste while eating slowly. Go on observing this again and again. When-

Cultivate the miraculous power of imaginative energy in yourself

ever you are performing any action, at that time stay with that thought for some time. In this awareness you will experience wonderful bliss and thoughtless state of mind. There are many benefits of this awareness towards different directions of action. You can sit for one hour on the bus and in a concentrated state an amazing power can be accumulated which will prove to be helpful in your work area. In this way any spare time during the day will fill you with wonderful powers by learning the art of accumulation

Positive thoughts

Positive thoughts mean to stabilise inspiring thoughts and hopeful thoughts at the time of harmful circumstances. In this book there are full details on various aspects of positivity. This can be called right thought. Always be a problem solver rather than a problem in the midst of obstacles. Suppose 15% is your problem then never extend it to 80%, but reduce it to 2%. Do not turn a mustard seed into a mountain but rather change it into cotton wool.

Elevated thoughts

This type of thought can be categorised under spiritual thought. This thought is related to higher consciousness. Spiritual thoughts are completely different from all the above-mentioned types of thought. On the one hand poisonous thoughts are most harmful to the human body, and on the other hand spiritual thoughts are the best nutrients for the body and mind. Deep sleep of two hours can relax your body's muscles and at the same time half an hour of spiritual thought can give you that much relaxation because of its blissful experience. When we meditate our resistance power of body and mind substantially increases by several times. Today this has been proven by medical science. Rajyoga meditation increases the secretion of morphin and endorphin chemicals.

No thoughts or freedom from thought

This stage is the highest spiritual state of mind which ranks after spiritual thoughts. This is that reactionless state where a person remains in a peaceful stage even in different dual circumstances like praise, insult, loss and profit, success or defeat, happiness or grief, etc. In this stage a person goes beyond all reactions and remains impartial and experiences higher soul consciousness by entering into the strongest mental divinity.

The Basis of a Stress-Free Life – Overcoming Fear

Yes, most of you are aware that a trembling mind due to fear cannot crate a vibration of bliss. How can a person who is trembling be stable? And a person who is unstable can never be at peace. The result is that life becomes a centre of bad thoughts and peaceless. Fear is one of the greatest obstacles in an auspicious path of devotion/medication.

The human mind becomes weak due to memories of different experiences of both happiness and sorrow which turns into nervous tension due to stress to make life unpeaceful. Stress weakens a person's thought power and action power. It also stops a person from reaching a higher rung on the ladder of spirituality.

Though we possess the true knowledge that the soul is immortal and imperishable and the body is perishable and whatever happens on this world stage happens for the best and God is Almighty and ever cooperative, still we are pessimistic about the future and this subtle fear persists every moment to make our life peaceless. What can be the reason behind this?

How to Overcome Anger

Today, the human culture is standing at the precipice of destruction and the fear of destruction has given an important role to anger. Human beings are facing many losses due to anger in almost every field. If people pay more attention to their health, then he alone will be more affected. That is why it is essential to keep in mind the losses that will arise out of destruction. There are basically four different types of health

that come under complete health. They are as follows:
1. Physical health
2. Mental health
3. Social health
4. Spiritual health

Physical health

Anger has a negative impact on different parts of the body. Some of the symptoms are as follows:
i. Excessive sweating; reddish colour of the face; stammering and trembling of the hands
ii. Reduction of stamina in the muscles due to stress
iii. Reduction in the functioning of the endocrine system
iv. Sympathetic system overflow

Mental health

Anger adversely affects the mental health of a person. Anger is exhibited in two different ways. Firstly, we either exhibit anger which is so called 'Anger Out'. This spoils your reputation and may spoil your plans. Secondly, anger can be consumed or digested which is called 'Anger in' Today, our well cultured society saves itself from defamation and guards its work from being spoilt. But this gives rise to a dual personality. You may be angry internally. A person who suppresses anger will cause more harm to himself. In this stage the suppressed anger may blast out severely or the person may become restless, sad, moody or feel inferior. This stage can cause an ulcer or heart attack.

Social health

Today whatever violence and terrorism that we have in society is the result of anger, which does not make us become an ideal person in society.

Spiritual health

Our spiritual health, i.e. meditation is impossible in a state of anger.

How to Reduce Stress

Stress which arises out of anger can be relieved by physical and mental relaxation. Some people believe that after having lunch there is a need to take rest which is nowadays known as post lunch nap, which is around 15-20 minutes. Some people give advice to meditate and pray in this time gap. Some say that if anger comes then hold both your hands tightly. Others have experienced that if you press your chin tightly, you can reduce anger. If you wish you can implement these tips such as:
1. Every day have food of health thoughts. Rajyoga meditation is the best device for this practice. Scientists have proved through research that Rayyoga meditation can cure heart patients, ulcer patients and stress.
2. Scientific research has proved that sattwic (pure) food helps in reducing stress, anger and violence. Fruit and vegetables are the best antioxidant coming under the category of sattwic food.

The Difference Between Knowledge and Being Knowledgeful

There are basically two things; one is true knowledge or laws or principles and secondly, implementation. But until you put in hard effort and practice it simply remains as a debt. The result is that you can never become successful in your behaviour.

There is always a devil of stress and tension waiting on the path of success and prosperity in your life. Stress and tension are both reciprocal. Fear alone can give rise to so much stress that all other reasons fail to do so. There are different types of thoughts associated with fear.

Two forms of fear in life

It would be wise for human beings to understand the subtle forms of fear and overcome them. Otherwise, time and energy would go to waste and man has to shed tears of guilt at the end of his life If you understand at least the subtle form of

fear you can overcome it in different ways. There are various forms of fear but here we are discussing broadly two forms;
1. Fear of death
2. Fear of debts of action

Fear of death

Every individual is deeply attached to life. Before fulfilling desires, this life should not slip out of our hands. Though a person may be detached from a material point of view, still he has a subtle fear that, "Whatever I wanted to do, why did I not do it?" People are nervous because they wanted to remember God, they expected to do Godly service, etc. All those desires are still not fulfilled. Thus if you wish to overcome this fear then never postpone anything but endeavour to do it on a daily basis. If you do not leave anything until tomorrow then will you be tense or fearful?

You must have observed that mental or physical depression can sometimes make a person so stressful that he starts thinking that death would be better. Thus, physical pain is more dangerous than the fear of death. One who wishes to attain a higher consciousness or has a burning desire, such people confuse karma philosophy. There is a controversial question amongst religion, divine vision and action-reward.

Fear of debts of action

Which is greater the power of the soul or the power of action? Which is invincible? All actions which are either performed in the past or present the effect will be felt in the future. How can anyone be free of this? The result is that a man cannot become neutral towards unlimited powers of the soul. But it is not like this. God said, "Meditation can dissolve all your impure debts." Meditation or the power of the soul can reduce a mountain into a mustard seed and a mustard seed into cotton wool. It is true that karma philosophy is strong but not so much that it can tie the divine energy of the soul within. Just as a person gets tied in the bondage of action due to ignorance, in the same way a person can get rid of it through meditation and true knowledge. The need of the hour is powerful meditation, which can destroy the bondage of action. There is no need to fear. Soul observes neutrally all different types of physical pain. In this world that person is courageous who has succeeded in gaining success over his inner enemy.

The second form of fear

Today we are so fearful that that we wish to create security through objects and people by worshipping them and this is full of uncertainty and struggle. This is not real power of the soul. The moment we start experiencing the powers of the soul, at that moment different types of fear end and on the other hand the necessity to hold on to material things also ends.

When you pay attention to material prosperity, then the centre of life becomes your self respect. This self respect is a self-made picture which is certified and accepted by society. To maintain this mask, a lot of struggle has to be done in order to hold on to different types of powers such as wealth, physique, relationships etc. which solely depend on fear of disclosing the mask. Whereas our original nature and form is peace, bliss, light, love, and courage, which is fearless from any challenge or insult, praise, etc.

When false respect and power is based on the mask, it degrades a person because the power also finishes. Wealth, position and fame are different powers of this mask.

On the other hand, the powers of the soul are unlimited and imperishable. These powers are attained due to one's own effort. In reality, the soul is knowledgeful and mighty. One simply needs to remember. All your steps of hard effort, meditation, dedication etc. are taken in this direction. You may remember yourself or you may hide yourself behind various masks which you have created but one day you will find you have come out of it. This power has its own specialty and can naturally attract an object or person towards itself. There is a magnetic attraction in this vast universe and due to this wonderful harmony it can produce the desired results in front of you automatically. This principle of nature and God's loving

cooperation is known as blessings. This stage gives rise to a loving attraction in your personality such that people come into a loving relationship with you and help to fulfill your desires.
1. Will I be unsuccessful?
2. Will I not be attacked by any disease?
3. Will I become poor?
4. The main cause of fear is ignorance of the unlimited capabilites within us.
5. People are also fearful because of suspicion, pessimism and blind faith. Some people think that the number 13 is unlucky. They are afraid to cross the road if they find a cat crossing their path.
6. If a person is suffering in pain for a long period of time, they fear being operated on because they believe they may die.
7. I may die on the road due to an accident, so I will not drive a scooter.
8. Negative emotions and thoughts such as depression, stress etc. arise due to fear and suspicion.
9. Fear of what will happen tomorrow.
10. Suspicion and an unstable stage can bring about stress and fear.
11. Fear of losing one's superior position in a hierarchy.
12. Fear of losing fame and self respect.

The Path of Fearlessness – Rajyoga Meditation

He whose companion is Almighty God, does he have any kind of fear? When we are in remembrance of God continuously, only then will we gain power. For this, the only path through which power can be attained is Godly love. The ghost of fear develops in the darkness of ignorance and weakness. When all powers are attainable, then why is there any fear? Thus, if you wish to be free from fear, then practise Rayyoga meditation. The greatest medicine to overcome fear is to experience the stage of soul consciousness. Rajyoga meditation means to remove the darkness from the soul. Then there would be no stress or fear. There will be only peace and happiness. Overcome all tensions and let only true peace dwell in your mind.

In reality the 'Soul' has its natural qualities, which is fearlessness and being beyond all inner bondage of threat and insult. It is full of bliss, love, peace, might and magical excitement. If you consider all elements of the material world against the emotions of this inner world, then you will find that all attachments are idols of your inner relationships. The remedy to be free from fear is not external wealth, position, fame, etc., but rather the experience of 'self' or 'soul'. This experience is the mysterious path of all success. This experience will finish all impulses to fulfill desires and a lack of wealth will not cause any tension. In this elevated stage one realizes that one is a king (ruler) of nature. The root of all attainments is inner soul power. Nature, soul and Supreme Soul create a wonders in this world drama.

The Difference Between Soul and Body, Knowledge and Experience, the Foundation of Fearlessness

We can become fearless by realizing the 'self or 'soul consciousness' and overcoming ego. There is only one elevated path to overcome fear, i.e. practice and experience of soul consciousness. Soul consciousness means to come into relationship with that indifferent authority, the soul. The way to practice is to develop an insight whereby you can easily keep yourself under control and awaken the intellect by the knowledge of the body and soul. Then the door of spirituality starts to open in which courage or fearlessness comes first. One whose body consciousness is destroyed can never become fearful.

In this way Rajyoga meditation helps a person reach the peak of subtleness which is a unique experience. He who forgets the difference between the physical body of male and female does auspicious actions, strives for spiritual prosperity by becoming soul conscious and spreads divine vibrations. Rajyoga

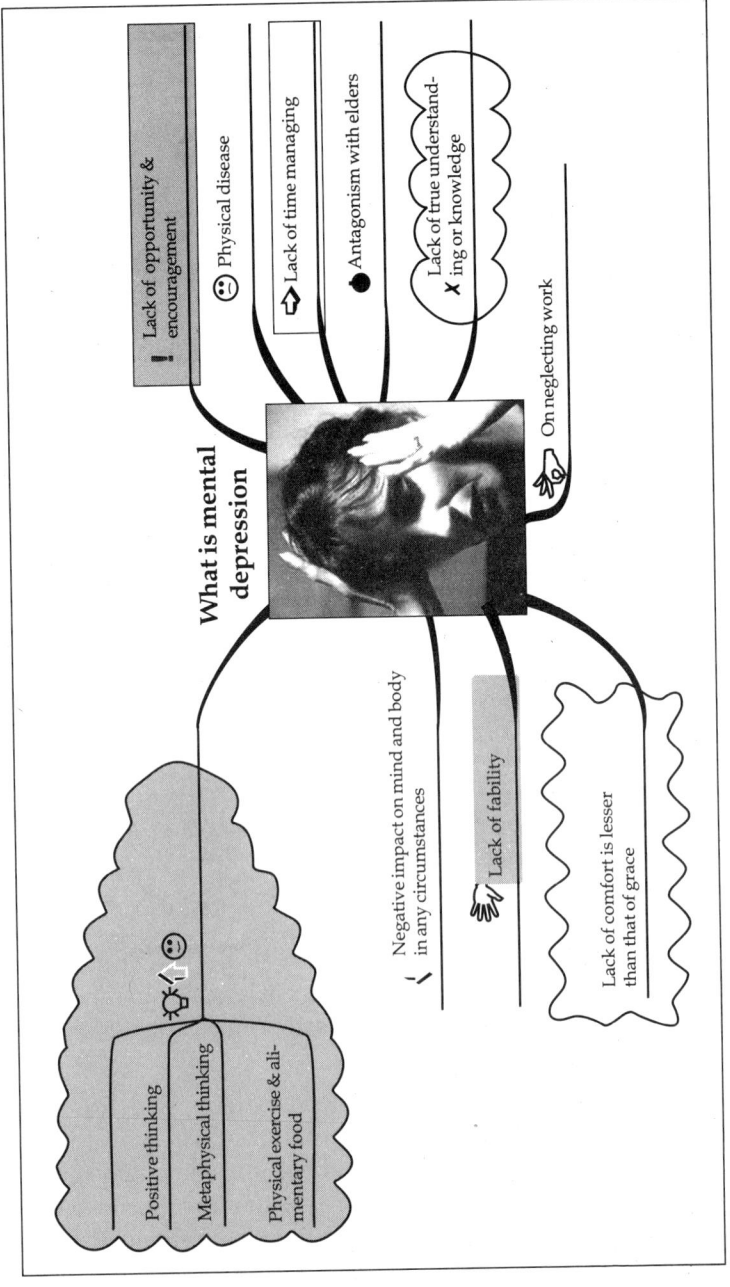

meditation means to conquer the fear of death in order to open the blissful door of nectar. Only then can man defeat all the wasteful thoughts of the present and the future and thereby create power of the soul within himself and overcome his fear.

Harmful effects of fear

It is due to fear that our work efficiency is destroyed and it is due to fear that you lose sleep. It is not wise to become fearful of fulfilling desires and expectations. Fear can also lead us to death and is the root cause of all disease.

There are many types of thoughts of a suspicious nature which can cause a person to become fearful and through this our physical and mental powers are destroyed. A lack of inner power prevents us from achieving our goals. We remain haunted by this depressive ghost throughout our lives.

If someone with determination and will-power decides to carry out an action, even if obstacles are in the way and he still goes ahead, then he definitely will succeed in attaining that goal. On the other hand the person who is filled with apprehension, doubt and uncertainty becomes fearful and loses his courage. He becomes misguided from his goal and never succeeds in attaining it. Thus, always inculcate self confidence and then perform the action.

A person having strong will-power can never accept defeat because he is always filled with strong self confidence and determination towards his creative work. He remains detached from his material happiness and he remains positive towards his success. He never allows fear, defeat, depression and stressful poisonous thoughts to dwell inside him. He is aware that fearful thoughts destroy mental powers in a man. Thus, the need of the hour is to be brave always and overcome such foolish suspicions.

The only certainty in life is death. Then why should people become nervous when one dies again and again? Will this be called intelligent or wise?

Golden Rules for a Stress Free Life

- If you observe neutrally all events of life you will find that it has many benefits, whether visible or invisible, but always see the positive side.
- Do not feel regret over your past mistakes and do not become tense due to future doubts because firstly they are like ashes and secondly events will not happen as you imagine. The present moment is in your hands. Let this moment be spent whole heartedly. Invest your physical power for creativity from this point onwards. The future is an indication of your present elevated actions.
- You are unique and incomparable in this universe. God never makes a carbon copy so it is a waste to compare yourself with others. Every individual is very special. Uniqueness is a specialty in this universe. There are unlimited possibilities so do not become tense by comparing yourself with others and thereby wasting your time and energy.
- Insult is that truth which always checks your purity of character. It tests your patience, forgiveness, love, tolerance and divinity. Thus always make an insulter your good friend who acts as a mirror in front of your inner state. If you have any weaknesses in your reflection then quietly improve them and if your reflection is perfect then relax. If you are happy and thankful in both stages, then there is no question of tension.
- Love, sympathy and forgiveness are the greatest human emotions of all. If others commit mistakes or hurt you then forgive them and this is a wonderful golden formula to experience happiness. If you do this just once you will feel like doing it again and again. Remember one thing, that if you forgive others a day will come when others will forgive you.
- Remember to use your power in solving problems until you reach the goal. Do not become like Abhimanyu who went into the trap of problems.
- There are many stressed people in this world who in a

real sense need your help. If you start serving others you will forget your own tensions and cooperate with others.
- A saying goes, "As your attitude, so the world". If you have a positive attitude towards any problem then you will find a solution and experience happiness even in difficult circumstances and vice versa. The former state of mind is better for stress free life.
- There are some circumstances which are very difficult and which cannot be changed even by hard effort. In this case this one needs to remember that change is a universal law of this universe. Only patience and courage is needed. Everything will change of its own accord. A saying goes, "Nothing happen before its time."
- The universe is a huge stage where all actors, whether heroes or villains, come down at their own time to play their part. If we perform as an actor by becoming neutral then would there be any question such as his acting is wrong or this is his fault, etc.
- Revenge has also affected human beings immensely. History is proof of this. It is difficult to change people or circumstances. Then why not change ourselves because to change ourselves is in our own hands. Where revenge increases stress, on the other hand the goal of changing oneself is to reach the peak of success.
- Jealousy takes us to hell and Godly thinking takes us to heaven. Jealousy burns the heart into ashes and Godly thoughts bring about bliss. So always save yourself from jealousy.
- One of the universal laws is that whatever we give, so we receive in return multifold. Then why not share happiness so that the stock becomes full. Never think of giving sorrow either intentionally or by mistake.
- Whenever you come across any painful circumstances or fall sick then accept the situation happily and understand that you must have made a mistake in the past and now have to pay off the debt.
- When you overcome different types of ego the darkness

of illusion is automatically destroyed. Today ego is one of the major obstacles on the path to happiness and peace. The moment you light the lamp of true knowledge, all obstacles of darkness are destroyed and all tensions go.
- Try to reduce your thoughts through Rajyoga meditation as much as possible throughout the day. Practise converting all thoughts into positive.
- Offer all your tension to God faithfully and become light.
- For complete health, whether material or spiritual, always remember God and connect yourself with that Supreme soul so that you take power to destroy all stress in your life and become a channel to donate this to others also.